With Presidents to the Summit

A. Denis Clift

GEORGE MASON UNIVERSITY PRESS
Fairfax, Virginia

Copyright © 1993 by
George Mason University Press
4400 University Drive
Fairfax, VA 22030

Distributed by arrangement with
National Book Network
4720 Boston Way
Lanham, MD 20706

3 Henrietta Street
London WC2E 8LU England

Library of Congress Cataloging-in-Publication Data
Clift, Denis.
With presidents to the summit / A. Denis Clift.
p.   cm.
Includes bibliographical references.
1. United States—Foreign relations—1969–1974.   2. United
States—Foreign relations—1974–1977.   3. United States—Foreign
relations—1977–1981.   4. Summit meetings—History—20th
century.   5. Presidents—United States—Journeys—History—20th
century.
6. World politics—1965–1975.   7. World politics—1975–1985.
I. Title.
E765.C57   1993   327.73—dc20   92–39588 CIP

ISBN 0–913969–51–6 (cloth : alk. paper)

 The paper used in this publication meets the minimum requirements of
American National Standard for Information Sciences—Permanence
of Paper for Printed Library Materials, ANSI Z39.48–1984.

For
Gretchen, Alexander and Tyrone

Also by Denis Clift:

Nonfiction: *Our World in Antarctica*
Fiction: *A Death in Geneva*

Acknowledgements

For permission to use copyright material, I gratefully acknowledge: Viking Penguin, a division of Penguin Books USA, Inc., for the quote from *On the Road* by Jack Kerouac, copyright (©) 1955, 1957 by Jack Kerouac, renewed (©) 1983 by Stella Kerouac, renewed (©) 1985 by Stella Kerouac and Jan Kerouac; Viking Penguin a division of Penguin Books USA, Inc., for the quote from *A Russian Journal* by John Steinbeck, copyright (©) 1948 by John Steinbeck, renewed (©) 1976 by Elaine Steinbeck, Thom Steinbeck and John Steinbeck; Simon & Schuster, Inc., for the quotes from *Hard Choices* by Cyrus Vance, copyright (©) 1983 by Cyrus Vance; Simon & Schuster, Inc., for the quote from *The Path Between the Seas* by David McCullough, copyright (©) 1977 by David McCullough; Little, Brown and Company for the quotes from *Years of Upheaval* by Henry Kissinger; Grosset & Dunlap, Inc., for the quote from *RN The Memoirs of Richard Nixon* by Richard Nixon; Houghton Mifflin Company for the quote from *A Thousand Days* by Arthur Schlesinger, Jr., copyright (©) 1965 by Arthur Schlesinger, Jr.; Greenwood Press for the quote from *General Wainwright's Story* by Jonathan Wainwright; Curtis Brown Ltd., for the quote from *Letters from Iceland* by W.H. Auden and Louis Mac-Neice, copyright (©) 1937, 1969 by W.H. Auden; W.W. Norton & Company, Inc., for the quote from *Thirteen Days* by Robert F. Kennedy; Doubleday, a divsion of Bantam Doubleday Dell Publishing Group, Inc., for the quote from *Silent Missions* by Vernon A. Walters; Doubleday, a division of Bantam Doubleday Dell Publishing Group, Inc. for the quotes from *Waging Peace 1956–1961* by Dwight D. Eisenhower; Bernard Grasset for the quotes from *Memoires d'Avenir* by Michel Jobert; Margaret Truman Daniels for the quotes from *Memoirs by Harry S. Truman* by Harry S. Truman; Henry Holt and Company, Inc., for the quote from *The Vantage Point* by Lyndon Baines Johnson, copyright (©) 1971 by Lyndon Baines Johnson; Houghton Mifflin Company for the quote from *Woodrow Wilson* by Arthur Walworth; Harper & Row for the quote from *The Public Papers and Addresses of Franklin D. Roosevelt 1941 The Call to Battle Stations* compiled by Samuel I. Rosenman; Russell and Russell for the quote from *The Public Papers and Addresses of Franklin D. Roosevelt 1944–1945* compiled by Samuel I. Rosenman; Harper Collins Publishers for the quotes from *A Time to Heal* by Gerald R. Ford, copyright (©) 1979 by Gerald R. Ford; Bantam Books, a division of Bantam Doubleday Dell Publishing Group Inc., for the quotes from *Keeping Faith: Memoirs of a President* by Jimmy Carter, copyright (©) 1982 by Jimmy Carter; W.W. Norton & Company for the quote from *Present at the Creation* by Dean Acheson; Chilton Book Company for the quote from *Willy Brandt Prisoner of His Past* by Viola Herms Drath; Doubleday Canada Ltd., for the quote from *The Presidents and the Prime Ministers* by Lawrence Martin; A.H. and A.W. Reed Ltd., for the quote from *Muldoon* by R.D. Muldoon; St. Martin's Press, Inc., for the quote from *The Canadians* by Andrew H. Malcolm, copyright (©) 1985 by Andrew Malcolm; Macmillan Publishing Company, a Division of Macmillan, Inc., for the quote from *By-Line: Ernest Hemingway* edited by William White, copyright (©) 1937 *The New York Times and North American Newspaper Alliance;* renewal copyright (©) 1967 by Mary Hemingway, copyright (©) 1967 by Mary Hemingway; Harvard University Press for the quote from *The Letters of Theodore Roosevelt,* edited by Elting E. Morison; Farrar, Straus Giroux for the quote from *Power and Principle* by Zbigniew Brzezinski; Harcourt Brace Jovanovich, Inc. for the quote from *Roosevelt: Soldier of Principle* by James McGregor Burns, copyright (©) 1970 by James McGregor Burns; William Morrow and Company for the quote from *Living with the Bible* by Moshe Dayan; Leona Schecter for the quote from *Mondale Portrait of an American Politician* by Finlay Lewis.

I thank James B. Fisher, Isabelle C. Gibb and Sharon Carser at George Mason University Press for the role each has played in bringing this work to publication.

Table of Contents

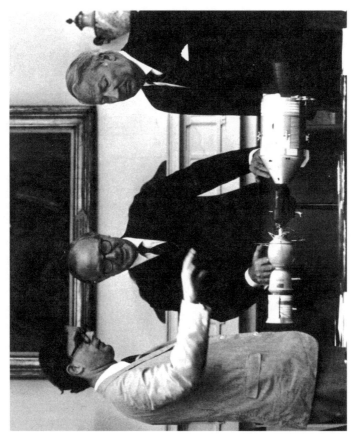

With UK's Edward Heath explaining the Apollo-Soyuz Space Mission in the Cabinet Room, the White House, 1975 (*White House*)

Preface

In the mid-1960s, some eight years after graduation from Stanford University, I deemed a sabbatical year in order and departed my editorship of the United States Naval Institute *Proceedings* for graduate study at The London School of Economics and Political Science.

Armed with eight library cards embracing the greater London area, and impressed by the near-cosmic wisdom of my tutor and lecturers, I plunged into readings of the international political system, foreign policy analysis and war and crisis in international relations. I grappled with stable elements and elements subject to constant change, with the stark rungs of the escalation ladder, and with the post-decisional stages. To enliven the year, I undertook research on international cooperation in the North Sea where discovery of massive quantities of natural gas had led to intricate division of seabed rights among the littoral states.

The pleasure I derived from international politics had been stimulated by my earlier years as *Proceedings* editor and by two expeditions earlier still to the Antarctic continent. There, as a naval officer on the Task Force Commander's staff, I had been in charge of protocol for the foreign observers visiting our scientific bases under the terms of the Antarctic Treaty. To a man, these observers were gentlemen. Beyond the routine, my greatest challenges were meeting their requirements for those rarest of polar treasures: an emergency 40-ounce jug of scotch or gin; an aspirin and water following a wearying trudge across the ice cap in the the thin air two miles high at South Pole Station; or a cooling lime refreshment as our icebreaker flagship rolled north along the coast of South America on the homeward leg of the five-month, 1961 Bellingshausen Sea Expedition.

That adventure in international relations coupled with the solemn readings required for my Master of Science degree at the L.S.E. told me that my future certainly lay in America's dealings with other nations. But nothing that I was then absorbing on behaviorist simulation, the cousins of crisis gaming and 'the holder of the balance' caused me to suspect that ten years later I would be inside Number 10 Downing Street shoulder-to-shoulder with the British Prime Minister singing an *a cappella* duet.

The academic readings in London—and my own drier papers—on interpreting the doctrine of power did not offer the clue that I would one day be studying a cyrillic and English-language dinner menu of bear ham with pickles, shredded sea slugs and roe deer saddle, then rising to clink my cut crystal glass of champagne with the President of the United States and General Secretary of the Soviet Union against the late afternoon light of November snow in Vladivostok to toast a new strategic arms accord. Nor at a time when Chinese students were being recalled *en masse* from London in the turmoil of the Cultural Revolution could I see myself in Beijing in the Great Hall of the People privileged to be passing leather-bound copies of formal treaty parchment for signature by the Vice President of the United States and the leader of the People's Republic of China.

From the early 1970s to the early 1980s, I would be privileged to participate in many such summits. This decade has already become a snapshot in the nation's history, embracing the end of the war in Vietnam, America's struggle to recapture its global leadership, to reinvigorate consultations and restore confidence among our most important allies. There were breakthroughs to peace in the Middle East, accompanied by the shock of new global problems—the soaring cost of energy foremost among them. Dedication to strategic arms control and to the shaping of new, more constructive relationships with major adversaries was central to the policies of the three Administrations of the time. Face-to-face meetings at the summit were employed with regularity by the three Presidents and their principal advisors.

As a senior member of the National Security Council and White House staffs, I would help to shape a succession of America's meetings with foreign leaders from the time of the 1971 preparations for the 1972 U.S.-Soviet summit to the 1980 meetings with the Presidents of Senegal, Niger, Nigeria, and Cape Verde. Give or take one or two, the calendar included the:

- U.S.—USSR Summit, Moscow, 1972;
- U.S.—French Summit, Iceland, 1973;
- U.S.—USSR Summit, Washington, 1973;
- Secretary of State's Visit to the USSR, March, 1974;
- France, the Pompidou Funeral, April 1974;
- NATO Summit, Brussels, June 1974;
- U.S.—USSR Summit, Soviet Union, July 1974;
- Secretary of State's Visit to the USSR, Romania, Yugoslavia and Italy, October 1974;
- U.S.—USSR Summit, Vladivostok USSR, November 1974;
- U.S.—French Summit, Martinique, December 1974;
- NATO Summit, Brussels, May 1975;

- President Ford's Visit to the Federal Republic of Germany, July 1975;
- Conference on Security and Cooperation in Europe, Helsinki, Finland, July–August 1975;
- President Ford's Visit to Poland, Yugoslavia and Romania, July–August 1975;
- Secretary of State's Visit to Canada, October 1975;
- NATO Ministerial Meeting, Oslo, Norway, May 1976;
- NATO Ministerial Meeting, Brussels, December 1976.

With President Carter's victory in the election of 1976 and my shift from the National Security Council staff to the Office of the Vice President, the odyssey continued with Vice President Mondale's:

- Visit to Belgium, Federal Republic of Germany, Berlin, Italy, The Vatican, Great Britain, France, and Japan, January–February 1977;
- Visit to Portugal, Spain, Austria, Yugoslavia and Great Britain, May 1977;
- Visit to Canada and Mexico, January 1978;
- Visit to the Philippines, Thailand, Indonesia, Australia, and New Zealand, May 1978;
- Visit to Israel and Egypt, July 1978;
- Visit to The Vatican and Italy, September 1978;
- Camp David Summit, September 1978;
- Inaugurations of the Presidents of Brazil and Venezuela, March 1979;
- Visit to Brazil and Venezuela, March 1979;
- Visit to Iceland, Norway, Denmark, Sweden, Finland, and the Netherlands, April 1979;
- U.N. Conference on Refugees in Indochina, Geneva, July 1979;
- Visit to the People's Republic of China and Hong Kong, August 1979;
- Yugoslavia, the Tito funeral, May 1980;
- Visit to Senegal, Niger, Nigeria, and Cape Verde, July 1980.

Our society today tends to accept as routine the images of our leaders with foreign leaders in overseas capitals, however remote, with television coverage of their encounters beamed live via satellite to the entire American nation, and often much of the world.

The glamorous, fleeting images of such coverage do not begin to do justice to the intricate business of summiting. We can learn as much from the successes and failures of practitioners of the summit as we can from readings, or at least most readings, of political theory, principle and doctrine. The lessons not only apply for those aspiring to a role in foreign affairs and international politics, whether in the Executive or Legislative Branches of government, but also to those seeking an understanding of the nature of the summit process. More broadly, they apply to any who seek to attain a goal through concerted effort with colleague or against competitor, for any who must prepare for such effort and carry it through with eyes always on the strategic objective and with mind always alert to the possibility of failure because of inattention to detail.

With Presidents to the Summit examines the anatomy of summits, the advancing, the staffing, the goals, the delegations, the grind, the perils, the excitement and the results. To capture the many dimensions, the book opens with the Reykjavik summit of 1973, the Nixon-Pompidou talks, my first on-the-road role in summit diplomacy. The second chapter then steps back a pace to offer a sketch of the prior history of our Presidents' summit travels, so as to place my decade's experience in the fuller historical American perspective.

These pages share the findings of one who has been privileged to participate in the business of summits. Of equal importance in an era when 'government work' is increasingly belittled and, accordingly, increasingly questioned as a career choice, *With Presidents to the Summit* gives ringing confirmation to the uniquely important responsibilities and experience of government service, and the very special sense of professional pride and satisfaction that flows from service to country.

Introductions

Gerald R. Ford

As the United States moves forward from the 1980s, to the 1990s, to the Twenty-first century, Americans will continue to look to each new President for national and world leadership that only the President can exercise. In the international realm, the President's management of the nation's security, our ties with allies and friends, and our dealings with adversaries shape not only the course that we as a people will take but also the image and the example that we will offer to the rest of the world.

America's image and responsibilities were foremost in my mind as President in the words I chose at Independence Hall, Philadelphia on July 4, 1976: "The world knows where we stand. The world is ever conscious of what American's are doing, for better or for worse, because the United States remains today the most successful realization of humanity's universal hope."

That Fourth of July truly was a splendid celebration. Three days later I had the distinct pleasure of welcoming Her Majesty Queen Elizabeth II, on the occasion of her visit to honor America's Bicentennial observance. Something wonderful happened in America on that Fourth of July, I told her. A spirit of unity and togetherness deep within the American soul sprang to the surface in a way that we had almost forgotten. People showed again that they cared, that they wanted to live in peace and harmony with their neighbors, that they wanted to pull together for the good of the nation and the good of mankind.

The Bicentennial visit of Her Majesty, of President Giscard d'Estaing of France, Chancellor Helmut Schmidt of the Federal Republic of Germany and the many other distinguished chiefs of state and heads of government marked a rich and deeply meaningful chapter in my years as President. Literally thousands of Americans worked behind the scenes, attending to issues large and small, pulling together to ensure the success of those visits. Among them, very few worked harder or with greater skill and fine results than the senior staff member on the National Security Council, Denis Clift. And his contributions to the Bicentennial marked just a small fraction of the part he played in the foreign policy of my administration.

During the final days in office, I took time to send him the following letter:

The White House
Washington, D.C.
January 19, 1977

Dear Denis,

I want to thank you for your outstanding and dedicated performance as NSC Senior Staff Member for Europe during the two and a half years of my Presidency.

In strengthening our ties with our friends and allies in Europe, in our progress toward more constructive relations with the Soviet Union and Eastern Europe, in our oceans policy and negotiations on law of the sea, and in the conduct of our diplomacy at a time of economic difficulty and political change in Europe, your role has been central.

I know of the enormous contribution you made in preparing for my meeting with foreign leaders and my visits abroad. Of my 124 meetings with foreign chiefs of state and heads of government, you were responsible for the substantive preparations for well over half. You accompanied me to Vladivostok for my meetings with General Secretary Brezhnev, and to Martinique for my talks with President Giscard d'Estaing; in 1975, you were a valued member of the delegations which I led to both the NATO Summit in Brussels and the Conference on Security and Cooperation in Europe at Helsinki. And in our Bicentennial year, during which so many European leaders visited the United States, you took personal pride in the success of this deeply symbolic dimension of our Bicentennial celebration.

Denis, for my entire term of office, you have devoted yourself to the Presidency and to your country in the finest tradition of public service. I am in debt to you for your wisdom, professionalism and skill. You have my admiration and lasting gratitude for a job very well done.

Sincerely,

s/Gerald R. Ford

Mr. A. Denis Clift
National Security Council
Washington, D.C. 20506

Now with *With Presidents to the Summit* we are able to step
behind the scenes to take a detailed look at the intricacies and
challenges of summit-level diplomacy not only in my administration but throughout the Nixon, Ford and Carter years. We look
at the historic meetings between and among Statesmen not
through the eyes of those who would sign agreements of importance to the entire world but rather throughout the keen, professional eyes of one who toiled in the preparation of those
agreements, the communiques and the statements to the
world's media. The insights are fresh, and there is an entire cata-
logue of lessons to be learned.

Many of the episodes in the chapters that follow brought back a
rush of welcome memories for me. *With Presidents to the Summit*,
while rich in well-crafted, often highly amusing historical moments, is far more than a reminiscence. Because we can learn so
very much from thoughtful interpretation of past events, this
book will be instructive reading for all who are interested in
international affairs. Of greater importance, *With Presidents to
the Summit* expands our knowledge of the summit process and in
so doing makes a lasting contribution to our study of the
Presidency.

Gerald R. Ford

Jimmy Carter

In *With Presidents to the Summit*, Denis Clift provides a special
perspective on global affairs, that of a White House staff
member who worked behind the scenes during numerous meetings of presidents of the United States with foreign heads of
state. During my administration, he served as Assistant for
National Security Affairs to Vice President Walter Mondale.
Because of my unique relationship with Walter Mondale, this
was a significant position. By the time I selected my running
mate in the campaign of 1976, I had determined that the Vice
President would play a larger role in my administration than any
previous Vice President had ever played, and that he would be

totally involved in the domestic, national security, and foreign policy decision-making process. The Vice President's office for the first time would be located in the West Wing of the White House, just steps from the Oval Office. The Vice President's staff would be integrated as a working team with my staff.

Vice President Mondale, supported by Denis Clift, not only served an my representative in many meetings with foreign leaders, but he also took part in deliberations and negotiations in which I was personally involved. Clift presents his account of the pioneering role played by the Vice President, as well as his personal viewpoint on the foreign policy activities of the administration. A notable episode in the book is the Camp David Summit with Israel and Egypt, in which he provided effective assistance.

This book is a valuable contribution to the understanding of official life in government and especially in the White House. It highlights the pitfalls and the tremendous rewards of the summit process. Scholars should benefit from this detailed account by a participant in the history of our times.

Jimmy Carter

Walter F. Mondale

In his memoirs, *Keeping Faith*, President Jimmy Carter described the excellent relationship, the partnership, he and I enjoyed from 1976 through 1980. The president broke new institutional ground making the Vice President "second in command," to use his words, "involved in every aspect of governing."

In *With Presidents to the Summit*, Denis Clift addresses the foreign policy dimensions of my years as Vice President and his role throughout as my Assistant for National Security Affairs. If the responsibilities of the Vice President were to increase so would the demands on his staff. From my meetings at NATO Headquarters and in allied capitals during the first week of the administration, to the talks with the Prime Minister of South Africa, to the Camp David Summit of 1978, to the many meetings with foreign leaders in the West Wing of the White House over the course of four years, the agenda was fast paced and the results often of lasting significance to the nation.

With Presidents to the Summit is an authoritative, very valuable account of business at the highest levels between and among nations. Mr. Clift chronicles his work for me in my missions on behalf of the President with the same fine professionalism and attention to detail that he brought to his responsibilities in the late 1970s.

Mr. Clift's wit and style are matched by his far-reaching insights. *With Presidents to the Summit* is at the same time splendid reading and an excellent contribution to our appreciation and understanding of the complex challenges and rewards of government service in international affairs.

Walter F. Mondale

The 1978 Camp David Summit: Prime Minister Begin, President Carter, President Sadat (*White House*)

CHAPTER ONE

Iceland — 1973

So I came here to the land the Romans missed,
Left for the Irish saint and the Viking colonist.
But what am I doing here? Qu'allais-je faire
Among these volcanic rocks and this grey air?

Letters from Iceland
W.H. Auden and
Louis Macneice, 1937

A stiff spring breeze carried its special Icelandic greeting—the pungent smell of fish works—when we stepped from our Air Force jet and crossed the tarmac at Keflavik International Airport. We were 20 strong, the pre-advance party for the Nixon-Pompidou summit of May 1973.

Fields of lava punctuated with ancient volcanic cones spread from either side of the two lane highway, Iceland's best, on the 32 mile drive into the capital city of Reykjavik. The two Presidents would soon be following this route. My thoughts went back to an earlier U.S.-French parade, 19 years before, to the cascading confetti, ticker-tape and cheering sidewalk crowds engulfing the young air force nurse who waved and smiled anxiously from the perch of her open limousine.

Hanging from the press truck rolling up Broadway directly in front of her, I had watched the angel of Dien Bien Phu, Lieutenant Genevieve de Galard Terraube, her gentle face, blue eyes turning toward the incessant shouts of the photographers; "Hey Jenny! Over here, Jenny! Big Smile...big smile! That's a kid...how 'bout a wave...another wave,...Jenny...that's a kid!" The blood, mud and torn bodies jamming the underground hospital through its 56-day siege had faded. America was pouring its praise on its new-found French heroine. Copy boy for the New York *Daily News*, I had clutched the film plates thrust at me by our photographer, jumped from the press

1

truck and made a dash for the subway. The angel's smile was in the next edition.

There were no angels, no heroines, only racks of drying fish and disinterested flocks of sheep along our route in 1973. As we had neared the southwest tip of Iceland, our pilot had flown low over the red and green roofs of the fishing community of Heimaey in the Westmann Islands. Lava from an erupting volcano had engulfed several homes and narrowed the vital approaches to the harbor. Volcanic ash and debris were everywhere. The danger of fresh eruptions and poisonous explosive gases had driven the islanders temporarily to the safety of Iceland. U.S. Navy personnel from the NATO Base at Keflavik had assisted in the evacuation. On the recommendation of our pre-advance party, the President's jet—Air Force One, the Spirit of '76 as Nixon had renamed it—would also pass low over the Westmanns, and the President would extend an offer of further U.S. assistance during the course of his summit visit.

As we began our pre-advance mission, the drumbeat in Washington was mounting that Watergate had already diminished the President's ability to drive the necessary hard bargain with the French. In Paris, word of Pompidou's illness, reinforced by his puffy appearance, brought into question his strength as a negotiator. On both sides of the the Atlantic there were more doubters than believers to the proposition that the United States could engineer the Europeans into signing a new Atlantic Charter.

Such considerations were for others to fret over. I was dedicated to achieving the charter, and I felt a spirit of tremendous adventure, rolling across this historic island nation scouting my first summit. Our pre-advance team included the head of the President's Secret Service detail, the head of the White House Communications Agency, military aides, doctors, National Security Council staff (i.e., me) and the lead and supporting advance men, specialists in the business of technical preparations for meetings between sovereign chiefs of state.

Summits involving U.S. leaders have never just come to pass accidentally, with the possible exception of an unscheduled chance encounter with a foreign leader on the fringe of a large multilateral gathering. The care that has gone into summit preparation has varied in degree, with the first spark of inspiration for the national result to be realized as the point of departure. From this have flowed the detailed planning for the substance of the talks, the structure and content of the desired documents and the accompanying substance for the private talks and public rhetoric of the summiters.

In parallel, planning and arrangements have proceeded on the technical side to provide the transportation, to shape the events to each President's advantage and convenience, to ensure that his program is fully provided for, to ensure his safety, to guarantee his official communications and to meet the critical, double-edged requirements of the press—a challenge of great dimensions given the flood of television, newspaper and radio coverage accompanying each summit. Poor arrangements at the technical level for talks between world leaders can undercut the finest of substantive achievements. Faulty interpretation, scheduling foul-ups, any of a thousand different snags, can result in flawed negotiations, in embarrassment for the leader and, accordingly, in setbacks ranging from minor to major proportions for the nation. To avoid such pitfalls, the check list has emerged as the summit staffer's constant companion. This list of essential needs to be met begins with the pre-advance.

The highway curved north at the approaches to Reykjavik. The bright greens, blues, reds, and yellows of the homes, each with its windows faced expectantly toward the south, dressed the drab landscape. Iceland's trees had been sacrificed centuries before during the 'Age of Settlement'—cleared for sheep grazing and consumed for fuel; not one was to be seen. I would find the grandest tree of all Reykjavik in the garden of the American Ambassador. Icelanders had long since captured their most precious natural resource, hot water fired by volcanic geothermal heat. White tanks perched above "the smokeless city", reservoirs for water, boiling at its source, coursing through pipelines throughout the city to heat each home and provide scalding hot tap water rich in the scent of sulfur. This geothermal heat on the fringe of the Arctic Circle also warmed greenhouses nurturing banana trees, vegetables, plants and flowers.

I asked about a large industrial plant forming part of Reykjavik's gateway, totally out of proportion to every other structure we had seen—a pioneering aluminum processing plant, importing bauxite from thousands of miles away, exporting aluminum thousands of miles away, eking a profit from nature's second gift, hydroelectricity almost free, fueling the energy-dependent industry.

Once in Reykjavik, we launched our pre-advance with a meeting with the U.S. Ambassador and members of his staff. Our ambassadors play a vital support role in America's summits. They are the President's full-time official representative on scene. A good ambassador informs himself fully as to the President's objectives as soon as he receives first word of a proposed visit—indeed, if he has not already proposed the visit. He forwards recommendations designed to contribute to those objectives, appoints a visit control office, marshals the entire embassy staff to support the summit, identifies problems that will have to be dealt with, and provides a continuing update on the maneuvering and the tactics of the President's foreign counterpart and of those who are helping to shape the positions that the other country will take.

A good ambassador helps to set the right tone for the summit talks through his pre-summit contacts with his host country. He and his staff can open almost every door for the pre-advance team, the advance team and, most importantly, the summit party. A good embassy is an integral part of the entire process of preparation. It is essential that those who are heading the pre-advance and those supporting the summit from Washington come to know the ambassador and his staff and work in partnership with them from the beginning. However, the staffer must guard against the rare but very real possibility that an ambassador, whether purposely or inadvertently, will turn out to be a problem maker rather than a problem solver.

I have worked with ambassadors who have refused to accept Washington's proposals for a visit, and who have tried to impose their own program and agenda on their distinguished visitor. It is a responsibility of the summit pre-advance to spot such a situation, to try to resolve it successfully on scene, and if unresolved, to advise Washington that the Embassy in question requires some gentle counseling. An expert pre-advance team leader seldom has to resort to Washington; however, he finds himself in a situation where he must maintain a constant vigil on his problem diplomat. I can recall one instance where our ambassador, having been repeatedly overruled, found a marvelous opportunity to compound the difficulties he was causing by drawing a speeding ticket on his way to the airport for the summit arrival ceremony. Needless to say, his actions were not lost on the local press. The following morning's newspapers gave front-page play to the incident.

In Iceland, the American Ambassador, Frederick Irving, was an absolutely superb professional. Our party drew fully on his expertise as we reviewed our planned sequence meetings involving bilateral talks with the Icelanders, meetings with the Icelanders and the French pre-advance party concerning the U.S.-French talks, and the social events that would involve the leaders from Iceland, France and the United States. Which raises a rather logical question—why a U.S.-French summit in Iceland?

Gaullist protocol still set an extremely formal tone for the U.S.-French relationship in the early 1970s. President Pompidou, who had succeeded the General in 1969 following six years as his Prime Minister, continued De Gaulle's reserve toward the United States. Pompidou had visited America in 1970, a visit during which he and his wife had been insulted by American demonstrators protesting France's sale of combat jet aircraft to Libya. There could be no question of his paying still another visit at least until America's President reciprocated with a formal return visit to France. President Nixon was looking forward to such a visit but not until the autumn of 1973.

This chessboard of summit maneuvering led to a series of island-hopping sessions between the U.S. and French Presidents: a quick Nixon-Pompidou consultation in the Azores in 1971, the Iceland summit of 1973, to be followed by December 1974 talks between President Ford and President Giscard d'Estaing in Martinique, the French West Indies. While the island strategy offered a convenient accommodation of U.S.-French interests, in 1973 it also unnecessarily complicated the Nixon-Pompidou talks by injecting Iceland's interests into the summit scenario. Those interests on the part of a usually reserved and gentle people were volatile and considerable. The experience would serve to underscore again the care that must be taken in the selection of a summit site, and the need to scrutinize the implications of that site—including the 'neutral site'—from every conceivable angle.

In 1973, the nation of Iceland was taking a stand, with all political factions and virtually the entire population of 209,000 people determined that British and other foreign trawlers should not fish within 50 miles of Iceland's coast. The British were not impressed, and the U.K.-Icelandic Cod War was in full heat of 'battle'. The issue went to the heart of Iceland's economy, with fish accounting for 85 percent of export earnings. The issue also went to the heart of the Icelanders' sense of justice. They cited the 1958 Geneva Convention on the Continental Shelf giving coastal states sovereign rights over their continental shelf's seabed resources, including the marine life on the shelf. They argued that the shelf and the waters above were, for Iceland, an organic unit. In 1972, they formally announced that their fisheries jurisdiction would be extended to 50 miles. They denied the World Court's jurisdiction in the matter and sent the *Thor*, the *Aegir*, and the *Arakvur*, their diminutive coast guard vessels, to cut the nets of the British trawlers and to engage escorting Royal Navy frigates in day after day of rammings, bumping and near collisions.

Iceland looked to the United States, to France and to other nations of NATO for support and protection from the British 'aggressor'. Iceland had only gained independence in 1944 after seven centuries of Danish and Norwegian rule. While fiercely jealous of this newly won freedom, Iceland was without her own armed forces, had joined the North Atlantic Alliance, and from 1951 provided Keflavik as the base for NATO's U.S.-manned Iceland Defense Force. Until May 1973, the United States had taken great pains to avoid being drawn into the Cod War, urging restraint on the part of the British and urging Iceland to forego unilateral claims and to pursue its fisheries interests in the ongoing U.S. Law of the Sea Conference. Such subtlety and distance would no longer be adequate with Presidents Nixon and Pompidou in Reykjavik. The Icelanders would press their case vigorously, detracting from the primary public purpose of the summit talks.

By early 1973, the United States and its Western European allies had taken to increasing squabbles—trade competition, monetary policies and differences over what constituted an equitable sharing of the collective defense were all part of the debate. In the wake of the 1972 U.S.-Chinese and U.S.-Soviet summits, the Europeans and Japanese were smarting over a feeling of grossly inadequate consultations on the part of the United States. These frictions had increasingly become part of my daily professional life as a member of the National Security Council staff for European affairs.

President Nixon signaled his heightened interest in Europe in his foreign policy report to the Congress in January 1973, then launched a fresh round of consultations with the leaders of Europe with the goal of quickly restoring the relationship to a more positive, cooperative spirit and to firmer footing. In April 1973, following the President's talks with Prime Minister Edward Heath of Great Britain and Chancellor Willy Brandt of the Federal Republic of Germany, Dr. Henry Kissinger, my boss and the President's National Security Adviser, sought to place this U.S. diplomatic effort in full conceptual perspective in an address entitled "The Year of Europe." It is not difficult, with the benefit of hindsight, to see how that title might have grated some Europeans. The text of the address, which both exhorted and chastised, catalogued the areas of difficulty, called for a high-speed concerted effort to set the U.S.-European house in order, and painted a vision of the benefits to be realized therefrom.

"The Atlantic nations must join in a fresh act of creation, equal to that undertaken by the post-war generation of leaders in Europe

and America...The United States proposes to its Atlantic partners that, by the time the President travels to Europe toward the end of the year, we will have worked out a new Atlantic charter setting the goals for the future—a blue print that:
—builds on the past without becoming its prisoner,
—deals with the problems our success has created,
—creates for the Atlantic nations a new relationship in whose progress Japan can share.

"We ask our friends in Europe, Canada, and ultimately Japan to join us in this effort.

"This is what we mean by the Year of Europe."[1]

In his press conference immediately before the President's departure for Iceland, Dr. Kissinger embellished the U.S. goals observing, "...the objective of the Administration is to lift the Atlantic debate out of the rut of purely technical controversies where for about a decade public attention has been concentrated." He underlined France's central role in reinvigorating the U.S.-European dialogue and, looking to the Reykjavik talks, said: "We will not, of course, be able to make any final decisions in a two day meeting in Iceland. What we hope to achieve is some agreement on procedures that might be followed in articulating the purposes we seek to define, procedures in which the role of France will be, of course, extremely important, so that by the time the President visits Europe toward the end of the year, we will be in position to conclude, or bring close to conclusion, the first phase of these negotiations."[2]

In Paris, the U.S. initiative was perceived quite differently. Michel Jobert, a long-time aide and confident of President Pompidou, had just been named France's Minister of Foreign Affairs. He believed that the Year of Europe speech and America's proposals were largely being driven by President Nixon's domestic political difficulties. The French had found portions of the speech both erroneous and patronizing, and had no interest in contributing to any suggestion that France wished to play a subordinate role falling in behind America's leadership in shaping some sort of collective U.S.-European relationship. "The French Government," Jobert would write, "kept its silence on the initiative of Dr. Kissinger, but made known its opposition both to the ideas and the calendar."[3] This nothwithstanding, the French pre-advance team was with our American party on May 10, in Reykjavik to prepare for the Nixon-Pompidou talks.

Pre-advancing a summit is a study in perpetual motion. Following an early morning huddle on May 9, our technical experts fanned out to begin weaving the supporting fabric of the summit, initiating contacts with Icelandic counterparts, surveying sites, launching the plans for every aspect of summit support that would be implemented by the members of the advance team who would follow us and remain in Iceland until the summit. These would include the Air Force personnel who would make the technical arrangements for the arrival, the handling and security for Air Force One—the 'Spirit of '76'—the various passengers, cargo and other supporting aircraft; the communicators who would ensure that that President and his party had the same swift, sure communications as in Washington; members of the White House medical staff who would survey the hospitals and clinics in Reykjavik and Keflavik to determine which facilities would be best equipped to handle the range of medical contingencies—from mild illness, to stroke, to gun shot; and the Secret Service who would track every aspect of the planning from the first day to provide for the President's security.

Eleven of our party crossed Reykjavik for the first round of planning with the French and the Icelanders. Our hosts had a number of pressing questions. When, precisely, would each of the Presidents arrive? How large would each Presidential party be? How many senior officials with each party? Where would the Presidents wish to stay (the visit was, in its way, unprecedented)? What would be the preferred meeting site? How did the United States and France wish to coordinate on security arrangements? Would we provide our own interpreters—every Icelander spoke English as a second tongue, or almost everyone— what were our preferences for translation of the French tongue? What program events did we anticipate in addition to the actual talks? Would there be sightseeing, salmon fishing? How many members of the press would accompany the parties? Where did we wish them to stay? Would President Pompidou and President Nixon wish talks with Prime Minister Olafur Johannesson? Would such talks be one trilateral meeting or two bilateral rounds? President Eldjarn would wish to receive the visiting Presidents; would a dinner at his residence be agreeable?

We carried specific instructions on most of these points. The Icelanders, led by their Under Secretary for Foreign Affairs, were thoughtful, solicitous, eager to be the best possible hosts. The morning session unfolded smoothly, and following a luncheon of rack of lamb garnished with local, hothouse vegetables, with spectacular spring snow squalls swirling in the distance against the long low face of Mount Esja, we departed on a tour of key locations.

Reykjavik is a spotless, trim city, with handsome residential streets built on the gentle hills overlooking the main harbor. It is a city of parks, ponds and gardens. Countless sculptures and statues adorn these greens apologizing for the absence of trees and offering testimony to the cultivation and the creativity of the people. Reykjavik is also a very small city, no more than 80,000 people. Its half-dozen hotels, while modern and comfortable, did not have facilities on the scale deemed necessary for the Presidents of the United States and France. This was more a matter of security and practicality than of comfort. We could not commandeer several floors of two entire hotels—the area required for correct support—when every hotel room in the nation would be at an absolute premium.

The American Ambassador's residence was a snug, refined townhouse adjoining the American Embassy on a narrow street in the heart of the city, a residence distinguished by an abnormally large dining room of recent vintage jutting out into the rear garden—an addition of the late 1960s constructed initially for a NATO Ministers' meeting. Our team decided that the President would best be accommodated at the official residence, as is often the case in summit travel. For their part, the members of the French pre-advance agreed; Pompidou and Nixon would stay at their official diplomatic residences. The Secretary of State, the Secretary of the Treasury and all the other members of the American Party, including Ambassador Irving and his family, would be housed in the Loftleidir Hotel overlooking the cross-runways of the old downtown airport. The French would take Hotel Esja, and the press—so many reporters and so few rooms—the bulk of the press would be quartered aboard a chartered cruise ship in the harbor.

As the plans took shape, we would recommend that President Nixon have his substantive talks with Iceland's leaders on the evening of his arrival, and that President Krisjan Eldjarn host a black tie dinner for the French and American leaders on May 31, at his 18th Century Bessastadir Bay residence, a pastoral setting overlooking the capital ten miles distant, the former home of Denmark's Governors. Additional pieces for the three days of talks fell into place; however, the site of the U.S.-French talks still had to be identified. Neither the hotels nor any of the government buildings offered what our pre-advance party was looking for. We had the requirement to provide not only for the two Presidents but also for concurrent meetings to be conducted at the Cabinet/Ministerial level on issues of international finance, trade and foreign affairs. Of greater importance, the site clearly would have to be *Presidential*!

By 1973, President Nixon's advance men had acquired a swashbuckling reputation. A year earlier, on the eve of the President's visit to Ottawa, they had proposed—albeit unsuccessfully—changing the color of Prime Minister Trudeau's office furniture and appointments from tan to blue to provide a 'more congenial' background for television coverage.[4]

Shortly thereafter, the advance men had won several duels with Soviet protocol over the complex scenario for the first Nixon-Brezhnev Moscow summit. Now, our highly capable, quick-witted, gregarious pre-advance leader, in charge of his own pre-advance mission carried this 'can do' spirit to Iceland.

Reykjavik had a newly constructed cultural treasure, the Kjarval Art Gallery, or Kjarvalsstadir, a handsome architectural success set apart on large grounds in the center of the capital. Security would be excellent, The Gallery's interior had a sparkling freshness and aura of good taste. A commodious office off the main floor offered the right setting for the Presidents' tete-a-tetes. However, the main floor was completely open, with no separate chambers for the contemplated meetings between Secretary of State Rogers, Foreign Minister Jobert and their aides, and the finance meetings between Secretary of the Treasury Shultz, Finance Minister Giscard d'Estaing and their supporting casts. Our pre-advance team huddled with our hosts and the French, and the solution emerged. The Government of Iceland would construct two large conference rooms within the Gallery—complete with walls, doors, conference tables and chairs—solely for the purpose of the summit. The Gallery would become a conference center for the last day of May and the first of June. This was the pre-advance; with our mission completed, we returned to Washington.

On May 27, the White House Advance Office distributed the detailed schedule, the 'bibles', for the trip. I was manifested aboard the second of the two Air Force Boeing 707s reserved for the President. The staff schedule reflected the key items in our pre-advance negotiations. It offers a useful introductory guide to any prospective summit sherpa.

THE WHITE HOUSE
WASHINGTON
ABBREVIATED STAFF SCHEDULE
TRIP OF THE PRESIDENT
TO MEET PRESIDENT POMPIDOU
Reykjavik, Iceland
May 30–31, and June 1, 1973

The final detailed schedule will be distributed on board 26000 upon boarding at Andrews Air Force Base on Wednesday, May 30, 1973.

Weather Forecast: For May and June, the average high temperature is 50 degrees, low overnight 30 degrees. More than half the days during these months are rainy, windy and overcast.

BLACK TIE will be required for dinner guests Thursday, May 31, 1973.

Wednesday, May 30, 1973

9:45 a.m. EDT	26000 departs Andrews AFB en route Keflavik, Iceland. (Flying time: 5 hours, 15 minutes) (Time change: + 4 hours)
10:00 a.m.	S'76 departs Andrews AFB en route Keflavik, Iceland. (Flying time: 5 hours, 30 minutes) (Time change: + 4 hours) NOTE: S'76 will fly over volcanic eruption on Westmann Islands.
7:00 p.m. IST	26000 arrives Keflavik
7:30 p.m. Advanceman:	S'76 arrives Keflavik
Dewey Clower	Arrival ceremony
9:00 p.m.	The President meets with President Eldjarn at State Council House.

Participants:

United States	**Iceland**
The President	President Eldjarn
Secretary Rogers	Prime Minister Johannesson
Dr. Kissinger	Foreign Minister Agustsson
9:30 p.m.	Talks conclude

OVERNIGHT
Thursday, May 31, 1973

9:40 a.m.	Staff motorcade departs en route Kjarvalsstadir.
9:53 a.m.	President's motorcade departs en route Kjarvalsstadir.

9:58 a.m.	Arrive Kjarvalsstadir (Head-to-Head Meeting Site). The President greets President Pompidou on his arrival.
10:00 a.m.	Meeting begins. Counterparts meet separately.

Foreign Policy
United States
Secretary Rogers
Assistant Secretary Stoessel
Ambassador Irwin
Denis Clift

Economic Policy
United States
Secretary Shultz
Under Secretary Volcker
Deputy Special Representative Malmgren

12:00 Noon	Meetings conclude. Return to residence/hotel.

PERSONAL STAFF TIME
2 HOURS, 44 MINUTES

2:50 p.m.	Staff motorcade departs for Kjarvalsstadir.
2:54 p.m.	President's motorcade departs en route Kjarvalsstadir.
2:59 p.m.	President arrives Kjarvalsstadir.
3:00 p.m.	Meeting begins. Same counterparts meet separately.

PERSONAL STAFF TIME
2 HOURS, 20 MINUTES

7:30 p.m.	Staff motorcade departs en route President Eldjarn's Residence.
7:40 p.m.	President's motorcade departs en route President Eldjarn's Residence.

U.S. Dinner Guest List
The President
Secretary Rogers
Secretary Shultz
Ambassador Irving
Ambassador Irwin
Dr. Kissinger
General Haig
Mr. Ronald Ziegler
Under Secretary Volcker

8:00 p.m.	Reception begins.
8:30 p.m.	Dinner begins. Toasts.
11:00 p.m.	Dinner concludes. President and party return to residences.

OVERNIGHT

Friday, June 1, 1973

9:50 a.m.	Staff motorcade departs en route Kjarvalsstadir.
9:53 a.m.	President's motorcade departs en route Kjarvalsstadir.

10:00 a.m.	Meeting begins. Same counterparts meet separately.
11:30 a.m.	Meetings conclude. Presidents, followed by their counterparts, proceed to plenary session.
12:15 p.m.	Bus will depart Loftleidir Hotel for those not participating in the meetings en route Keflavik Airport.
12:35 p.m.	Plenary session concludes.
12:40 p.m.	Motorcade departs en route Keflavik Airport.
1:25 p.m.	Arrive Keflavik Airport, Departure ceremony.
1:35 p.m.	S'76 departs Keflavik en route Andrews AFB. (Flying time: 5 hours, 50 minutes) (Time change: – 4 hours)
3:25 p.m. EDT	S'76 arrives Andrews AFB.
3:40 p.m.	26000 arrives Andrews AFB.

As reflected in the schedule, the entire focus of the summit was on those hours set aside for the substantive talks, with an absolute minimum of ceremonial events. What, in fact, transpired?

Of the May 30, 40-minute session with Prime Minister Johannesson and his colleagues, Secretary Kissinger would write: "We found them polite but only slightly interested in the Franco-American Summit. Their overwhelming concern was the war they were about to start with Britain over cod fish...The Icelandic Ministers were uttering dire threats of escalating military action while Nixon and Rogers implored them to withhold the final sanction."[5] While he was far more diplomatic at the time, telling the press that the United States was pained by this dispute between friends and would do its best to contribute to a constructive solution, the U.S. position was seen by a disillusioned Icelandic public as one of indifference. The summit presence of the President in Iceland in the middle of the Cod War did not advance U.S. interests. The dispute, however, would eventually be resolved. Iceland and America are today the best of friends, and Great Britain and Iceland remain allies in the NATO Alliance.

The U.S.-French talks produced a result which on the surface was minimal but which, in fact, would make a very positive contribution to the Year of Europe process. The French, of course, had arrived in Iceland determined to make no concessions to the Year of Europe initiative. Following the first day of talks, Pompidou would only authorize the U.S. side to state that in the course of the day's review of relations within the Atlantic Alliance, the French President had stressed the important role played by U.S. forces in Europe and the danger of unilateral reduction of those forces.

In his toast at President Eldjarn's dinner, Pompidou continued to steer a very general course not veering from the status quo: "As world relations alter, Europe gradually and patiently discovers the road towards unity, a unity which is necessary but not thereby easier to achieve. There again there is marked progress.

"Would it mean that relations between the U.S. and Europe, and more specifically between the United States and France, have lost some of their urgency or interest? Certainly not. We know the place of Europe in your concern. For our part, however favorable may developments be in the world situation, we believe that it is still too fraught with uncertainties for the need for our alliance to decline."[6]

Jobert would triumphantly sum up his assessment of the summit in a single sentence: "On the issue of money, of Europe, the Atlantic Charter and international commerce, the agreement which they awaited from the President of France did not come."[7]

Behind the closed doors of the Kjarval Art Gallery on May 31 and June 1, the U.S.-French talks had covered considerable ground. In their private sessions, the two Presidents had ranged across developments relating to Europe, South East Asia, the Middle East, monetary and trade matters and the SALT and MBFR negotiations. Secretary Shultz and Minister Giscard d'Estaing had dealt at a greater level of specificity with the international balance of payments situation, the question of Special Drawing Rights, and the need for overriding political will on the part of western democracies to overcome the prickly problems of international trade. Foreign Minister Jobert and Secretary of State Rogers had spent considerable time in their counterpart talks examining Middle East developments. They had also talked at length on Asian developments—Vietnam, Cambodia, the role of China—and here the newly appointed White House Chief of Staff Alexander Haig had offered a careful assessment based on his most recent visit to South Vietnam.

The art gallery arrangements, so carefully crafted, had provided the fact and the public appearance of the broadest most substantive possible discussions. The three-chambered arrangements had given Nixon the maximum opportunity for one-on-one talks with Pompidou without distracting or counterproductive interjections by subordinates from either side. In Kissinger's words: "This gave Nixon a pretext for excluding Bill Rogers and Pompidou for doing without Valery Giscard d'Estaing. At Nixon's request, I joined the two presidents as note-taker. No doubt this added to Jobert's resentment. Having been 'elevated' to Foreign Minister, he now found himself relegated to a secondary forum."[8] From my vantage point at Secretary Rogers' left hand during those talks, I had observed Jobert treat the situation with drole good grace. Each time the American Secretary of State had attempted to pursue one of the central U.S.-European issues, Jobert would smile and turn the discussion aside with the comment, "But, of course, Mr. Secretary, that is being discussed down the hall."

The front-page headline of *The New York Times* of June 2, 1973, would proclaim; "Nixon, Pompidou Conclude Talks; Some Gains Seen." President Pompidou would repeat to the press the same encouraging line that he had delivered to the summit's concluding plenary session, noting that "We haven't given birth, but we have conceived, and conception is usually more pleasant that delivery." The press was further informed that Dr. Kissinger and Foreign Minister Jobert had already agreed to meet in Paris on June 7, to follow up on the meetings at Reykjavik.

Despite French satisfaction over lack of agreement on specifics, the very fact of the summit was its success. With the Iceland summit, the United States had taken another highly visible step in the larger process of re-asserting its influence on the direction of U.S.-European relations. With the commitment of the prestige of the President to this process, the United States was dramatizing the increase in priority being accorded to the U.S.-European relationship. With each new step in this process, the United States was underlining to the Governments of Europe that the U.S. voice would be heard and that U.S. influence would be increasingly felt. While the original Year of Europe calendar would not be met in every specific, by 1974 the United States would have reinserted itself as a full partner with Western Europe in the shaping of U.S.-European relations. The NATO Ministers would reach agreement on a Declaration of Principles to guide the relationship, new U.S.-European mechanisms would be developed to grapple with the mounting energy crisis, and new summit-level multilateral forums—the very forums so resolutely opposed by France in 1973, would be established with the first of the new, annual Economic Summits of the seven most influential industrialized democracies to be held at Rambouillet, France in 1975. For America, with the launching of the process, the U.S.-French summit at Reykjavik had accomplished its most important objective.

On the flight back to Washington aboard 26000, I had the pleasure of entertaining Haraldur Kroyer, Iceland's Ambassador to the United States. Kroyer was about to be reassigned to Geneva. This would mean a sacrifice for his family; his son would have to surrender a prized possession. As the 1973 Reykjavik summit drew to a close, the Ambassador and I toasted the conclusion of final agreement. My family would adopt the Kroyer's four-foot yellow rat snake Tiger Eye.

There would be other serpents in my sherpa's travels. Before recounting those adventures and the lessons they offered, it is useful first to take a very quick look at the history of official travels abroad by U.S. President, and at the evolution of summit diplomacy as an instrument of America's foreign policy.

End Notes

1. Kissinger, Henry A., *The Year of Europe*, address to the Associated Press Annual luncheon, Waldorf Astoria Hotel, New York, April 23, 1973.

2. Kissinger, Henry A., Press Conference, The White House, May 29, 1973.

3. Jobert, Michel, *Memories d'Avenir*, Bernard Grasset, Paris, 1974, page 232.

4. Martin, Lawrence, *The Presidents and the Prime Ministers*, Doubleday Canada Limited, Toronto, 1982, page 20.

5. Kissinger, Henry A., *Years of Upheaval*, Little Brown and Company, Boston, Toronto, 1982, page 172.

6. Address by the President of the French Republic, Reykjavik, May 31, 1973.

7. Jobert, Michel, *Memories d'Avenir*, Bernard Grasset, Paris, 1974, page 232.

8. Kissinger, Henry A., *Years of Upheaval*, Little Brown and Company, Boston, Toronto, 1982, page 175.

CHAPTER TWO
Head-to-Head

When a chief of state or head of government makes a fumble, the goal line is open behind him. This I was to learn in my first experience with this dangerous diplomatic method, which has such attraction for American Presidents.

Present at the Creation
Dean Acheson, 1969

Tucked in the garden at the front steps of Syracuse University's Maxwell School of Citizenship there is a statue of Lincoln so deep in thought that the enormity of his Presidential burden at once stirs inspiration and compassion. "No one can experience with the President the glory and the agony of his office," Lyndon Johnson has observed, "...the President represents all the people and must face up to all the problems."[1]

As the international involvement of the United States has grown through the 20th Century, the President's absolute responsibility for the conduct of U.S. foreign policy has placed mounting demands on his time in office. The drive for achievement and success; the need to lead public opinion and at the same time to be responsive to key domestic interests; the acute need for precise timing of decisive action to capitalize on opportunity or to stem the adverse have singly or in combination led Presidents increasingly to bypass traditional diplomatic practice. To attain critical foreign policy goals in war and peace, American Presidents have turned to the direct application of the unique powers of their office at the summit.

The evolution of summitry as a diplomatic practice favored by American Presidents has been accompanied and accelerated by the unceasing, expanding rush of new technology since the turn of the century. Increasingly efficient summit cocoons have been spun for successive Presidents permitting all technical and staff support required to conduct the operational business of the White House—a fully effective traveling White House—anywhere in the world.

The first foreign travel by any American President was not until 1906, and that was not to the summit but to the ditch. Teddy Roosevelt sailed from Norfolk, Virginia aboard the USS *Louisiana* on November 9, 1906, for a first-hand inspection of the digging and building of his bold creation, the Panama Canal. On the journey south, he reflected on his pioneering journey in a letter to Kermit Roosevelt, with his words capturing the pace of the voyage that would land him in Panama on the 14th, with departure on the 17th and return to the United States on the 26th:

On Board USS *Louisiana*, November 1906

Dear Kermit:

So far the trip has been a great success, and I think Mother has really enjoyed it. As for me I of course feel a little bored as I always do on shipboard, but I have brought on a great variety of books, and am at this moment reading Milton's prose works, Tacitus and a German novel called *Jorn Uhl*. Mother and I walk briskly up and down the deck together or else sit aft under the awning or in the after cabin, with the gun ports open and read; and I also spend a good deal of time on the forward bridge and sometimes on the aft bridge, and of course have gone over the ship to inspect it with the Captain. It is a splendid thing to see one of these men-of-war, and it really does make one proud of one's country...We are now in the tropics and I have thought a good deal of the time over eight years ago when I was sailing to Santiago in the fleet of warships and transports. It seems a strange thing to think of my now being President, going to visit the work of the Panama Canal which I have made possible...[2]

If it was good enough for Roosevelt, it was good enough for William Howard Taft who would make the second foreign voyage of a President, traveling to Panama in early 1909 to check on the progress of the Canal and to meet with the President of Panama. Taft would also make the third foreign excursion, a one-day, cross-border meeting in Ciudad Juarez with President Diaz of Mexico on October 16, 1909.

A decade then passed before the first of America's true summiteers, President Woodrow Wilson, headed the U.S. Delegation to the Paris Peace Conference at the end of World War I. In examining the anatomy of summiting, the foreign policy practices of Wilson, his staffing, and his technique for gaining information and for diplomatic probing over a period of years prior to his unprecedented journey are as noteworthy as the peace conference itself.

In the person of Colonel Edward Mandell House, Wilson would for the first time entrust the role of White House personal diplomatic emissary and foreign policy advisor to the President, a role which later would be Harry Hopkins' under Franklin Delano Roosevelt, would become institutionalized by successive national security advisors to the President following enactment of the National Security Act of 1947, and would achieve its greatest prominence as played by Henry Kissinger under Presidents Nixon and Ford.

House had made himself known and valuable to Wilson before the election of 1912. Following the election, he had become the President-elect's closest adviser. "Wilson knew that he could trust both the information and the judgment of the "Little Wizard" in New York. House could see so much more than other men and report it so much better, always getting the right point! The hand of the Colonel was constantly on the shaping of the President's Cabinet."[3] That shaping included the naming of William Jennings Bryan as Secretary of State.

In this century, while Presidents have relied totally on the professionals of the Foreign Service and the Department of State for the day-to-day management and implementation of foreign policy, they have to greater or lesser degree tended to shy away from the Department of State in the shaping and launching of critical initiatives. This has not been a complicated determination. Presidents take seriously their right to lead. Presidents believe seriously in their right to weigh alternatives—indeed, alternatives to the status quo being tended by their governmental departments. They believe they have the right to take their own decisions following the weighing of options, and to enact those decisions at the time and place of their choosing. In practice, this is not an easy business.

This is not to say that the government bureaucracy is not most times well-intentioned. The fact is that a President's word carries unbelievable authority, and unless that word is delivered to the desired audience with precision, it can be subject to the most counterproductive misinterpretations. My first taste of this goes back to my Antarctic days.

I had listened to Jack Kennedy's inaugural address via the BBC at a friend's home in Wellington, New Zealand while the icebreaker USS *Glacier* was in dry dock completing her refitting for the 1961 Bellingshausen Sea Expedition. The *Glacier* and the USS *Staten Island* set sail on January 29, 1961. As part of my official duties, I was responsible for writing the sole news dispatches from the expedition; they ran regularly in the New Zealand press; and were picked up by the wire services for release in the United States. And, there were some exciting stories. The headline and lead sentence on February 17, in *The New York Times*: "4 SCIENTISTS SAVED IN ANTARCTIC STORM—Navy helicopters have rescued four scientists trapped in the Antarctic by a blizzard with freezing winds of more than 100 miles an hour..." Another dispatch reported our ships momentarily locked in the Antarctic ice.

As the story eventually would be told to me, the new President took an interest in the drama of the expedition and asked his Naval Aide to keep him abreast of developments. This expression of interest rippled downward through the Navy's chain of command, and by the time it reached our two ships it had been distorted into a stern, clipped message ordering the expedition's Commodore to get his two ships out of the Antarctic pack ice immediately to avoid being trapped for the winter. We had been biding our time, as polar seamen must, awaiting a shift in the winds that would produce open leads of water in the sea permitting us to exit. However, the order just received sent officers and men over the side and onto the ice with dynamite to blast a path through the ice to open water. We blasted away for more than a day with little effect; ice is elastic and easily absorbs the force of an explosion. Then the winds shifted and we were again underway and free.

Misinterpretation of a President's instructions is not always accidental. Those who are entrusted with carrying out existing policy are not always inspired by the possibility of a change of direction, and those who are opposed may do their best to block or undercut a directive or even a testing of the waters. Woodrow Wilson looked to his State Department for the government's daily foreign policy business, but he looked to Colonel House as his instrument of initiative. From 1914–1917, House would undertake repeated overseas missions personally directed by the President who was searching for a way to mediate the end of the war.

Wilson dedicated more than half a year to the Treaty of Versailles, setting sail for Paris on December 4, 1918, for negotiations preliminary to the Paris Peace Conference; visits to Great Britain, Italy and The Vatican; the Peace Conference; a brief return for business in the United States in February 1919; and then again to Paris from March through mid-June and the signing of the treaty that would bring an uneasy peace and would create the League of Nations. Before his return to the United States and the exhausting challenge to his achievements in Europe he visited Belgium on June 18–19, to address the Parliament. Wilson's brilliance as a statesman had been matched by his innovations in diplomacy and summit staffing.

Presidents Harding and Coolidge reverted to an earlier style, with Harding paying the obligatory visit in 1920 to the Canal and touching foot in Canada in 1923, en route home from Alaska, and Coolidge venturing only once abroad—to Havana, Cuba for a hemispheric conference in 1928. President Herbert Hoover also limited his travels to this hemisphere with a pioneering good-will visit to several nations, a summit practice that would gain increasing popularity with his successors. On November 26, 1928, while still President-elect, he departed for Central and South America on an odyssey that would take him to Honduras, El Slavador, Nicaragua, Costa Rica, Ecuador, Peru, Chile, Argentina, Uruguay, with a final call at Rio de Janeiro, Brazil on December 21–23, 1928. The First, tentative chapter on American summitry was coming to an end.

August 9–12, 1941, marked the beginning of a totally new, dramatic, decisive personal involvement by an American President in the shaping of world affairs—the first of the wartime summit talks between President Franklin Delano Roosevelt and Prime Minister Winston Churchill at Argentia, Newfoundland. These talks also saw further refinement to the art of summiting.

In terms of foreign visits, Roosevelt's first two terms, from 1932 through 1940, had been no more than routine: informal stops in the Caribbean and the Canal Zone en route to and from visits to the East Coast and Hawaii; two trips to Canada in 1936 and 1938; more vacation trips to the salubrious Caribbean and Gulf with stops in Panama; and an official swing through Brazil, Argentina, and Uruguay in the autumn of 1936.

The world had changed drastically by the summer of 1941. Roosevelt dispatched his White House Assistant Harry Hopkins to London on "the pre-advance." On August 3, 1941, the President departed Washington for New London, Connecticut where he boarded the Presidential yacht *Potomac* for a fishing trip. Under cover of darkness, he transferred to the cruiser USS *Augusta*, which proceeded with wartime destroyer escort to Argentia harbor to await Churchill who was steaming across the Atlantic aboard the *Prince of Wales*, the Royal Navy's prized battleship fresh with the scars of her encounter with Hitler's *Bismarck*.[4] Using an emissary to set the stage, and resorting to secrecy on the voyage, for reasons of both security and international politics (secrecy so contrary to the ideals and so difficult to the practice of American democracy), had gained status that would be lasting as accepted options in the business of summitry.

"Before embarking for his meeting with Churchill, the President had mapped out his ideas in the form and spirit of a joint declaration of the English-speaking democracies. By emphasizing that any postwar order should be based on principles of freedom, justice, security and access to raw materials and natural resources, the President felt that the peoples of the world would derive new hope in their resistance to Nazism."[5] By August 11, Roosevelt and Churchill, working with their senior advisers, had reached agreement on a statement of common principles guiding the policies of the United States and the United Kingdom. The Atlantic Charter, as it would be known, was a document that would become a model for many subsequent summit declarations in the post-World-War-II era. Broad in its carefully crafted language, far-reaching in its vision, the Charter was a document that advanced the national political needs of each leader, declaring to the world the spirit of unity between the United States and the United Kingdom, while at the same time addressing issues still to be resolved between the two countries in language that could be interpreted to suit the domestic political exigencies of either leader. The Charter was a shared commitment to a shared future goal that also left U.S.-U.K. negotiations and agreements on detailed commitments and undertakings to the future. A bond, not a treaty, the declaration of principles was now a part of U.S. summit practice.

The drafting of the Atlantic Charter at Argentia launched a succession of important summit meetings between Roosevelt and Churchill, with increasing inclusion of other allied leaders as World War II progressed. The second in this series of meetings was at Casablanca in January 1943, which marked the introduction of a truly revolutionary new instrument of summitry, the aircraft.

Even before America's formal entry into the war the United States had begun to fly lend-lease war supplies across the Atlantic in support of the British and other allied forces. In her chronicle of the war, *Journey Among Warriors*, Eve Curie captured the dramatic history of Pan American Airways pioneering flight of the flying boat Clipper *Cape Town* across the South Atlantic to Africa en route to the war zone. It was a lengthy journey for Curie and the plane load of mechanics and pilots going to West Africa to begin ferrying warplanes to the front. The *Cape Town* departed New York on Monday, November 10, 1941, refueled at Bermuda, arrived that evening at San Juan, Puerto Rico, departed at one o'clock the following morning for Port of Spain, Trinidad, then down across the Equator and the Amazon River to the nighttime landing off Belem, Brazil. After another rest overnight, the Clipper departed for Natal on Brazil's easternmost cape jutting far out into the South Atlantic—the jump-off point for Africa—and on Thursday morning, November 13, the *Cape Town* delivered its passengers to a British motor launch off the port city of Bathurst, British Gambia.[6]

On January 11, 1943, President Roosevelt boarded Pan American Airways *Dixie Clipper* in Miami, following a train trip from Washington, and the big flying boat honored to be making the first Presidential flight overseas arced south and east from Port of Prince, to Belem, to Bathurst. There, the cruiser USS *Memphis* quartered the President before his departure for Morocco aboard a C-54 on January 14, 1943. Following Roosevelt's strategy sessions with Churchill on the invasion of southern Europe, their meetings with the estranged French Generals De Gaulle and Giraud, and the President's meeting in the field with U.S. forces, Roosevelt again returned to Bathurst for the hospitality of the *Memphis* prior to his return flight to the United States via Liberia, Brazil, and Trinidad, with the last leg on January 29. "He was hollow-eyed and tired by now; the long hours in the air had been distressing, for flying 'affects my head just as ocean cruising affects yours' he wrote his wife."[7] The summit trip had spanned 17 days, three continents, safely above the threat of Nazi U-boats. The *Dixie Clipper's* historic mission did not mark the end of the warship's role in overseas Presidential transportation, but it signaled that the shift to the air was already on the horizon.

1943 was to be a year of extremely heavy summit travel for Roosevelt: a round of good neighbor talks with President Avila at Monterrey, Mexico in April; a resumption from August 17–25, of the face-to-face strategic discussions with Churchill in Canada; then another arduous trip across the Atlantic from mid-November to mid-December for the Cairo Conference with Churchill and Stalin, follow-up talks with Churchill in Cairo in early December, consultations with General Eisenhower and visits to the troops in Malta and Sicily before re-boarding the battleship USS *Iowa* for the voyage home. In the midst of global conflict, the 1943 meetings served to highlight still another unique dimension of power that any American President brings to the summit table—the power of Commander-in-Chief of all U.S. Armed Forces.

Following D-Day and the success of the allied landings in Europe, Roosevelt and Churchill met again in Quebec in September 1944. With the continued advance of allied forces against the Germans and the Japanese, the need to grapple with looming post-war international political problems again sent the American President to the Mediterranean and on to the Soviet Union for the Yalta conference with Churchill and Stalin from February 3–12, 1945. In his report to the Congress on March 1, 1945, just weeks before his death, Roosevelt described the agreements the summit leaders had reached to bring the war to an end as quickly as possible, and the results of his efforts with Churchill and Stalin to provide for international order and security with the return of peace.

Roosevelt's report on Yalta illuminated both the personal dimension of summit negotiations and the underlying sharing of responsibility in the United States among the President, the Congress, and the American people. Of his role—the personal role that only a President can bring—he said: "There was on all sides at the Conference an enthusiastic effort to reach an agreement. Since the time of Tehran, a year ago, there had developed among us—what shall I call it—a greater facility in negotiating with each other, that augurs well for the peace of the world. We know each other better." And, of the implications of Yalta for the United States, he said: "Speaking in all frankness, the question of whether or not it is entirely fruitful or not lies to a great extent in your hands. For unless you here in the halls of the American Congress—with the support of the American people—concur in the general conclusions reached at Yalta and give them your active support, the meeting will not have produced lasting results."[8]

The next two Administrations included powerful, extremely influential Secretaries of State: Marshall and Acheson in the Truman years and John Foster Dulles at the right hand of President Eisenhower. President Truman slowed the pace on summit travel dramatically, with his first and only overseas voyage to Germany for the 1945 July–August Potsdam Conference. He continued the work of the difficult transition to peace with Stalin and Churchill—then, midway through the talks with Prime Minister Attlee following the British elections. Truman's subsequent meetings with foreign leaders were limited to visitors to the United States and to summit sites in the Western Hemisphere, and three sets of 1947 talks: Mexico City in March, Ottawa in June and Rio de Janeiro in September.

Truman had departed for Potsdam aboard the cruiser USS *Augusta*. As lead escort ship, the cruiser USS *Philadelphia* broke and smoothed the seas for the President and his party, and provided additional security. Truman's memoirs captured the advances in communications support for the President and the nearing of the final crossover from sea to air for overseas summitry. In describing his passage from Newport News, Virginia to Antwerp, Belgium he wrote: "During the nine days I had spent at sea I had been in constant touch with developments at home and in other parts of the world through the unique facilities which had been set up aboard ship. The office of the First Lieutenant of the *Augusta* had been made over into a communications center and was complete in every detail. This was designated as the Advance Map Room, corresponding to the Map Room in the White House. Here messages were received and transmitted in virtually the same volume and with the same dispatch as at the White House itself. For all practical purposes, the Advance Map Room was the White House during the time the *Augusta* was underway."[9]

The laconic, literary days of Teddy Roosevelt's first passage to the Panama Canal were now distant history; full White House support was gaining increasing mobility. The surface pace was now the principal, limiting factor. As Vice President, Truman had witnessed the introduction in June 1943 of FDR's first presidential aircraft, the *Guess Where II*, and then a year later, the second more famous Douglas DC-4 *Sacred Cow*. When Truman arrived in Europe as President, the *Sacred Cow* had preceded him and would fly him from Belgium to Germany and support him throughout the summit conference. On July 30, as Potsdam drew to a close, he commented on his return by ship to the United States in a letter to his mother and his sister Mary: "I'd rather fly...I could be home a week sooner. But they all yell their heads off when I talk of flying."[10] The war had accelerated the thrust of aviation and the continuing introduction of incredibly good new aircraft. By 1947, President Truman would exchange the two-engined *Sacred Cow* for the four-engined *Independence*, with its increased margin of safety and more domestic travel by air. Following Potsdam, however, the President would subordinate his meetings with foreign leaders to concentrate on towering internal organizational decisions. These decisions would affect the structure of the U.S. government, and shape the character of summitry in the decades to come.

Eighty years before, at the close of the Civil War, an inward-looking United States was suddenly so deeply absorbed with industrialization and the development of the American West that there was neither time nor enthusiasm for foreign affairs. In 1947, the United States, now a nuclear superpower, found itself responsible for the security and well-being of the entire 'Free World', and there was an urgent requirement to streamline and modernize the foreign policy and defense structure of the Executive Branch to give the President and the nation the mechanisms required to play America's new global role. The wartime, largely independent operations of the military services had to be meshed with the peacetime requirements of civilian control in the nuclear era. The world, although at peace, had become a far more dangerous place, and the United States felt a pressing need for more and more information about the activities and the intentions of other nations. U.S. Cabinet departments could no longer proceed independently with major decisions. The actions of one impacted on the actions of others and on the interests of the nation.

In 1947, the National Security Act was passed creating the Cabinet position of Secretary of Defense, in addition to the Service Secretaries. The Act created interdepartmental munitions, resources, and research and development boards, a Central Intelligence Agency, and a National Security Council to steer overall coordination.

In 1949, the Congress at Truman's request passed the National Security Act of 1947, as amended, consolidating and strengthening the role of the Secretary of Defense over the military services and trimming the membership of the National Security Council to the President, the Vice President, the Secretary of State and the Secretary of Defense, with a full-time civilian Executive Secretary and supporting staff. The Director of Central Intelligence and the Chairman of the Joint Chiefs of Staff would serve the Council as advisers. The Act provided that: "The function of the Council shall be to advise the President with respect to the integration of domestic, foreign, and military polices relating to the national security so as to enable the military services and the other departments and agencies of the Government to cooperate more effectively in matters involving the national security."[11] In President Truman's words: "The creation of the National Security Council added a badly needed new facility to the government. This was now the place in the government where military, diplomatic and resource problems could be studied and continually appraised. This new organization gave us a running balance and a perpetual inventory of where we stood and where we were going on all strategic questions affecting the national security."[12]

The NSC system did far more for the President. It placed the reins of foreign, defense, and international economic and resources policy effectively in his hands. It harnessed State, Defense and other Executive Branch departments, and on a continuing basis kept them pulling in the traces, willingly or not, however and for whatever required. It provided the President with a professional national security staff producing a continuing flow of professional assessments and other substantive support. This enabled the President to absorb and master the details of complex issues, often under tremendous time pressure, and to digest the range of options required for decision in a manner more thorough and objective than might otherwise have been possible had the information been coming directly from the Cabinet Secretaries.

Successive Presidents would exercise the capabilities of the National Security Council to differing degrees. As his memoirs reflected, President Truman used the NSC to consider all major national security issues. President Eisenhower, former Supreme Allied Commander, applied the staffing philosophy and experience of his military career, directing the expansion of the NSC committee and staff structure until the NSC system became the single, central mechanism for the consideration of all national security issues, with different elements of the staff supporting the decision-making and the implementation of decisions taken. "Under President Eisenhower, the NSC was a form of super department placed atop the traditional structure of executive departments and agencies to solve the problems that individual departments were unable to handle. Under Kennedy, the Council became one of several means by which problems might be solved."[13]

President Kennedy dismantled much of Eisenhower's extensive NSC committee structure. President Johnson cut back even further on the size of the staff and formal use of the Council, keeping the NSC structure in place but preferring to address national security issues—particularly those relating to Vietnam—in less formal White House settings with his principal foreign policy, defense and intelligence advisers. The National Security Council would be revived as a major instrument of Government under President Nixon. And, as I would immediately appreciate when I joined the NSC staff in 1971, the NSC system would enable the President to control the pace and direction of foreign affairs, and of his meetings with foreign leaders, no matter how complex or contentious the issues might be within the U.S. government.

As the NSC system evolved and matured from the late 1940s on, it reinforced successive Presidents' confidence in their ability to take charge of thorny foreign policy and to pursue them in face-to-face contact with other leaders. As the Cold War deepened through the

1950s and 1960s, each in turn would go for the ultimate brass ring—a summit with the leaders of the Soviet Union.

While President-elect, Dwight David Eisenhower moved swiftly on his promise to end the Korean War with a visit to the Korean war zone from December 2–5, 1952. By the end of his second administration in 1960, Ike had traveled the world in the cause of peace and friendship. In December 1959, he welcomed the introduction of the first four-engine jet to the Air Force's fleet of Presidential aircraft with the pioneering, whirlwind, 'barnstorming' summit swing through several nations that would retain popularity with future Presidents in the 1960s, 1970s, and 1980s—a tete-a-tete, a speech, a banquet; 24-hours here, 36 hours there—Rome, Italy; The Vatican; Ankara, Turkey; Karachi, Pakistan; Kabul, Afghanistan; New Dehli, India; Tehran, Iran; Athens, Greece; Tunis, Tunisia; Paris, France; Madrid, Spain; Casablanca, Morocco; then the homeward dash back across the Atlantic. The big jets could set a dazzling pace, a pace their powerful passengers longed for and strove to master.

President Eisenhower underlined his firm belief in the power of personal diplomacy: "Experience both before and after becoming President had confirmed my instinctive feeling that at all levels of government, face-to-face, friendly discussions offer advantages that can scarcely be realized through written communication and secondary representations."[14] The war years had given Eisenhower, while still in uniform, a wealth of political experience. He was at ease with foreign leaders. He had gained the admiration and respect of Presidents, Prime Ministers and crowned Heads of State. He appreciated both the ways and the imperatives of international politics.

President Eisenhower understood the complete responsibility a summit leader must bear for the success or failure of such personal diplomacy. His approach to the 1959 Camp David Summit with Premier Nikita Khrushchev, and related meetings with allied leaders exhibited the particular attention he gave to the fine points of summitry. Eisenhower appreciated the need for careful preparations for meetings with an adversary, as he underscored in his letter to British Prime Minister Harold Macmillan on June 3: "As you know, I adhere to my position that a summit meeting based on nothing more than wishful thinking would be a disaster. The world would interpret such a move as being virtual surrender, while Soviet prestige would be enhanced...."[15] He appreciated the need for genuine consultations with America's most important allies, the need to engage them as diplomatic partners, not to relegate them to bystanders with the resulting negative impact on their domestic political positions, and on relations with the United States.

In August 1959, Eisenhower flew to Bonn, London, and Paris for a week of consultations with Chancellor Adenauer, Macmillan, and President De Gaulle. He was alert to the possibilities of progress reaching beyond the stated purpose of such a visit: "For sometime I had been searching for an opportunity to renew personal contact with General Charles De Gaulle, who had returned to power in France only the previous year. His unfavorable stance toward certain Western problems was caused by an unwavering and understandable purpose: restoring the prestige of France. I hoped that by renewing old associations and revealing my sympathetic understanding of his purpose, I possibly could encourage him to become more flexible in his views respecting NATO's command arrangement."[16]

Through summitry, Eisenhower had learned the value of face-to-face dialogue, consultations with allies, and the possibilities of positive side-results (spin offs) from such talks. He also recognized the requirement for precise, professional tactics and strategy with the Soviets. This was augmented by his philosophic approach to the question of a President's prestige at the summit in the broader context of the need to avoid nuclear war, and to provide genuine leadership. As he told reporters: "I emphasized that the search for some break, some avenue of approach, as yet unexplored, through which we might move to a better relationship between East and West, was truly vital. The costs Americans bore every year for armaments were staggering. If this went on indefinitely, we could reach a breaking point. Consequently, any President who recoiled from using the last atom of his own prestige or energy in the attempt to find an acceptable approach to the dilemma should be condemned by the American people."[17]

The Camp David summit could be measured a success, with Khrushchev exposed both to the President's resolve and, during his visit to the U.S., the incredible achievements of the American nation. However, the following year, American prestige again was on the line. Khrushchev scuttled the U.S.-U.K.-French-USSR quadripartite summit in Paris by demanding—the unacceptable demand—that the American President apologize for the U-2 reconnaissance flight just downed on Soviet territory. In January 1961, the quest for better relations with the Soviets passed from Ike to JFK.

President John F. Kennedy set a moderate pace for summit travel during his brief Presidency: in 1961, an address to the Canadian Parliament in May; talks with de Gaulle in Paris, with Khrushchev in

Vienna, and with Macmillan in London during the last week of May and the first week of June; and flights to Caracas, Bogota and Burmuda during the course of December for meetings with the Venezuelan and Colombian Presidents and a second round of talks with Macmillan.

In June 1962, the President paid a State Visit to Mexico, and that December he again met with Macmillan, in Nassau, the Bahamas, to conclude an agreement on future U.S.-U.K. nuclear cooperation. By 1963, a splendid new Boeing 707, tail number 26000 and still part of the Air Force fleet today, had become Air Force I. Kennedy attended the Conference of Presidents of the Central American Republics in San Jose, Costa Rica that March. In late June and early July, he undertook his final, most memorable overseas mission: to the Federal Republic of Germany for talks with Adenauer; on to West Berlin to deliver his famous "Ich bin ein Berliner" speech underlining America's commitment to the divided city; on to Ireland to address the Parliament and to visit the land and the home of his ancestors; to Great Britain for talks with Macmillan; to Rome for meetings with the Italian President; and to the Vatican City on July 2, 1963, for an audience with Pope Paul VI.

The President had entered the White House eager to break the Cold War stalemate with the Soviet Union. "Kennedy had a natural curiosity about Khrushchev; what Isaiah Berlin once called the royal-cousins approach to diplomacy has an allure, sometimes fatal, for all heads of state. Moreover, Kennedy, unlike [Secretary of State] Rusk, had no doctrinaire opposition to the idea of summitry. 'It is far better,' he had observed in 1959, 'that we meet at the summit than at the brink.' "[18]

The 1961 Vienna talks did not produce the desired break-through. During his subsequent stopover in London, Kennedy sought to play down the event when he was asked by a BBC correspondent if Macmillan's absence was a reflection on the U.K.'s diminished stature: "Oh no—this was not intended to be a summit meeting. Mr. Macmillan himself, the Prime Minister, has seen Mr. Khrushchev on several occasions. But I bear the responsibilities as President of the United States, and I felt it important to have an exchange of views with Mr. Khrushchev, and also to make clear our position; and particularly I was—after that conversation I was anxious to see the Prime Minister.

"But this was this not a summit meeting, but it was an opportunity to make a more precise judgment as to our future course."[19]

In summitry, the risk of international miscalculation accompanies national calibration of judgment. In August 1961, the Soviets proceeded with the erection of the Berlin Wall, necessitating the President's trip to reassure the divided city the following summer.

With the deepening, black shadow of the Cuban missile crisis in October 1962, there was no longer any illusion that face-to-face diplomacy alone would provide the solution. Late in the evening of October 23, 1962, with Soviet ships steaming toward Cuba, only hours before the U.S. quarantine went into effect, the President, his brother the Attorney General, and Ambassador Ormsby-Gore of Great Britain conversed in the White House, informally weighing the President's tactical choice. "The President talked abut the possibility of arranging an immediate summit with Khrushchev, but finally dismissed the idea, concluding that such a meeting would be useless until Khrushchev first accepted, as a result of our deeds as well as our statements, the U.S. determination in this matter. Before a summit took place, and it should, the President wanted to have some cards in his own hands."[20] The United States prevailed; the Soviet missiles were withdrawn; the crisis passed.

The occasion did not arise for a summit with the Soviets in 1963. The final weeks of Kennedy's Presidency did include the successful culmination of eight years of exploration and negotiations with the signing of the Limited Nuclear Test Ban Treaty in October 1963. This marked an important step forward. However, the burden of attempting the next step now fell to Lyndon Johnson, who held his first face-to-face, get-acquainted talk with Soviet Deputy Premier Anastas Mikoyan on the fringe of the Kennedy Funeral.

From late 1963 through 1968, President Johnson's foreign summit travel was heavily influenced both by the tragic circumstances of his accession to the Presidency and by the war in Vietnam. As Vice President during the Kennedy years, Johnson had taken numerous official overseas trips. Now as President, with no Vice President until the elections of November 1964, Johnson stayed close to home concentrating on domestic issues and making only one, brief cross-border visit to Vancouver for talks with Canadian Prime Minister Pearson, and the Columbia River Treaty ceremonies in September 1964.

Following another domestic year in 1965, Johnson made trips first to Mexico and Canada, and then in October–November 1966, as both President and Commander-in-Chief, undertook the first of his far-reaching jet swings through the Pacific for talks with America's allies and to the war zone to visit the troops at Cam Ranh Bay. In 1967, he returned to the front on a whirlwind global flight that took him to the funeral of Prime Minister Holt in Canberra, Australia; to Thailand and Vietnam for visits with the troops; on to Karachi, Pakistan for talks with President Ayub Khan; to Rome; to Vatican City and back to Washington—all in one week's time. 1967 had also included flights to Punta del Este, Uruguay for a multilateral Latin American Summit; to Bonn for Chancellor Adenauer's funeral, and bilateral discussions with foreign leaders also in attendance; and the year had included an additional visit to both Canada and Mexico. The time still was not ripe, however, for meaningful summit discussions with Soviet leadership. Johnson's memoirs reflect the sensitivity he felt to criticisms that his almost total attention to Vietnam had meant squandered opportunities for easing Cold War tension. He underlined the energies he had devoted to the negotiation of the Treaty on the Nonproliferation of Nuclear Weapons, signed in the final year of his Presidency, and the progress realized on a number of bilateral fronts, fisheries, consular, civil air and cultural agreements, for example.[21]

By early 1967, the President and his principal NSC advisers were agreed that new developments in the strategic arms race demanded the most urgent attention: "We had known for some time that the Soviets were installing an antiballistic missile system around Moscow. Pressure rose for us to follow suit to protect our major cities and ICBM emplacements with an ABM system. It was time, if not past time, for mature men to take stock together of how to achieve mutual security without the huge added costs of elaborate protective systems and the expanded offensive systems they would trigger into being."[22]

Johnson wrote Chairman Aleksei Kosygin. An exchange of letters between the two leaders led to agreement on a summit to be held on June 24–25, 1967, when Kosygin would be in the United States for a meeting of the United Nations. In keeping with the fine points of summit protocol, they would meet at a point midway between the nominal home bases of the American and Soviet leaders—at Glassboro State College, Glassboro, New Jersey. When Johnson and Kosygin parted at the end of the second day of the talks, there was absolutely no progress to report. Johnson would conclude his summit travels with informal visits to Nicaragua, Costa Rica, Honduras, and Guatemala in July 1968.

The effort to find a more constructive road of U.S.-USSR cooperation to increase security and ease world tensions continued to prove exceedingly difficult. From the time of the division of Europe at Yalta and the coming of the Iron Curtain, successive Presidents had experienced tensions, repeated crisis, failures, and only an occasional positive step forward with the Soviets. The 1940s, 50s, and 60s had seen the Berlin airlift, the rejection of the 1955 open skies proposal, the invasion of Hungary, the collapse of the 1960 summit, the flawed Vienna talks, the Berlin Wall, the Cuban missile crisis, the invasion of Czechoslovakia and the stalemate of Glassboro.

Progress during the same era had included the post-Cuban missile crisis introduction of the U.S.-Soviet Hot-Line, the signing of the Limited Test Ban Treaty in 1963, and of the Nonproliferation Treaty of 1968. This was the sobering legacy that the two superpowers brought to the new era—the summitry of detente in the early 1970s.

End Notes

1. Johnson, Lyndon Baines, *The Vantage Point*, Holt, Rinehart and Winston, New York, 1971, page ix.

2. *The Letters of Theodore Roosevelt*, Elting E. Morison, ed., Harvard University Press, Cambridge, MA, 1952, page 495.

3. Walworth, Arthur, *Woodrow Wilson*, Houghton Mifflin Company, Boston, 1965, page 258.

4. Burns, James MacGregor, *Roosevelt, The Soldier of Freedom*, Harcourt Brace Jovanovich, Inc., New York, 1970, pages 125–26.

5. *The Public Papers and Addresses of Franklin D. Roosevelt 1941 The Call to Battle Stations*, compiled with special material and explanatory notes by Samuel I. Rosenman, Harper & Brothers Publishers, New York, 1950, page 316.

6. Curie, Eve, *Journey Among Warriors*, Doubleday, Doran and Co., Garden City, New York, 1943, pages 1–12.

7. Burns, *Roosevelt, the Soldier of Freedom*, pages 316–24.

8. *The Public Papers and Addresses of Franklin D. Roosevelt, Vol. 13, Victory and the Threshold of Peace 1944–45*. Samuel I. Rosenman, ed., Russell and Russell, New York, 1969, pages 570–71.

9. Truman, Harry S., *Memoirs, Vol. One, Year of Decisions*, Doubleday and Company, Inc., Garden City, New York, 1955, page 337.

10. Ibid., 402.

11. Section 101 (a) National Security Act of 1947, as Amended, Section 2, Public Law 216, 81st Congress, August 10, 1949.

12. Truman, Harry S., *Memoirs, Vol. Two, Years of Trial and Hope*, Doubleday & Company, Inc., Garden City, New York, 1956, page 59.

13. Falk, Stanley L., Bauer, Theodore W., *The National Security Structure*, Industrial College of the Armed Forces, Washington, D.C., 1972, page 44.

14. Eisenhower, Dwight D., *Waging Peace 1956–1961*, Doubleday & Company, Inc., Garden City, New York, 1965, page 485.

15. Ibid., 399.

16. Ibid., 413.

17. Ibid., 415.

18. Schlesinger, Arthur M., Jr., *A Thousand Days*, Houghton Mifflin Company, Boston, 1965, page 305.

19. *Public Papers of the President of the United States, John F. Kennedy, 1961*, United States Government Printing Office, Washington, 1962, page 440.

20. Kennedy, Robert F., *Thirteen Days*, W.W. Norton & Company, Inc., New York, 1969, pages 66–67.

21. Johnson, Lyndon Baines, *The Vantage Point*, pages 475–76.

22. Ibid., 479.

CHAPTER THREE
Detente

We suggested that curtains were a prelude to war, and that if war should come it could be for only one of two reasons—either through stupidity, or through intent, and if it was through intent on the part of any leaders, then those leaders should be removed, and if it was through stupidity, then the causes should be more closely inspected.

A Russian Journal
John Steinbeck, 1948

"Can you keep your mouth shut?"

Secretary of State Henry Kissinger was to the point, if not endearing, as he moved from me to other members of the U.S. Delegation in the foyer of his Lenin Hills guest house quarters overlooking Moscow. Before my mild protest and reassurance could register, he had already left the room, a whirlwind of intense professional action. In fact, his words were more a positive caution than a negative question. At the end of the third day of talks with the leader of the Soviet Union, on October 26, 1974, the door had been opened and the way prepared for a promising summit meeting between General Secretary Leonid Brezhnev and America's new President, Gerald R. Ford.

Discretion was imperative. The results of our delegation's talks in Moscow now had to be weighed formally by the President and the National Security Council. Following the President's decisions, consultations had to be held with the Congress and the Allied leaders; following that, final negotiating strategy, tactics and specific positions had to be set, together with the launch of the pre-advance and the mass of the detailed planning required for the summit.

Both sides wanted to build on the important progress of the 1972, 1973, and 1974 U.S.-Soviet summits. In his Moscow luncheon toast on October 24, 1974, Foreign Minister Andrei Gromyko pointedly commented on the first round of talks between Kissinger and Brezhnev that morning; his words, which would be carried across the USSR by the official Soviet press, reflected the USSR's anxiety over the forced resignation of President Nixon and the USSR's desire to move ahead with the United States: "Achievements of great importance have been registered in Soviet-American relations. They are well known, and I will not go over them again. But now the main task is to continue the line jointly taken in these relations and develop and encourage these relations. The Soviet Union is still firmly in favor of continuing that line.

"Leonid Brezhnev during the conversation expressed his satisfaction with the statements made by President Ford who is in favor of developing Soviet-American relations and who is in favor of continuing that line. This is fully in accord with our own line of policy."[1]

On October 25 and 26, the tentative outlines of a mutually acceptable formula had painstakingly been developed for a new long-term Strategic Arms Limitation Agreement, to replace the interim SALT Agreement of 1972. A month later, at Vladivostok, Ford and Brezhnev would agree to a 'ceiling' limiting offensive strategic nuclear weapons. They would meet again in Helsinki, Finland, in 1975. However, the Vladivostok Accord marked the end of a half-decade of the most prolific and productive cycle of summit negotiations ever between the United States and the Soviet Union.

When I joined the National Security Council staff in the spring of 1971, preparations were already underway for the 1972 U.S.-Soviet summit still more than a year away. Having served on interdepartmental committees in the Executive Office of the President from the time of the Johnson Administration in 1967, I brought a deep appreciation of the draining, time-consuming, contentious business of shaping national positions for international negotiations. Now, with the NSC, I became a staff-level practitioner of interagency coordination as never before. The first major assignment, in addition to the daily staff routine, was to work with the Department of State and the Department of Defense, preparing the United States for negotiations with the Soviets aimed at ending the Cold War confrontation very much in existence between U.S. and Soviet warships and military aircraft.

Unlike the strategic arms talks that addressed the extremely complex, sometimes theoretical, potentially cataclysmic issues relating to the curbing of the nuclear arms race, the incidents at sea negotiations had a much more tangible, immediate purpose. Destroyers, cruisers and other surface units of the U.S. and Soviet navies steamed at close and dangerous quarters. Patrol and reconnaissance aircraft of the two nations were buzzing each other's warships mast high. Soviet warships and intelligence collectors were tailing U.S. aircraft carriers, harassing, maneuvering to cross the carrier's bows when the U.S. ship was required to hold steady course and speed during aircraft launch and recovery operations.

The Mediterranean and the Sea of Japan were two of the principal arenas of challenge. U.S. and Soviet warships would deliberately set courses that would require one or the other to fall off to avoid collision. On occasion, neither commanding officer would give way in this 'chicken of the sea'. On occasion ships would collide—a hostile, unyielding relationship between the two navies that was symptomatic of the far larger Cold War stalemate existing between the U.S. and the USSR.

Today's senior Senator from Virginia, John W. Warner, first as Under Secretary than as Secretary of the Navy, chaired the interdepartmental team developing the U.S. position under the aegis of the NSC, and led the U.S. delegations to two rounds of talks in October 1971, and mid-May 1972 with Soviet naval counterparts. As the talks progressed, the structure of a mutually beneficial agreement began to emerge. First, the agreement would deal with the operations of surface warships and military aircraft on and over the high seas. Submarine operations would not be involved, except to the extent that either U.S. or Soviet surface warships signaled that they were conducting exercises with submerged submarines. And, the operations of the merchant ships and fishing vessels of the two nations were exempt from the agreement.

Secondly, as the talks neared conclusion, the two sides agreed to be guided by the letter and the spirit of the International Rules of the Road—the maritime code of conduct already in place and accepted by the world's mariners—in the drafting of the agreement. This point was significant, for early in the talks the Soviets had proposed establishing specified stand-off distances—in hundreds or thousands of feet or meters—to provide for ship and aircraft encounters. The issue was stoutly debated both within the U.S. Government and with the Soviets. Finally, it was agreed that the potential for conflict between fixed distances and the provisions of the International Rules increased rather than lessened the chances of an incident at sea. Accordingly, the International Rules were accepted as the basis for the specifics of the agreement.

On May 25, 1972, with Secretary Rogers and Foreign Minister Gromyko in attendance, Secretary Warner, and Admiral of the Fleet Gorshkov signed the U.S.-Soviet Incidents at Sea Agreement as one of the first formal actions of the 1972 Moscow Summit.

The Agreement's ten articles defined the ships and aircraft to be included, and prescribed the new code of conduct to be observed by the two navies in clean, specific language. For example:

> Article III., 1. In all cases ships operating in proximity to each other, except when required to maintain course and speed under the Rules of the Road, shall remain well clear to avoid risk of collision.

> Article III. 2. Ships meeting or operating in the vicinity of a formation of the other Party shall, while conforming to the Rules of the Road, avoid maneuvering in a manner which would hinder the evolutions of the formation.

> Article 111. 6. Ships of the Parties shall not simulate attacks by aiming guns, missile launchers, torpedo tubes, and other weapons in the direction of a passing ship of the other Party, nor launch any object in the direction of passing ships of the other Party, and not use searchlights or other powerful illumination devices to illuminate the navigation bridges of passing ships of the other Party.

> Article IV. Commanders of aircraft of the Parties shall use the greatest caution and prudence in approaching aircraft and ships of the other Party operating on and over the high seas, in particular, ships engaged in launching and landing aircraft, and in the interest of mutual safety shall not permit: simulated attacks by the simulated use of weapons against aircraft and ships, or performance of various aerobatics over ships, or dropping various objects near them in such a manner as to be hazardous to ships or to constitute a hazard to navigation.[2]

The Agreement also provided that each nation's Naval Attaches would serve as the channel for communications on alleged incidents or violations, and that delegations of the U.S. and USSR would meet annually to review implementation of its terms. It was a solid agreement that brought immediate, positive results at sea and that continues today to serve the interests of the parties. It augured well for the broader objectives of the 1972 summit.

At this point in my career as sherpa, I had not yet matriculated to summit delegate or summit participant in these important new contacts with the Soviets. I was a laborer behind the scenes helping to guide the lengthy, thorough, multi-faceted preparations for both the 1972 and 1973 summits. The President, his National Security Adviser

Dr. Kissinger, and the NSC system controlled the pace and direction of these preparations. National Security Study Memorandums, the formal NSC directives, specified the work to be undertaken and the channels in which it would flow, and the flow was through the White House. The President's decisions and the guidance for implementation by the Departments of government emerged from the NSC system in the form of National Security Decision Memorandums. Cabinet Members were involved, but the President and his staff guided the process, dealing directly with the Soviet leadership whenever required.

Dr. Kissinger described the nature of this process for the SALT I negotiations during a meeting with reporters at the Intourist Hotel during the 1972 summit: "Of course, we have now developed what we believe to be a rather good system for conducting these negotiations; that is to say, we have an extremely able delegation, and a very able negotiator who conducts the ordinary business of the negotiations. We have in Washington a series of committees that make the technical studies and that back up the negotiator.

"Over the last two years, when the negotiations have reached a deadlock, we have used the mechanism of Presidential exchanges with the Soviet leaders to break the deadlock, in each case by compromise that turned out to be fair to both sides...."[3]

Members of the U.S. team turned their attention to SALT, the ABM Treaty (that had eluded Johnson at Glassboro), and to a statement of the Basic Principle of Relations Between the United States of America and the Union of Soviet Socialist Republics—the most important documents of the first summit. Meanwhile, I was concentrating on the accompanying bilateral agreements that were intended to take U.S.-Soviet relations from stalemate to an interconnecting web of mutually beneficial bilateral programs. Building on the new spirit of relaxed tensions and cooperation, the work culminated in Moscow with the signing of agreements on environmental protection, a joint commercial commission, cooperation in the field of medical science and public health, cooperation in science and technology, cooperation in the exploration and use of outer space for peaceful purposes, and the incidents at sea agreement.

None of these agreements came easily; the bureaucracies of both nations scrapped for advantage. On May 20, 1972, following the departure of the Presidential party from Washington for the summit, the stream of messages began to flow between Air Force One and the White House. The final touches, the final wrangles over language were still continuing. A message from Kissinger to Haig directed that I arrange a meeting that Saturday morning with the Department of State and the National Aeronautics and Space Administration to examine the most recently proposed Soviet language for the Space Agreement. Draft revisions continued back and forth between Washington, Moscow, and the Presidential party still en route to the Soviet capital; the agreement was signed on May 24.

In 1975, I would be at Cape Canaveral to witness the lift-off of the Saturn rocket carrying America's astronauts to the rendezvous of the Apollo-Soyuz mission with Russia's Cosmonauts. I had learned as sherpa, as I would again in 1973 and 1974, that the deadlines and imperatives of summits would drive the bureaucracies of the participated nations to unaccustomed speed and proficiency—contributing in 1972 to the newly emerging detente.

Following the conclusion of the summit, on the President's flight from Kiev to Tehran, Dr. Kissinger summed up the mood of the President's party; "We are leaving with a very positive attitude. We are not trying to be sentimental. Looking at all the dangers, all the things that can go wrong, nevertheless we believe it may have turned a page in our relationship. We leave open the possibility that this may be a stratagem on their part, but that is not our assessment."[4]

Nixon flew on for two days of talks in Iran with Shah Mohammed Reza Pahlavi, and then to Warsaw for a formal East-West dialogue with First Secretary Gierek of Poland, before the return flight to Washington. Indeed, in the goldfish bowl of world summitry, it was important not to segregate or regulate to a markedly inferior political status other important Warsaw Pact members pressing to be included in the detente process. Regular consultations with both Poland and Romania moved forward in parallel with the Soviet summits.

1972 proved to be one of the most dramatic years in U.S. history for presidential personal diplomacy—the Moscow summit, the 'break-through' visit to Shanghai, Peking and Hangchow to resume contact with the People's Republic of China, as well as a State Visit to Ottawa in April, and an informal round of talks with Chancellor Bruno Kreisky in Salzburg, en route to Moscow. Nixon's extensive foreign travel experience, including eight pathfinding years of overseas missions as Eisenhower's Vice President, launched him on the summit trail early in his first years as President. His travels included repeated consultations with European and Asian allies, with the leaders of Canada and Mexico, and with South Vietnam's President Thieu.

In 1973, President Nixon went abroad only once, to Iceland for the talks with Pompidou. While construction materials were still being assembled for the Year of Europe, the main effort of summitry was on the next structural additions to detente, with General Secretary Brezhnev's visit to the United States, June 18–26, 1973. In early May, Dr. Kissinger flew to the USSR for four days of preparatory talks with the Soviet leader and Foreign Minister Gromyko. In mid-May, the Soviet advance party, which had studied its U.S. counterparts the year before, arrived in the U.S.. On the morning of Brezhnev's arrival in Washington an enormous Soviet flag festooned the north side of the Old Executive Office Building facing Brezhnev's Blair House guest residence, and the entire block of Pennsylvania Avenue between Blair House and the White House, normally teeming with six lanes of traffic, had been closed for the duration of the visit to help assure the Soviet Leader's security.

The 1972 summit had signaled a dramatic departure from the confrontation that had enveloped U.S.-Soviet relations since the final days of World War II. The Interim SALT I Agreement marked the first step toward significant limits on offensive strategic nuclear arms. The ABM Treaty provided limits that might nip in the bud an enormous, multi-billion dollar strategic defensive arms. And the Declaration of Principles not only codified the approach to be taken to achieve more constructive bilateral relations, but muted competition and channeled U.S.-Soviet contacts at all levels to more productive ends. The bilateral agreements on which I had labored began the process of codifying the opportunities for increased bilateral cooperation.

Between the 1972 and 1973 summits, additional agreements had been signed—a Trade Agreement, a Maritime Agreement, and an understanding covering payment of the remainder of the USSR's World War II Lend-Lease obligations. On the NSC staff, we monitored the results of the initial deliberations of the new bilateral committees and commissions at the same time that we helped to steer the preparations for Brezhnev's 1973 visit.

Throughout this period, I was struck by the way that the Soviets—in whatever field of proposed bilateral cooperation—lived up to their negotiating tactics: these tactics, clearly understood by us, consisted of holding out until the last moment before agreeing to terms even possibly acceptable to the United States. Dealings under the new Maritime Agreement offer a choice example. Implementation of the agreement involved the hard-nosed, real-world business of cargo shares and cargo rates, in addition to all of the accompanying political language. During one such negotiating session in Moscow, our Maritime Administrator pushed away from the conference table at the end of the last scheduled session telling his Soviet counterpart that there could be no agreement since the Soviets insisted on holding to clearly unacceptable positions. The Soviet side still did not budge. Our negotiator departed for his hotel to pack; there were no calls or messages. At the airport, at the ramp of the aircraft that would take the Administrator back to Washington, his Soviet 'colleague' intercepted him with an offer of acceptable terms.

In June 1973, at the White House, at Camp David, and at the Western White House in San Clemente, California, the second full story of the structure of detente sprung into place in a crowded week of summitry. President Nixon and General Secretary Brezhnev signed an agreement on Basic Principles of Negotiations on the Further Limitation of Strategic Offensive Arms, setting a target date of 1974 for the completion of a more permanent agreement. Expanding on the 1972 interim accord, this agreement set both quantitative and qualitative limits on strategic offensive arms, and open the negotiating trail to further reductions in 1975 and beyond.

On June 22, in the East Room of the White House, the two leaders signed an Agreement between the United States of America and the Union of Soviet Socialist Republics on the Prevention of Nuclear War. Building on the 1972 Declaration of Principles, this carefully worded document—though shy on concrete specifics—set forth agreed objectives and conduct. These objectives aimed at avoiding exacerbations in relations, in avoiding military confrontations, conduct that would exclude the outbreak of nuclear war between the U.S. and the USSR and, indeed, nuclear war between either nation and any unnamed third party. Thus the framework of detente continued to grow. No longer were the two sides struggling to eliminate ship collisions; the agreement now had progressed to an overall code for the avoidance of nuclear war.

Nixon and Brezhnev extolled the progress they were realizing in a banquet at the White House. President Nixon proclaimed: "Our two peoples want peace. We have a special responsibility to insure that our relations—relations between the two strongest countries in the world—are directed firmly toward world peace. Our success will come to be measured not only in years, but in decades and in generations, and probably centuries."[5] And, Brezhnev's response was couched in visionary terms no less than the President's: "Naturally the development of good relations between the Soviet Union and the United States will have, and already has, no small bearing on world affairs. But this influence is one that promotes the strengthening of peace, security and international cooperation. In building through joint effort a new structure of peaceful relations, we have no intention of turning it into a secluded mansion completely fenced off from the outside world. We want to keep this spacious edifice open to all those who cherish the peace and well-being of mankind."[6]

The summit included the signing of many other new agreements, agreements on which I had labored with my colleagues in Washington and Embassy Moscow for several months, promoting cooperation in additional functional fields of mutual interest: cooperation in areas such as in the studies of the world ocean, the field of agriculture, the field of transportation, scientific and technical cooperation in the field of peaceful uses of atomic energy. Also included was an augmented civil war agreement, a U.S.-USSR tax convention, and a general agreement on contacts, exchanges, and cooperation to provide an improved framework for the expanding bilateral contacts.

The Soviet side, even more than the U.S., was intensely interested in fostering increased bilateral trade. My first personal introduction to General Secretary Brezhnev took place in Blair House at the opening of an informal meeting between Brezhnev and leaders of U.S. business and industry to discuss the opportunities for such trade. Secretary of the Treasury George Shultz was the American host for that event. As I came through the receiving line, he introduced me and gave a brief description of my role as a member of the NSC staff. Brezhnev kept a firm grip on my hand, his eyes looking up studying my face as the words were translated by the USSR's premier U.S. interpreter, Victor Sukhodrev. In turn, Brezhnev smiled, nodded and said, "I envy you your youth."

On June 24, prior to his return flight to the USSR, Brezhnev delivered a television and radio address to the American people—as had Nixon to the Soviet people the year before—expressing full satisfaction with his visit and optimism for the future of U.S.-Soviet relations. The summit, despite the growing domestic problems of Watergate, had gone well. Soon after Brezhnev's departure, I received a fine silver dish from Dr. Kissinger, inscribed:

A.D.C.
U.S.-USSR SUMMIT
18–25 JUNE 1973
H.A.K.

To me, this thoughtful gift symbolized the successful completion of my behind-the-scenes apprenticeship.

By March 1974, with the Western world reeling from the jolts of the 1973 Arab-Israeli war and the global energy crisis, U.S.-European cooperation had become a necessity more than ever. Multilateral talks continued between East and West on the possibility of force reductions in Europe, and on broader understandings to bring enhanced security and cooperation in Europe. Dr. Kissinger had become Secretary of State as well as the President's National Security Adviser. I had become the NSC's senior staff member for Eastern and Western Europe. It was in that capacity that I traveled with the Secretary and his party through the night across the Atlantic, aboard Tail Number 86970, a special mission U.S. Air Force VC-137, for the March 24–28, 1974, U.S.-USSR negotiations in Moscow.

The momentum of detente summitry had brought with it a momentum of expectations. The agenda for the talks was headed by SALT, the complications of bilateral trade—that is to say, the linkage we had created between normal trade and the human rights issue of freedom of immigration—as well as the requirement for continuing dialogue on the Middle East. Other agenda items for the 1974 Moscow Summit, among them the new bilateral negotiations I was also monitoring, were proceeding in parallel channels. In discussing his trip with the press prior to his departure, Secretary Kissinger had touched on the anatomy of summit SALT preparation. He cited the initial exchange of essential detailed strategic arms proposals between the two sides, the 'conceptual breakthrough', and then the grinding work required to bring the agreement in principle forward to the final stage of a formal agreement. Kissinger had hinted that progress might be possible, and the press had committed him in advance to realization of the 'conceptual breakthrough'.

The refueling stop in the Federal Republic of Germany provided a stark reminder of the fragile, unfinished process of detente. One of the embarked journalists, Strobe Talbott, a talented diplomatic correspondent for *Time*, had to abandon the trip. His translation and editing of Nikita Khrushchev's oral memoirs, *Khrushchev Remembers*, had angered the Soviets, and now they had denied his final efforts to gain visa approval for the Moscow visit.

Foreign Minister Gromyko was on hand at Vnukovo-2 Airport to meet our party. Stands of white birch stood out prominently against the film of soot covering the late winter snow along the highway leading to Moscow. Soon, tall, gray high-rise apartment slabs replaced the woodland, reminding me of the return to New York City from Long Island after leaving the fields and parks for the first of the apartments of Queens. However, there was a difference. The apartments of these gray Soviet buildings had to be tiny, judging by the close vertical and horizontal spacing of the windows on each concrete face.

Our motorcade sped into the city, climbing up into the hills past Moscow University. Motorcades are another of the countless special components of summitry. The summit staffer must learn, and learn quickly, that each motorcade is geared to the precision movement of one person, the summit principal. Keeping track of schedules, gauging descent times in crowded foreign hotel elevators, knowing the vector and distance to your staff car or bus in the standing procession prior to departure are essential elements of the good staffer's survival. Motorcades do not wait for staff. Once they have swept away under full-sirened police escort, local traffic will close in behind and it is not easy to regain the summit party.

I have never missed a motorcade, but I have borne good bruises from bangs taken while leaping into already moving cars. I have also developed an eye over the years for the different techniques of the police, security, and military forces of various nations providing security for the motorcades. For example in Lagos, Nigeria, soldiers standing in escorting jeeps and trucks used their rifle butts to bang on the roofs of cars not quick enough to clear a path. In the Netherlands, helmeted police in fluorescent orange and white Porsches would dart like birds of prey ahead of our speeding convoy. In Moscow, the KGB's security cars would swerve out into the oncoming lanes at the sight of an approaching car and head straight for it until the motorist dove for the safety of the far curb or shoulder.

Our motorcade swept through the gates of the Lenin Hills guest complex; half a dozen neo-Victorian pink stone mansions with an adjoining banquet hall, resting in a hilltop setting of formal gardens, looked down across the tops of white birches and evergreens to bridges crossing a bend in the Moscow River. These luxurious buildings, I was told, had been built by Stalin for his senior ministers. However, with his demise members of Moscow's ruling elite had deemed it politically inadvisable to establish residence therein. The deep carpets, the high gloss of the varnished woods, the cut glass and the lace were decidedly non-revolutionary in their opulence.

Soviet hospitality was generous and continuous throughout our stay. Each morning the dining room's breakfast table, served by uniformed waitresses, were laden with cucumbers, tomatoes, cold meats and fish, as well as breads and the hot, customary western breakfast fare. Apart from negotiations or drafting records of the day's talks, or the formal social events that are part of such visits, the appointment that remains in my mind from that first stay in Lenin Hill's Guest House Number Four was the movie and billiards room across the hall from my bedroom on the second floor. It contained a splendid pool table with pockets so narrow that it was virtually impossible to sink a shot. I have had the lingering suspicion that this was a deft psychological touch on the part of the host government to place its distinguished visitors on the defensive.

Secretary Kissinger's Secret Service detail was always present. There was even an agent at the door to General Secretary Brezhnev's Kremlin Office when the Secretary and his delegation entered for each session of the talks. The hospitality continued inside the conference room with island trays of mineral water and other soft drinks running the length of the center of the conference table, and with occasional banter between Brezhnev and Kissinger to lighten the weight of the deliberations. The talks were heavy going. Neither side was yet prepared to make the concessions required for the development of a mutually acceptable formula for the detailed drafting of the new, permanent strategic arms agreement. Neither side saw the Moscow round as a failure, which it was not. Both termed it business-like and constructive in the official communique. However, despite the fact that negotiations would continue from the respective capitals, the news media reported the lack of a 'conceptual breakthrough' as failure. Kissinger would later write of this lesson in summit preparations: "The media never lets you forget a failed forecast....One final rule for aspirants to high office: if you cannot resist the urge to make a prediction, use turgid and impenetrable prose; you will never escape your mistakes if you have a talent for aphorisms."[7]

At 11:30 a.m., March 28, 1974, our Air Force jet taxied to a stop at a secured parking area at London's Heathrow Airport after the three and one-half hour flight from Moscow. A far more genteel British motorcade parried with local traffic on the drive into White-hall for Luncheon and talks with Foreign Secretary James Callaghan, and then a courtesy call by the Secretary of State on Prime Minister Harold Wilson before our return that evening to Washington. A debrief on the meetings with Brezhnev and Gromyko, an exchange on Middle East developments and on ways to broaden and quicken the pace of new U.S.-European initiatives were the focal points of the London stopover. The Foreign Secretary listened carefully and probed professionally in his cheerful, informal engaging manner. This was the first of several meetings I could look forward to having with "Sunny Jim" Callaghan during his years first as Foreign Secretary and then Prime Minister.

On June 25, 1974, His Majesty King Baudouin I, King of the Belgians, greeted President Richard Nixon on his arrival in the glow of a summer's evening at Melsbroek Military Airport on the fringe of Brussels. Nixon had just completed his penultimate summit swing of importance, to Austria, Egypt, Syria, Israel, and Jordan. Now he was on the final lap: a NATO Summit with accompanying bilateral talks with Prime Minister Tindemans of Belgium, Chancellor Helmut Schmidt of the FRG, Harold Wilson of Great Britain, and Rumor of Italy; and the third of the summits of detente with Brezhnev in the the USSR.

In his arrival statement to King Baudouin, President Nixon captured the essence of the evolutionary change the United States was striving for in advancing Western interests while negotiating improved relations with the East: "As you have noted, this visit comes between two other visits, the first to the Mideast and the next to the Soviet Union. It is significant that this is the case because this symbolizes the central role that the Atlantic Alliance plays in pursuing our goal of a lasting peace in the world. Without the Alliance, it is doubtful that the detente would have begun, and without continuing a strong alliance, it is doubtful if detente would continue."[8]

The gathering of Atlantic Alliance leaders at the NATO Summit on June 26, marked the 25th anniversary of the Alliance with the signing of a Declaration of Atlantic Relations affirming anew the commitment of the United States, Canada, and our European partners to the principles and purposes of the trans-Atlantic relationship, of which the Alliance formed the heart.

This Declaration, in effect, marked the formal culmination of the Year of Europe initiative that the United States had launched 18 months before. A fresh statement of purpose was to be welcomed a quarter-century after the Alliance's founding, the fact that the pace of world events had already brought renewed momentum to U.S.-European relations notwithstanding. More specifically, the Declaration was to be welcomed as a fresh statement of unity on the eve of another round of U.S.-USSR summitry that would, as ever, have considerable impact on the interests of each NATO member nation.

In mid-1974, the East-West swing from Cold War to detente was reaching its most pronounced, if short-lived, phase. This was captured in Nixon's address to the NATO Council, in which he played on the combined opportunity and danger posed by detente, the changes in European politics since 1949, and his belief that NATO members, "had to accept the fact and the fear of Communism was no longer a practical motivation for NATO; if NATO were to survive, it would need other binding motives to keep it together."[9] At the NATO Council meeting, President Nixon promised close consultation with Alliance members on the results of his upcoming meetings with Brezhnev. And, while in Brussels, the President held more thorough tete-a-tetes on his plans for Moscow with Prime Minister Wilson, Chancellor Schmidt, and Italy's Prime Minister Rumor.

The U.S.-USSR Summit of June 27 through July 3, 1974, marked the grand finale to the show, if not the substance, of detente in the early 1970s. U.S. support aircraft—for security, communications, and logistics support—preceded the President. The glossy English-Russian language booklet of U.S. participants ran 25 pages long. General Secretary Brezhnev, President Podgorny and Premier Kosygin were ramp-side at Vnukovo-2 Airport to greet the President and Mrs. Nixon when they stepped from the 'Spirit of '76'.

Once inside the capital city, President Nixon took residence in the elegant apartments of the grand Kremlin Palace, within the Kremlin walls. Our NSC staff offices were in the same wing; an interior of graceful design, with halls luxuriously carpeted with oriental rugs so long they almost reached the vanishing point. Occasional oil lamps punctuated the egg-shell walls with brass and crystal fittings. White lace curtains, hanging from the countless long windows, blew gently inward along the halls in response to the warm late-June breeze. In the early evening we met for a reception in the chandeliered opulence of St. Vladimir Hall. (Here I would note, summit sherpa's family and friends strain to spot 'their man' in the live international television coverage and subsequent news photography of such events.) In the 15th Century Chamber of facets of the Grand Kremlin Palace, an official dinner of the highest rank was given in honor of the President by the Presidium of the USSR Supreme Soviet and the Soviet Government. Moving from one event to the next on that first day, I was struck by the fact that the Soviets continued to treasure the very Czarist contributions that they so resolutely condemned. The President spoke that evening of the transformation of relations from confrontation, to coexistence, to ever-expanding bilateral cooperation. The talks on core issues of strategic importance were difficult and moved slowly; the President and Brezhnev met twice the following day. To mark the progress already achieved by the occasion and the deadline of the third summit, the U.S. and Soviet delegations assembled in St. Catherine's Hall on the afternoon of the 28th for the signing of still more bilateral agreements, which had involved my staffing efforts. Those included were the U.S.-USSR Agreements on Cooperation in the Field of Energy, Cooperation in the Field of Housing and Other Construction, and Cooperation in Artificial Heart Research and Development. The bilateral agreements had by now grown to some 15 in number, and created the new web—barring the unforeseen—of cooperative ties between important elements of U.S.-Soviet society, designed to draw the two nations into increasingly productive cooperation. With an agreement on housing, given the inferior quality of Soviet efforts in the field, there could be no doubt that we had neared the absolute limit of such undertakings. As the President prepared to sign the Artificial Heart Agreement—a very technical undertaking negotiated between the U.S. Department of Health, Education and Welfare, and the USSR Ministry of Health—Secretary Kissinger could not resist turning to those in attendance and quipping, "my most difficult negotiation."

The first days in Moscow produced only sparse bulletins on the strategic arms negotiations, consisting of little more than the fact that Nixon, Brezhnev and their delegations were continuing to address SALT and, in that context measures to limit further Anti-Ballistic Missile deployments, and to narrow further the scope of permissible nuclear weapons tests. On the evening of the 28th, we attended a performance at the Bolshoi in honor of the President and Mrs. Nixon. On the 29th, the President and the General Secretary signed a Long-Term Agreement to Facilitate Economic, Industrial and Technical Cooperation Between the U.S. and USSR. Our delegation then departed for the two-hour flight south to Simferopol, and the hour's motorcade to Brezhnev's vacation complex in Oreanda, a suburb of Yalta, on the Black Sea.

The Crimea was at its most luxuriant as our cars, buses and supporting trucks snaked their way down through green, flower-dressed mountainsides to the sea. Vacationing Soviets—the men in shirtsleeves, the younger women in mini-skirts—paused in their sidewalk strolls to watch our procession as it rolled through Yalta and on to the VIP retreats. The President's residence was a seaside villa. The majority of our delegation was housed in two sanatoria—the Soviet workers' high-rise health-vacation resorts. Mine, the Parus Sanatorium, which belonged to the All-Union Central

Council of Trade Unions, perched on a cliff. From my balcony, the sun was strong and hot. Tour boats were churning the off-shore water. Tiny figures were sunbathing on the beach far below. The Swallows Nest, a castle built for Czar Nicholas II, was below, off to the right gracefully atop a promontory jutting above the sea.

My summit staffing obligations were minimal during the weekend at Oreanda. To ensure that I was not bored, a new-found companion emerged in the form of a rather senior Soviet diplomat with well-established KGB connections. He appeared at the bar for evening cocktails, was at my table for dinner, and bright and cheerful as ever, in the dining room to greet me at breakfast the following morning. The summit sherpa should always bear in mind, as I did on the occasion, that you are never off-duty or on vacation however pleasant and salubrious certain days may be in summit travel. Foreign governments are intensely interested in each member of high-level American delegations, observing, learning what they can, filing personality reports that are added to larger files to be drawn on as required in dealings with the United States.

To reach the Parus Sanatorium's private beach, one descended by elevator 240-feet through a shaft cut in the granite cliff, then walked another hundred feet to the seaside face of the shaft's lower horizontal arm. As I followed this route for a swim on the morning of the 31st, I was brought up short by an incredible reminder of the proficiency of the U.S. technical support accompanying American Presidents on foreign travel. Here, on a stand at the edge of the beach's worn and rounded granite rocks, stood a telephone with the symbol of the White House Communications Agency and the words Oreanda White House on its dial. To reach almost anyone, almost any place in the world, I would only have to pick the receiver and identify myself and the connection invariably would be in seconds, not minutes.

I had experienced the proficiency of this White House communications system only two weeks before when I had been rolled out of bed at home by a 2:00 a.m., call from the White House operator. The President was in Salzburg, Austria, en route to the Middle East, and at the moment of the call was behind closed doors in official conversation with the Austrian Chancellor. A hard-charging assistant White House press secretary came on the line to advise that she needed a text that the press secretary could draw on an hour later in reporting the highlights of the President's conversation to the awaiting, traveling press corps. It had been so easy to pick up the phone in that staff room in Salzburg and to say "I want to talk to Denis Cift, NSC staff, at his residence." It had been a bit harder to peel my eyes open and to pound out some cogent highlights of the President's emerging conversation. I was back on the phone in half-an-hour to dictate the recommended press guidance, which met the requirement. Now, on the beach at Oreanda, I had no occasion to pick up the phone, but I did tell the Director of White House Communications later that day that I had been disappointed not find another phone floating on a rubber sea horse when I had taken a swim that morning.

From 11:00 a.m., until 4:00 p.m., that Sunday, Nixon and Brezhnev had continued arms control discussions. The shape of the progress that might be possible during the President's stay in the USSR had begun now to emerge. At mid-afternoon I and a few other staff members joined the principal members of the two delegations for a three-hour Black Sea cruise aboard the General Secretary's two, near-identical 115-foot yachts. When I arrived, Nixon and Brezhnev were seated at the pool-side terrace of the Soviet leader's villa, with the sound of surf breaking along the granite rock sea wall just beyond. The mirrored surface of the pool's long, rounded rectangle reflected the diving platform, and the bottom side of a high, modernistic roof extending the entire length and breadth of the pool, with tracks for sliding glass walls that could be drawn in the event of inclement weather.

The yachts were tied to a pier perpendicular to the shore, and lay with their engines running. The President and the General Secretary took their places at upholstered seats around a table on the open upper deck aft of the enclosed bridge on 'Boat One'. My colleagues and I, accompanied by the Soviet Deputy Chief of Protocol and several other members of the Soviet party boarded the 'Back-up Boat'. With 'Boat One' in the lead we were underway, moving slowly at first in the waters immediately off Yalta to permit the reporters, photographers, and television crews aboard another chartered tour boat to capture the summit party's departure. The U.S. and Soviet flags flew from the yardarms of the leaders' yacht. Both yachts flew the naval ensign of the KGB Frontier Forces from their fantails— green and blue with the red hammer and sickle in the block of white.

The two yachts were as powerful as they were impeccably maintained. Varnished bridgework and fine, blue trim set off the white hulls, the large, rectangular windows of the curved main deck saloons forward, as well as the upper decks. Oriental carpets ran the length of both the open passenger decks and the interiors. Brezhnev's love for big, fast cars had been well reported in the course of the summitry of detente, and his pleasure for speed was as true on the water. Throttles were opened, and the two yachts, charging against white-capped waters, were soon tearing across the black sea at 30 knots. The two sailors at parade rest at the stern of each yacht locked the long black ribbons of their caps in their teeth to avoid a punishing whipping from the wind. Wakes kicked twice the length of our hulls as we flew along the coast. Far in the distance, the faint gray shapes of Soviet warships on station for the summit visit, broke the Black Sea's southern horizon. The wood paneled interiors of each yacht, with their crystal and mirrors engraved with contemporary Soviet art, bore tables heavily laden with a late afternoon lunch. To my mind, the cruise that afternoon marked the high point in the friendship and ease between the U.S. and Soviet leaders in the detente of the early 1970s. The relationship was not one of deep friendship or enduring bond, but rather one of comfortable, professional familiarity borne of intensive negotiations and face-to-face contacts over a period of several years.

On July 1, the President flew to Minsk for a ceremonial visit to the Belorussian Soviet Socialist Republic. There, in keeping with the formal protocol of summitry, he paid honor and respect to the Soviet nation by laying a wreath at the Khatyn Memorial—a towering statue of a village blacksmith with his dead child in his arms—a lasting memorial to a village massacred, an atrocity of World War II.

The bulk of the American delegation returned directly to Moscow, where I once again was boarding my Russian staff car for the short drive from the Rossiya Hotel, through the Kremlin Wall, past the 4-ton Czar Cannon, and the enormous 200-ton Czar bell, to a modest doorway in an internal Kremlin courtyard. With a glance at my summit credentials, Soviet guards waved me through, and I was again striding along the long halls of the Czars' apartments to our staff office to resume my share of the work of the President's speeches, toasts, and the culminating Joint U.S.-Soviet Communique of the summit. The permanent SALT agreement on offensive strategic arms was not to be at the 1974 Moscow summit. Nixon and Brezhnev could only agree to a Communique underscoring the importance of such and agreement; that it should run until 1985 and that the U.S. and Soviet SALT Delegations should re-convene in Geneva to resume negotiations. Against this pronounced stall, the summit did mark limited strategic arms control progress: a protocol limiting both the U.S. and USSR to a single deployment area for anti-ballistic missile systems (the 1972 Treaty had specified two areas for each); and an agreement limiting underground nuclear explosions—a Threshold Test Ban prohibiting explosions above 150 kilotons. Added to this, the summit had permitted the continuation of critical international political discussions addressing continuing, crucial points of friction and contention including those in the Middle East and in East-West relations more generally. On July 2, President Nixon again addressed the Soviet people, and the tone of his words clearly reflected his awareness of the closing of a chapter. He reflected on the progress achieved since 1972 in the context of his own career-long experience with the Soviets: "It was exactly 15 years ago next month when I was here in Moscow as Vice President that I first spoke to the people of the Soviet Union on radio and television. In that speech, I said, let our aim be not victory over other people, but the victory of all mankind over hunger, want, misery and disease, wherever it exists in the world."[10] He pointed to the web of new bilateral agreements contributing to that objective. And, in recognition that he would no longer be at the summit to guide the work still undone, he concluded with a reference to a story to by Tolstoi: "A very old man was planting apple trees. He was asked: what are you planting apple trees for? It will be a long time before they bear fruit, and you will not live to eat a single apple. The old man replied, I will never eat them but others will and they will thank me."[11]

A formal diplomatic reception beneath the massive chandeliers of St. George Hall in the Kremlin brought the 1974 Moscow summit to a close. Following honors for the President at Vnukovo II Airport, I boarded Air Force One for the ten-hour flight back to the United States. As we taxied toward the main runway for take-off, the President moved casually through the big jet, quipping about its American comforts, shaking hands and thanking each of us for our part in the summit.

Four and one half months later, the cold air of late November stung the nostrils as I stood informally with General Secretary Brezhnev, Foreign Minister Gromyko, Ambassador Dobrynin, and other members of the Soviet and U.S. delegations on a snow-covered taxiway at Vozdvizhenka fighter base waiting for President Gerald R. Ford to disembark from Air Force One. Brezhnev, in high humor, bantered with the traveling press corps. "What's in those, Mr. General-Secretary," a reporter asked pointing to the closed-door interceptor aircraft hangers. Brezhnev absorbed the translation and immediately shot back, "tomatoes...vegetable cellars where we store tomatoes." Everyone laughed. The General Secretary quickly stepped forward to greet the new American President; then a long motorcade rolled into position to take us a thousand feet or so to the luxury train that would carry us to the summit site on the outskirts of Vladivostok.

Following the Moscow summit, Gromyko had come to Washington in September on the fringe of the Foreign Minister's address to the U.N. General Assembly. Those talks had set the stage for our October visit to Moscow. It was clear that there was a reasonable chance of further progress on strategic arms limitations, based on the tentative understandings of October. The new President's schedule—extremely crowded both domestically and with foreign visitors to reinforce the fact of continuing U.S. strength and leadership—called for visits to the Republic of Korea and Japan in November. The U.S. and USSR agreed to a meeting at the summit, in the Far East, at Vladivostok. President Ford was deliberately cautious about its prospects—a get-acquainted visit, and opportunity to discuss bilateral relations, nothing more.

At the staff level, the preparations for Vladivostok were intensive. Over the span of weeks, if not months, background papers, personality studies, positions papers on each of the issues the President could expect to address with the Soviets were compiled. President Ford devoured this information. While the public's expectations were not prematurely raised, the President and his staff prepared for full realization of the potential of Vladivostok.

To be a summit sherpa one should enjoy travel, whatever the form, the mode, the pace. The Soviets had brought the best train in the entire USSR across the nation to be available for the 90-minute run. And it was a beauty, replete with the rail-borne version of the same rich paneling, mirrors, carpeting and crystal that I had last seen on the Black Sea. The staff cars were of the continental layout—windowed compartments with sliding doors opening onto a corridor running the length of each carriage.

The President and the General Secretary were in the dining car, engaging in essential, preliminary small talk: "Looking out of the dining car window at the snow-covered terrain, I mentioned the difficulty we had clearing the streets of Washington and how snarled the traffic became when the weather went sour. Brezhnev's bushy eyebrows arched, and he leaned forward across the table that separated us. 'We'll send you snowplows.'"[12] I was one or two carriages behind this discussion leaning against a chrome rail, studying the passing landscape; small rural homes, whisps of chimney smoke, outhouses, an occasional figure. My eyes caught a black car that was keeping pace with our train, several black cars speeding along the road paralleling the tracks. It was our VIP motorcade on a break-neck race that would bring it to the train platform at our destination only seconds before our arrival!

There was another feature that caught my eye. Several heavy cables were underfoot in the train carriage corridor. I followed them the length of the carriage, past the ajar door of the toilet compartment, where they plunged through the open flap at the base of the toilet bowl to the exterior of the train.

Once again, the White House Communications Agency had preceded us. Rumbling through the far-Pacific reaches of the USSR, the President of the United States had secure communications leaping from the roof of the train to a global link of communications relays. The communications support available to the President and his party included not only regular telephone service at Vladivostok, but also secure voice communications, secure teletype service, a two-way staff radio net available to any member of the official party requiring such support, and a paging system for each member of the party. Such communications support is almost always available to the U.S. summit party—as it is increasingly to other high-level delegations. It is the staffer's responsibility to become familiar with the range of such support and how to use it most effectively. Once a summit is under way, there is insufficient time for on-site training.

Upon arrival of cars and trains at the Okeanskiy Sanatorium summit site, a 100-acre health spa and recreation area 10 miles north of Vladivostok, the two sides proceeded to the conference building and immediately convened the first session of the SALT discussions. The conference room, a warm, almost steamy greenhouse lounge bordered with palms and flowing plants, provided an unique atmosphere that proved conducive to progress. The first session ran from 6:15 to 8:15 p.m.. Ford and Brezhnev decided to push ahead. An elaborate dinner was postponed until the following day. The second session ran from 8:45 to 11:30 p.m.; then a third from midnight until 12:30 a.m., on the 24th. During the breaks, the President, Secretary Kissinger and General Brent Scrowcroft conferred while strolling the grounds, or behind the closed doors of the President's own limousine, which had been flown ahead to be available to him in the USSR.

When I entered the talks the following morning, spirits were high. The discussion had switched to East-West relations and the prospects for the Conference on Security and Cooperation in Europe. The President was euphoric; the talks the night before had far exceeded his expectations.[13] Now, as he and Brezhnev continued their discussions on CSCE, MBFR and the Middle East, the delegations' SALT experts were closeted elsewhere at the conference site putting the final touches to the language of the new understanding.

The conceptual breakthrough suggested the preceding March had now been realized. The Vladivostok Accord of November 24, 1974, established the principle of strategic parity between the United States and the Soviet Union, placing a ceiling of 2,400 as the number of strategic delivery vehicles—ICBM launchers, SLBM launchers and heavy bombers—permitted to each side; and a sub-ceiling of 1,320 on the number of ICBMs and SLBMs to be armed with multiple, independently targetable warheads, or re-entry vehicles. It was further agreed that the new agreement should run until 1985, and that U.S. and Soviet delegations should re-convene in Geneva in January 1975, to negotiate the details of the formal permanent agreement text with the Vladivostok Accord as their guide.

With the talks successfully completed, the Soviet chefs produced their banquet:

Fresh and Red Caviar
Fish Puff Pie
Assorted Fish
Bear ham with Pickles
Vegetables

Taimen Salmon Soup
Borsh Flotskyi Style

Shredded Trepang
Roe Deer Saddle with Cowberry

Ice Cream with Jam
Coffee and Tea
Fruits

At the General Secretary's invitation, the President and our delegation then boarded the Soviet motorcade for a tour of Vladivostok—*vladet* (master), plus *vostok* (east)—the primary naval base for the Soviet Pacific Fleet. A handsome city of hills much like those of San Francisco, its harbor crowded with the gray hulls of Soviet warships. A city that, until our summit visit, had been closed to Americans since 1948.

At twilight, I re-boarded the VIP train for the run north to Vozdvizhenka and the return flight to the United States with the President aboard Air Force One. In his informal address that afternoon at the luncheon that had, in effect, marked the culmination of progress for the detente summitry of the early 1970s, President Ford addressed the General Secretary in the words that had played on the theme struck decades before by Steinbeck in his Russian journal: "As nations with great power, we share a common responsibility not only to our own people, but to mankind as a whole. We must avoid, of course, war and the destruction that it would mean. Let us get on with the business of controlling arms, as I think we have in the last 24 hours."[14] The challenge, as our two nations would find, would lie in the observance not only of the letter, but also of the undertaking between nations—the spirit—of such agreements.

End Notes

1. Press Release No 436, *Department of State*, October 24, 1974.

2. Agreement Between the Government of the United States of America and the Government of the Union of Soviet Socialist Republics on the Prevention of Incidents on and Over the Sea, Moscow, May 25, 1972.

3. Press Conference of Dr. Henry A. Kissinger, Assistant to the President for National Security Affairs, Intourist Hotel, Moscow USSR, May 27, 1972.

4. Pool Report, aboard Air Force One, Kiev to Tehran, May 30, 1972.

5. Exchange of toasts between President Nixon and General Secretary Leonid I. Brezhnev, the State Dining Room, the White House; *Office of the White House Press Secretary*, June 18, 1973.

6. Ibid.

7. Kissinger, Henry A., *Years of Upheaval*, Little Brown and Co., Boston, Toronto, 1982, pages 1020–21.

8. Exchange of remarks between King Baudouin I and President Nixon, Melsbroek Military Airport. *Office of the White House Press Secretary*, Brussels, Belgium, June 25, 1974.

9. Nixon, Richard M., *Memoirs of Richard Nixon*, Grosset & Dunlap, New York, 1978, page 1027.

10. Address by President Nixon to the People of the Soviet Union, The Green Room, Grand Kremlin Palace, *Office of the White House Secretary*, Moscow, USSR, July 2, 1974.

11. Ibid.

12. Ford, Gerald R., *A Time to Heal, The Autobiography of Gerald R. Ford*, Harper & Row, New York, 1979, page 213.

13. Ibid., 218.

14. Toast by President Ford at a luncheon with General Secretary Leonid I. Brezhnev, *Office of the White House Press Secretary*, Vladivostok, USSR, November 24, 1974.

CHAPTER FOUR
The West's New Watch

The world is all so changed; so much that seemed vigorous has sunk decrepit, so much that was not is beginning to be!

The French Revolution
Thomas Carlyle, 1837

A steady rain fell on the Presidential motorcade moving through the night on the half-hour drive from Orly Airport to the American Ambassador's residence in Paris. Through the arcs cleared by the staff car's windshield wipers, I could see gendarmes at attention, lining the entire route, their glistening white gauntlets captured in the beams of our headlights.

BULLETIN...

FLASH...PARIS...POMPIDOU DEAD...FLASH.

The wire story flash had been brought to my desk in the Old Executive Office Building within seconds of its receipt in the White House Situation Room on April 2, 1974. Having just returned from the Secretary of State's negotiating session in Moscow, I had been working down through a stack of NSC staff papers requiring reading and action, and at the same time shaking off the remnants of a nasty flu that had attacked at least half of our Moscow traveling party. The bulletin brought instant change.

On the morning of April 2, President Nixon issued a statement in behalf of the American people expressing profound personal regret at Pompidou's death. Shortly thereafter, the White House Press Office announced that the President would fly to France for the Pompidou Memorial Service. By the time of that announcement, a White House advance team was airborne, en route to Paris to make the myriad, detailed arrangements for the President's visit; and I was preparing at the Washington end to accompany the President on that somber mission.

When I boarded Air Force One at 9:45 a.m., on April 5, I already had the pocket-sized, detailed staff schedule for the visit. These 5"x3" schedules, the 'bibles' of American summitry, are an essential part of the staffer's kit. They provide details that are not readily available anywhere else for the precision, fast-paced events of overseas travel: the weather at the flight's destination; the time, location, and security instructions for baggage call; transportation instructions for each member of the party to Andrews Air Force Base. Our schedule for Paris called for a 10:20 a.m., departure from Andrews—Air Force One rolls as soon as the President is aboard—and a 10:30 p.m., arrival at Orly. It provided the debarkation arrangements for each member of the party; identified the French reception committee; and gave the scenario that would take the President past the French Honor Guard to a Pavilion d'Honneur, where he would observe a moment of silence before a portrait of Pompidou and then make brief remarks.

The schedule provided the car by car assignment for each member of the party from Orly to Paris; and the rooming list— those who would be with the President at the Ambassador's residence and those, room by room, who would be at the Hotel de Crillon for the first overnight. Invariably, before a departure, my eyes would trace a schedule through to the first berthing assignment—the first day and the first night. I always knew I would have time to study the rest of the 'bible' during the long, overseas flight.

When President Nixon boarded Air Force One that morning, there was no casual visiting with staff. The morning press' headlines were still crowded with the news of an Internal Revenue Service ruling that would require the President to pay almost $500,000 in back taxes. The atmosphere aboard the jet was extremely reserved, almost glacial. The traveling party was not large: the President, his Chief of Staff Alexander Haig, his press secretary, appointments officer, the Deputy Assistant to the President for National Security Affairs Lieutenant General Brent Scowcroft, the President's physician and his military aide, two or three other members of the professional White House staff, myself, Deputy Assistant Secretary of State Wells Stabler, and three secretaries. Additionally, the President had asked Lieutenant General Vernon Walters, then Deputy Director of Central Intelligence, to accompany him as his personal interpreter for the mission. State Department representation on the delegation was lighter than usual given the fact that the Secretary of State had just remarried and was vacationing with his wife in Mexico.

The initial schedule included two principal events, the Memorial Service at Notre Dame Cathedral at 11:00 a.m., on April 6, to be followed by a formal diplomatic reception for the visiting foreign leaders at the Quai d'Orsay at 5:00 p.m., with departure for Washington immediately thereafter. Even prior to our departure from Washington, I had begun the staffing for another event. While our pre-trip planning had called for no bilateral meetings between the President and any other foreign leader attending the memorial service, we were certain that the President would wish to call on Alain Poher, President of the French Senate. Under the French Constitution, Poher would serve as interim President of France until the results of the next Presidential elections, to be held between 20 and 35 days from the date he took office. We also began to assemble the biographies of the Kings, Queens, Presidents, and Prime Ministers—more than 60—who had already announced their plans to pay last respects to the late French President.

Shortly after we were airborne for Paris, our Air Force One communicators received a message indicating that one of the most important leaders of the Western Alliance had advised that he would welcome a meeting with the President after the Memorial Service. Within two hours, this message had been followed by other similar requests, and work began in earnest on the staffing of an entirely new schedule of informal, bilateral summit tete-a-tetes for the afternoon of April 6. The President would require papers for each meeting, each in his preferred NSC/White House format, each presenting the priority issues before the United States and each of the other nations, the likely specific interests of the other leader, and recommendations as to the points the President would wish to make.

The list grew rapidly: in addition to Poher, President Leone of Italy, Prime Minister Wilson, Chancellor Willy Brandt, Prime Minister Hartling of Denmark, a breakfast meeting the morning of April 7, with the USSR's Podgorny, to be followed by a meeting with Prime Minister Tanaka of Japan. The flight to Paris made clear that the summit staffer does not always have the luxury of ample time. Instead of the months available for careful preparation of my part of the U.S.-Soviet summits, I was now operating on a margin first of hours, then minutes. Messages were sent from Air Force One to Washington requesting additional information from State and other departments on key political and economic issues, to be cabled to Embassy Paris and available to us on our arrival. As Air Force One neared its European landfall, I was already dictating the introductory pages for each of the meetings to Nancy Meinking, the NSC staff secretary on the flight, and she was 'building' the set of meeting folders that we would continue to add to once in Paris.

A member of the advance team guided us to the NSC staff office in the U.S. Ambassador's residence at 11:30 p.m.. Coffee and State Department telegrams were our diet for the next four hours. By 3:30 a.m., we had each of the President's papers in its folder, ready for General Scowcroft's review, approval, and initialing forward to the President. "That's Saturday," I said to Nancy; "we'll do Sunday in a few hours." Bleary-eyed, we surveyed the four walls of the staff office. "We're in Paris," I thought, " could just as easily be Pittsburgh." My bedroom in the residence was without doubt the fanciest I had ever been in in my life. I was asleep instantly. In what seemed a matter of seconds, I was sitting bolt upright! There had been the crash of a door. I saw the silhouette of helmet and rifle against the night sky between open french doors leading to a balcony. It was 4:00 a.m.; Marines guarding the President were changing watch.

At 10:30 a.m., on April 6, I had been closeted again for several hours in our NSC staff office, capturing recommendations from the most recent State Department messages, drafting the last of the papers for the upcoming meetings. The faint wail of sirens told me that the President had departed en route to Notre Dame. Shortly thereafter, I was able to emerge from the 'staff bunker' to discover a sunny, spring day. I reconnoitered the formal rooms of the three-storied, eighteenth century residence at 41 Rue du Faubourg Saint-Honore, just off the circumference of the Place de la Concorde. Ambassador John Irwin's collection of original oils added to the elegance of the interior, the marble floors, the grand white stone staircase serving the three floors of the mansion. The structure was further enhanced by its grounds, a formal garden of lawn, trees and planting running from the rear of the mansion toward the Champs-Elysees.

The afternoon talks went smoothly. At 5:00 p.m., the President departed for the diplomatic reception, accompanied by staff, the American Ambassador to France and General Walters, his interpreter. Walters was—and is—a phenomenal linguist, fluent in eight languages. By his own account, he was already proficient in French, Spanish, Italian, and German, in addition to his native English, by the age of 16.[1]

He had traveled extensively with Richard Nixon during both the Vice Presidential and the Presidential years. He would later reflect on this final overseas assignment with the President and its significance in terms of Nixon's view of summitry: "President Nixon greatly enjoyed these trips abroad and the contact they gave him with foreign leaders. He believed that much could be done by such contacts and that leaders who know one another personally were less likely to react rashly to what the other might do."[2]

On April 7, immediately following the President's breakfast with Chairman Podgorny and his meeting with Prime Minister Tanaka, which had included a strolling conversation along the tan pebbled paths of the residence's gardens, our delegation departed for Orly, and we were again airborne for the United States. General Walters, in an aisle seat immediately across from me on Air Force One, fished into a carry-on satchel for book and began to read. A half-hour or so later, he fished again for another. He had my admiration—finding relaxation as he was on the long flight reading foreign dictionaries.

The tete-a-tete between Chancellor Brandt and President Nixon would soon take on historical significance. In early May 1974, the international wires were carrying a new flash: "BLITZ—UNOFFICIAL—BRANDT RESIGNED—REUTER HZ/GBA 0100 5/7/74."[3] Gunter Guillaume, Brandt's personal aide for several years had been arrested and had confessed to being a spy for the East German Ministry of State Security and an officer in the East German Army. Brandt had taken responsibility and resigned. Within a matter of weeks, the leadership of France and the Federal Republic of Germany had changed. Giscard d'Estaing, former Minister of Finance, was now President of France. Helmut Schmidt, former FRG Minister of Finance was now the West German Chancellor.

On August 9, 1974, at 11:35 a.m., President Nixon had a one-sentence letter delivered to the Secretary of State: "Dear Mr. Secretary: I hereby resign the office of President of the United States. Sincerely, Richard M. Nixon."[4] Scandals and death had now completed a stunning change in the leadership of the West. Pompidou, Brandt, and Nixon were gone. And, perhaps because fate had brought Giscard d'Estaing, Helmut Schmidt, and Gerald R. Ford to power near-simultaneously, the three leaders, with Harold Wilson of Great Britain, seemed to share a special affinity and a fresh dedication to cooperation.

I had been among those in the East Room of the White House for President Nixon's farewell to his Cabinet and staff at mid-morning, August 9. Less than three hours later, I was in the Roosevelt Room with Secretary Kissinger and the new President for his first meeting with the NATO nations' Ambassadors to the United States. In President Ford's words: "The Nixon resignation, of course, had been just as profound a shock internationally as it had been in the United States. Henry impressed upon me how essential it was that I become identified in the minds of the diplomatic corps as someone knowledgeable about and involved with the conduct of American foreign policy. Thus, on my first day as President, I met with some 60 envoys from nations all over the world—some privately, such as representatives of the Soviet Union, the People's Republic of China, Israel, several of the Arab nations and South Vietnam. Others—the envoys of our NATO Allies—we received as a group."[5]

In his address to a joint session of the Congress on August 12, President Ford set a theme of *continuity* as his approach to the nation's foreign policy: continuity in collaboration with America's allies in the Atlantic and Pacific, continuity of dialogue aimed at improved relationships with our neighbors in Central and South America, continuity—in the wake of the Vietnam War—to friends and allies in Asia, continuity in building on the achievements of the 1972–74 summits in relations with the Soviet Union, continuity in following through on the opening to the People's Republic of China, continuity to negotiations for a lasting peace among all parties in the Middle East, and continuity to a stable structure of trade and finance among all nations.[6] The theme, which made great sense to me, given my labors since 1971, had, of course, been shaped by Secretary Kissinger. Even before taking the oath of office, Ford had announced that he would urge Kissinger to continue both as Assistant to the President for National Security Affairs and as Secretary of State. And, with the new President looking to Kissinger in this dual role for guidance at the outset of his presidency, the Ford Administration got off to a running start in summitry.

The foreign policy flavor of the new President's schedule was captured by the official record of his first full week in office. Included were the following: a statement of support for the independence of Guinea-Bissau; the address to the Congress; announcements of nominations of the new U.S. Ambassadors to Greece and the Republic of Korea; a message to the Congress on U.S.-U.K. atomic energy cooperation; a White House visit by King Hussein of Jordan; telephone conversations with the U.K. Foreign Minister and Prime Minister; a meeting with Soviet Ambassador Dobrynin; announcement of the acceptance of an invitation to visit Japan; a White House meeting with Egyptian Foreign Minister Fahmy; a White House breakfast with

Senate Members to discuss the link between trade and freedom of emigration in America's relations with Communist countries; and several meetings on national security issues.[7]

With the coming of September and the opening of the U.N. General Assembly, the annual surge of high-level foreign visitors—Ministers, Heads of Government and Chiefs of State—began again, with intense diplomatic pressure for calls on the President either before or after each leader's U.N. address in New York. From October 8–13, Edward Gierek, First Secretary of the Central Committee of the Polish United Workers Party—that is to say, the leader of Poland—paid an official visit. For at least four months before, representatives of the Polish Embassy in Washington had been discreetly, nervously taking soundings of me and my U.S. Government colleagues on the prospects for this visit, given the mounting domestic problems faced by President Nixon. My counsel had not been complex. Whatever the outcome of those problems, Poland could expect that the United States would continue on a steady course, honoring its international commitments. They should assume that the First Secretary's visit would proceed as planned.

The results of Gierek's visit reflected the interests of both nations in extending the benefits of detente beyond U.S.-USSR bilateral relations. Indeed, the President and the First Secretary presided over the signing of a string of documents in the finest tradition of the 1972-74 summits: a Joint Statement of Principles on U.S.-Polish Relations; a Joint Statement on the Development of Economic, Industrial and Technological Cooperation; a Joint Statement on the Development of Agricultural Trade; and bilateral agreements on cooperation in the fields of coal research, health, environmental protection, science and technology, and the avoidance of double taxation. However, there was a difference, as the Polish First Secretary reminded the President during the course of his lengthy, formal reply to the President's toast at the White House dinner on October 8. Reviewing Poland's long history and its current place in the world, he said: "The people of Poland found it in its new Socialist homeland, *in its consciously chosen alliance with the USSR* and other Socialist nations, in its active foreign policy of international security and peaceful cooperation."[8]

Within two weeks, we were in Moscow, preparing for the Vladivostok summit, then on to Romania, Yugoslavia, and Italy with the Secretary of State on missions that both contributed to the foreign policy requirements of the moment and set the stage for more intensive, future involvement by the President. In fact, President Ford's first summit travel was to Mexico for a day's talks and ceremony with President Echeverria on October 21, 1974.

A month later, the President was in Tokyo on a State Visit, with a ceremonial call on Emperor Hirohito (a call which, while entirely cordial, involved incorrect staff advice to the President on his diplomatic attire, an important checklist item for any summit sherpa), and talks with Prime Minister Tanaka. The central focus of the latter was on the energy crisis and the requirement for intensified cooperation among consumer nations. Air Force One then carried the President to Seoul, South Korea where a welcoming crowd of two million cheered him on his 12-mile motorcade from Kimpo International Airport to the Blue House for talks with President Park Chung Hee. Here, Ford assumed the dual role of both President and Commander in Chief, pledging further American cooperation in the development of South Korea's defense industries, and pledging that American troops would remain on the peninsula in the shared defense of the nation. Ford then traveled by helicopter to meet with the soldiers of the U.S. Army's Second Division only a few miles from the Demilitarized Zone separating North and South Korea. Having made that firm recommitment to American allies in the Pacific, the President was again airborne for Vladivostok.

True to the foreign policy commitment made in this first address to the Congress, President Ford continued an extremely fast pace of summit-level consultations throughout 1974 and early 1975—a White House meeting in mid-November with Chancellor Bruno Kreisky of Austria, and White House talks and dinner with Prime Minister Trudeau of Canada less than two weeks after the return from Vladivostok. While the President was continuing to open important personal lines of contact to other world leaders, at the staff level earnest preparations were underway for one of the most important summits of the new President's first months in office.

On October 10, 1974, the White House and the Elysee Palace simultaneously announced that President Ford and President Giscard d'Estaing would meet on the island of Martinique, the French West Indies, in December. There was a tone and spirit to the new French President's communications and actions that offered the potential of positive results, still undefined, at Martinique. Dr. Kissinger, as Secretary of State and National Security Adviser, geared up preparations within the NSC system to ensure that the President would be able to capitalize on any opportunities for progress at Martinique.

President Ford would grow tremendously and become a highly accomplished statesman during his Presidency. In the autumn of 1974, he was working hard to learn and to master this complicated craft and he placed the highest value on Kissinger's recommendations and guidance. Ford wrote: "Kissinger kept stressing how important it was that we attempt to improve our relations with the French, so on December 14, I flew to meet Giscard for two days of talks on the French West Indies island of Martinique."[9] To that point, Ford had never met Giscard d'Estaing. "Photographs showed him to be a tall, balding elegantly attired man with sharp eyes, a prominent nose and an aristocratic bearing, and he had a reputation for aloofness."[10] The staff papers for Martinique provided the President with great detail on d'Estaing—his background, the policies of his new government, the interests forming the very heart of the enduring U.S.-French alliance, the current differences and difficulties in the bilateral relationship, and U.S.-French relations in the context of regional and global issues. For example, the Middle East, East-West relations, the continuing energy crisis, and the attendant economic difficulties of the democracies; as well as papers analyzing those issues susceptible of progress.

I have mentioned that the Martinique Summit was announced simultaneously in Washington and Paris. Proper execution of such announcements marks the first, formal, public step toward a successful summit. As the prestige of each participating nation is committed when leaders meet at the summit, it is important that neither be seen as capturing a political advantage through unilateral revelation of a planned meeting. Summits announced or leaked in advance by one side may be postponed or canceled by the other. No leader, however small his or her nation, however miniscule its role, can afford the domestic political perception of having been treated as a subordinate or an inferior. France, of course, was second to none in insisting on the correctness of this procedure, and indeed it was successfully carried out in 1974. Given the splendid checks and balances of the U.S. democratic process, given the need to engage several departments of government as part of the careful preparation of any major summit, the business of managing simultaneous announcements is never less than nerve-wracking.

"Un Grand Honneur Pour Cette Terre Francais des Antilles," the newspaper *France-Antilles* announced in red and black banner headlines; "Le Monde Entier Regarde la Martinique."[11] Giscard d'Estaing alighted from his white Puma helicopter at 4:30 p.m., at

Lamentin Airport on the outskirts of Fort de France to receive formal military honors. At 4:45 p.m., President Ford's scheduled arrival time, Air Force One rolled to a precision stop, with the plane's forward door, from which the President would deplane, aligned precisely with the foot of the long red carpet the French President was traversing to greet his American guest. The Star Spangled Banner and La Marseillaise were played. The greens of the island's tropical foliage were brilliant in the fresh sunlight of a receding sea squall. As I watched the colorful arrival ceremony, savoring the warm, thick Caribbean air—with the snows of Vladivostok still a new and vivid memory—I was impressed as I would continue to be by the very special privilege I enjoyed as a participant in America's summit diplomacy.

Even before his first meeting with Ford, Giscard d'Estaing had signaled a desire for greater cooperation with the United States. His experience as Finance Minister had taught him that the international monetary and energy problems were global in scale, that France could not afford the posture of Gaullist aloofness with the United States if her own interests were to be served. In early October, Secretary Kissinger had remarked on the new tone of the relationship, in the context of his dealings with France's new Foreign Minister Jean Sauvagnargues and Giscard d'Estaing: "He said that president Giscard doesn't have the same theoretical bias as his predecessors and is prepared to proceed on a more pragmatic 'basis.'" that with Sauvagnargues "we now talk about problems and not about form."[12]

Now, first at Lamentin Airport and later at that evening's state dinner at the French Prefect's residence in Fort de France, Giscard's words captured the new tone and projected the new personal style: "It was a real pleasure for me to extend to you and to all those accompanying you, a most cordial welcome. As soon as you came into office, we both felt that we should establish a direct and personal contact. Such contact is in keeping with the traditional relations between France and the United States and under the present circumstance, we thought this would be especially useful....All this points to the importance of our meeting, as stressed by our partners in the European Community, and sincerity—the frankness and cordiality with which I trust our talks will start and be concluded."[13]

That evening, in the elegant ambiance of the Caribbean, tropical flowers, torchlight and Martinique rums at the Prefect's residence, Giscard continued his stage-setting welcome for the summit talks of the following day: "Freedom and friendship have stamped their mark on the relations between our two countries. Freedom allows for their frankness and independence; friendship demands mutual under- standing and cooperation." And, in the same spirit in his return toast, President Ford said: "Let us continue our historic relationship with renewed spirit and redoubled effort as good and responsible friends. Our common heritage gives me confidence that we will continue our joint endeavors for peace and stability in the world. Mr. President, it is with this objective that I look forward to our discussions tomorrow. I have every hope that our talks will strengthen the friendships between us, both in a bilateral sense and also as members of the alliance which Americans regard as the cornerstone of our foreign policy."[14]

The drafting of proposed toasts is part of the summit staffer's responsibilities—anecdotes, gentle humor, historical vignettes, spe- cific goals of the summit, and the significance of the event not only for the participating nations but also for international relations in the broader sense, are among the preferred ingredients. The toast should contribute not only to the spirit of the occasion but also to the flow of the summit, to the media's coverage and from that coverage to the public's appreciation of the event. The toast should be drafted to cap- ture the summit leader's cadence and manner of speech. It should also be organized so that even a quick advance reading permits the leader to capture its themes and outline to facilitate smooth reading; or better still, to facilitate departures from the prepared text for extemporaneous delivery based on prior study of the text. Toasts are part of the substance and the record of a summit, and Presidents— particularly during jet travel to several nations in quick succes- sion—rely on their staffs for carefully drafted remarks. And, it is not uncommon in summit suites to have a last minute flurry among a delegation's speech writers, NSC and foreign policy advisers at a Pres- ident's request to produce new or revised language that better captures the dynamics of a summit in progress. Such was not the case on the evening of December 14. The two Presidents were relaxed and seemed to enjoy each other's company thoroughly. There was a 'posi- tive chemistry', which they had captured in the friendly, easy delivery of their toasts, and, more importantly, in their dinner conversation. As my colleagues and I re-boarded a launch from the French aircraft carrier *Foch* for the return trip to our hotel across the harbor, the omens for the following day could not have been better.

On December 15, the two Presidents and their Foreign Minis- ters retired by helicopter to the secluded, informal setting of a mountainside villa to course across the agenda of U.S.-French interests in the fresh, positive spirit established so publicly the day before. In parallel, their financial experts, Secretary of the Treasury William Simon and Minister of Finance Jean-Pierre Fourcade closeted themselves at the U.S. delegation's hotel. These dialogues continued through the day. And, in the process, one of my tasks served to underscore that an American President engaged in overseas summitry continues to exercise the full responsibilities of his office. General Alexander Haig, Ford's first Chief of Staff, had been nominated by the President to serve in the extremely important dual-hatted position as Commander-in-Chief U.S. Forces Europe, and Supreme Allied Commander Europe. Already in Belgium serving in the first of these capacities, he received formal approval from the NATO Governments as SACEUR, while President Ford was in Martinique. My draft of a message of congratulations from Ford to Haig, penned in the setting of my seaside hotel room balcony, went forward to the President for review and approval. That evening, the President repaid French hospitality with a dinner equal in relaxed cordiality to that of the night before.

The summit communique was released at 11:00 a.m., December 16, before the two Presidents took their leave. *Le Figaro* would report that the summit had marked the end of an era of U.S.-French quarrels. *L'Aurore* would agree saying that Ford and d'Estaing had eliminated the "surliness, friction, and misunderstandings which for a long time crippled Franco-American relations." Giscard d'Estaing, interviewed in Martinique by French radio, ascribed much of the success of the summit to the friendship, the frankness, and the "quality of human relations" he and Ford had established. He expressed the belief that the talks in Martinique would lead to continuing, very friendly cooperation. In introducing the communique in a press conference at the Meridien Hotel, Secretary Kissinger had characterized the talks: "Having attended many similar meetings between French and American leaders, I must say I found this atmosphere the most positive between the two leaders, and one in which as far as the United States in concerned—the French President will undoubtedly speak for himself—we will continue in the exchanges that will be necessary to implement the various aspects of the communique, as well as the cooperation that is foreseen in the communique."[15]

The international energy crisis of 1973–74 occupied a central place in the results of Martinique. Ford and Giscard d'Estaing stated their agreement on the need for an early conference of oil exporting and oil importing nations. Under Pompidou, France has kept her distance from the newly established International Energy Agency struggling to find common ground among the Western consumer nations whose economies had been assaulted by the continuing leap in the oil producers' prices. Now, France under Giscard d'Estaing was skillfully moving closer to an agreed consumer position.

With the advice of their Finance Ministers, the two Presidents agreed that the time had come to move from a fixed price for gold to a market price, easing one of many international monetary strains and tensions.

The communique went on to present the essence of the summit discussions on East-West relations, again, the prospects for the Conference on Security and Cooperation in Europe, discussions with the People's Republic of China, with the USSR, progress within Western Europe on the process of European unity, developments in Vietnam, Laos, and Cambodia, and developments in the Atlantic Alliance, Here, the results of the summit moved from the desirable to hard, positive accomplishment. Giscard D'Estaing, moving to eliminate a U.S.-French friction of almost a decade had told Ford that France would agree to pay the United States $100 million as a financial settlement for the relocation in 1967 of U.S. forces and bases committed to NATO from France and other allied nations. "Initially," Ford would write, "we had wanted a payment four times the amount the French were offering. But Bill Simon and I agreed that any settlement after so many years of deadlock was more important for the future course of our bilateral relations that the sum involved. We told the French they had a deal."[16]

The Martinique summit marked a major step forward both for U.S.-French relations and U.S.-European relations, and for this the Federal Republic of Germany's new Chancellor deserved great credit. Helmut Schmidt had pronounced his intense concern over the threat that the international energy and economic problems posed to the well-being of the Western democracies in his first NATO summit appearance as Chancellor in June 1974. Throughout the summer and fall, he stayed in close consultation with his friend Giscard d'Estaing, now the leader of France. Schmidt knew beyond a shadow of a doubt that if the oil consumer nations were to emerge successfully from the crisis, they would need maximum unity in their dealing with the oil producers. This meant that France would have to abandon the positions of Pompidou and Jobert, and would have to work more closely with the United States and the other members of the International

Energy Agency. This, in turn, meant that skillful, flexible diplomacy would be required on the part not only of France, but also on the part of the new U.S. President to ease the change in the position of France.

With the groundwork laid, Schmidt came to Washington for his first talks with President Ford on December 5–6, 1974. The two days enabled Schmidt skillfully to advance his views on the range of economic and energy problems not only with the President, but also with Secretary Kissinger, Secretary Simon, the Chairman of the President's Council of Economic Advisers, and the Chairman of the Federal Reserve Board. The talks produced a detailed, lengthy U.S.-FRG statement of agreed positions on both political and economic issues, in language helping further to set the stage for Martinique. At the same time great care was taken, of course, in all public statements relating to the U.S.-German talks to underscore that France's decisions would be for France to take and that Ford and Schmidt did not presume to speak for France.

The tone of Schmidt's words during the course of the summit underscored both the importance of the issues and the fullness of his satisfaction over the understandings being reached. He expressed his thanks "for this free exchange of analyses and talks and of the plans we might put into operation in the next time, because we do really feel that your great country, five times as big—I mean in economic size—than ours, and our second biggest in terms of foreign trade, we do really feel that both our responsibilities, vis-a-vis the world's economy as a whole and the other partners of the free world economy, request from us that we try as much as one can to coordinate our economic policies as we have coordinated our defense policies, as we have coordinated our detente policies, as we tried to coordinate our policies all over the globe. Now, at this present stage I think in the economic field there lies a greater part of our faith, not only of your people, also of ours, also of other people."[17]

As would be the case with the President's meeting with Giscard d'Estaing, Ford's down-to-earth, congenial, forward-looking manner produced an immediate bond and friendship with the Chancellor. Schmidt liked the President's style, his willingness, for example, to depart from normal summit formality and to stroll from the White House over to Blair House for a continuation of the talks begun earlier that day in the Oval Office. Ford, in turn, took great satisfaction in his relationship with Schmidt. He noted that after the first State Dinner of December 5, the two had continued their discussion in the White House residence until 2:00 a.m.. In Ford's words: "This underscores a point often overlooked in discussions for foreign policy—the importance of personality. Relations between the U.S. and West Germany were excellent throughout my administration, primarily because Schmidt and I got along so well. As we became better acquainted, we called each other by our first names, we joked with each other and we saw eye to eye on almost everything."[18]

Following the very successful meeting with Schmidt and Giscard d'Estaing, Ford invited Prime Minister Harold Wilson to Washington in late January 1975, to continue his head-to head talks with key allied leaders. Shortly after having taken office, the President had met briefly at the White House with British Foreign Minister Callaghan. Now, he and the British Prime Minister pressed ahead with the international agenda of energy shortages, inflation, balance of payment deficits, regional tensions around the world and the central security interests they shared as allies. Harold Wilson was 'an old pro' at summitry, having served as Prime Minister from 1964 to 1970. That said, he also shared the experience of Ford, Giscard and Schmidt in that he had again taken the reins of power in 1974—a *bona fide* member of the Big Four's Class of '74. On top of that, he and Ford were both dedicated pipe-smokers. They got along famously.

President Ford had indeed found attraction in the dangerous diplomatic method of summitry, to use Dean Acheson's words; it had paid him, quick, valuable dividends early on in his dealing with America's allies and the USSR; and it had set the stage for more intensive summitry still throughout 1975.

End Notes

1. Walters, Vernon A., *Silent Missions*, Doubleday & Company, Inc., Garden City, New York, 1978, page 5.
2. Ibid., page 574.
3. Drath, Viola Herms, *Willy Brandt, Prisoner of His Past*, Chilton Book Company, Radnor, Pennsylvania, 1975, page 5.
4. *The New York Times*, New York, August 10, 1974, page 1.
5. Gerald R. Ford, *A Time to Heal*, Harper & Row Publishers, New York, 1979, page 129.
6. *Presidential Documents*, The President's Address Delivered Before a Joint Session of the Congress, August 12, 1974, Administration of Gerald R. Ford, August 19, 1974, Vol. 10, Number 33, page 1034.
7. Ibid., pages 1029-41.
8. Exchange of Toasts Between the President and Edward Gierek, State Dining Room, the White House, *Office of the White House Press Secretary*, October 8, 1974.

9. Ford, Gerald R., *A Time to Heal*, page 222.

10. Ibid., pages 221–222.

11. *France-Antilles*, December 15, 1974.

12. Farnsworth, Clyde H., *The New York Times*, October 7, 1974, page 4.

13. Exchange of Remarks Between the President and President Valery Giscard d'Estaing, Lamentin Airport, *Office of the White House Press Secretary*, Martinique, F.W.I., December 14, 1974.

14. Exchange of Toasts between the President and President Valery Giscard d'Estaing, The Prefect's Residence, *Office of the White House Press Secretary*, Martinique, F.W.I., December 14, 1974.

15. Press Conference of Henry A. Kissinger, Secretary of State and Assistant to the President for National Security Affairs, Meridien Hotel, *Office of the White House Press Secretary*, Martinique, F.W.I., December 16, 1974.

16. Ford, Gerald R., *A Time to Heal*, page 223.

17. Exchange of Toasts Between the President and Helmut Schmidt, Chancellor of the Federal Republic of Germany, the White House, *Office of the White House Press Secretary*, December 5, 1974.

18. Ford, Gerald R., *A Time to Heal*, page 221.

CHAPTER FIVE

Europe—1975

I am not ignorant that it is, and has been of old, the opinion of
many people, that the affairs of the world are so governed by
fortune and Divine Providence that man cannot by his wisdom
correct them, or apply any remedy at all; from whence they would
infer that we are not to labor and sweat, but to leave everything to
its own tendency and event.

The Prince
Machiavelli, 1513

For those of us in the State Dining Room of the White House on
the evening of May 14, 1975, there was a highly unusual atmosphere
of distraction. As President Ford continued a flow of small talk with
his official guest, Johannes den Uyl, the new Socialist Prime Minister
of The Netherlands, members of the President's Cabinet and staff—
Secretary Kissinger, Secretary Schlesinger, General Scowcroft—variously would excuse themselves, leave the room and then return a few
minutes later. While den Uyl and his Dutch delegation maintained a
reserved politeness, conversations among the American participants
at the stag dinner intensified. Following the toasts, the serving of
liqueurs and a final few moments of conversation, the President bade
farewell to his guests and walked swiftly along the Rose Garden
colonnade from the Residence to the West Wing Oval Office.

In the wake of America's withdrawal from Vietnam, the President was faced with a crisis challenging U.S. prestige and testing U.S.
resolve. On May 12, naval patrol boats of the Armed Forces of
Cambodia had seized the U.S. merchant ship SS *Mayaguez* and her
crew in international waters, in violation of international law. U.S.
demands for the return of the ship produced nothing. A U.S.
Navy-Marine Task Force built around the aircraft carrier USS *Coral
Sea* had immediately been ordered to the waters off Cambodia. On
the afternoon of May 14, the President ordered the Marines to retake

the *Mayaguez*. As the U.S.-Dutch dinner wore on in the White House, at 9:00 p.m., Washington time, the Marine engagement half-a-world away reached a bloody, successful climax with the ship and her crew again safely in U.S. hands, but with the loss of two-score Marine lives, one Marine for every American crew member saved.

While costly, the retaking of the *Mayaguez* served to confirm dramatically that a new chapter had been turned in the diplomacy of the Ford Presidency. If 1974 had produced a fresh unity of purpose among the West's Big Four, challenges to the the United States and Europe continued to multiply. Nowhere was this more evident than within the North Atlantic Alliance. Two member nations, Greece and Turkey, were engaged in a continuing crisis-level feud over Cyprus. Portugal, for so many years a 'sleepy', little-noticed member of the Alliance was in the throes of revolution, swinging sharply from right to left with the possibility of Communist domination. Adding to the political problems of NATO's Southern Flank, the Communists were threatening to replace the Christian Democrats as Italy's largest parliamentary party. The smaller NATO nations, smitten by the five-fold increase in the price of oil, were wavering in their commitments both to maintain and to improve their contributions to the Alliance's common defense. Beyond Europe and NATO, the problems of the Middle East, of relations between the world's industrialized North and developing South, and the threat of loss of momentum in the efforts to build on a mutually beneficial detente between East and West all demanded attention.

Acutely aware of the need for action and of the need to demonstrate fresh American global leadership, President Ford moved in the spring of 1975 to engage the dynamics of summit diplomacy on several international fronts. On April 18, the White House—in coordination with spokesmen in other NATO capitals—advised the White House press corps of an upcoming NATO summit. I have earlier mentioned the importance of adhering to the practice of simultaneous announcements. It is also the summit staffer's responsibility to ensure that the spokesman making the announcement not only has the announcement text but also additional guidance in the form of questions that may be anticipated from the press and recommended answers. The objective is to keep the initiative and the direction of the announcement with the spokesman, and not to permit follow-on questions by any reporter to detract from the media's coverage of the intended message.

The announcement of the 1975 NATO summit involved the preparation of a very brief, straightforward document by my office, to be forwarded by Secretary Kissinger's NSC front office to the White House Press Secretary. Text of Press Guidance:

"An announcement was made today in Brussels that the North Atlantic Council has decided that the next Spring meeting May 29–30 will take place with the participation of heads of state or governments. As the President indicated on April 10, he will attend this meeting and looks forward to it as an opportunity for further consultations among the leaders of the Atlantic Alliance and to affirm once again the cohesion and common destiny of the members of the Alliance.

****

Q. What will be the purpose of this meeting?

A. At the meeting the leaders will review the full range of security issues of common concern within the Alliance. They will also review the new steps achieved in recent months in promoting cooperation to meet economic and energy problems. The pace of recent international developments suggests that the time is at hand for the Western leaders to take stock and consult on this agenda of common concerns.

Q. Do you have anything more specific on the agenda or arrangements for the Summit meeting?

A. Now that a date has been set for the meeting, I am certain that preparations for the summit and work on detailed arrangements will begin promptly.

Consulting and taking stock with the Western leaders involved far more than the multilateral colloquy around the NATO conference table. The tightly scheduled hours in Brussels would permit the President not only to deliver a formal address to the North Atlantic Council but also to conduct separate bilateral talks of equal importance with the majority of the summit's participants. Further, the fact of the President's presence in Europe provided him with the springboard for additional summit stops—a path-finding visit to Spain, on onward stop in Austria for a rendezvous with President Sadat of Egypt on the Middle East agenda, and final important leg to Italy and the Vatican City for talks with President Leone, Prime Minister Moro, and His Holiness Pope Paul VI.

At the NSC staff level, I monitored preparations for the visit with a long checklist including each of the European trip's events to be staffed, listed vertically in chronological order on the left-hand side, and the status of each event's staffing in a lateral set of boxes running form left to right beneath the heading, with HAK indicating Kissinger in his NSC role:

EVENT	Drafts Received from State Dept. and Others	Cover Memo Drafted	Forwarded to HAK
A. Departure Remarks Andrews AFB			
B. BRUSSELS May 29–30			
1. Arrival Statement			
2. Toasts			
3. Book for Meeting with King Baudouin I			
4. NATO Summit Book			
5. President's Address to NATO Summit			
6. Book for Giscard d'Estaing[1]			
7. Book for Tindemans, Belgium			
8. Book for Thorn, Luxembourg			
9. Book for Caramanlis, Greece			
10. Book for Demirel, Turkey			
11. Book for Schmidt, FRG			
12. Book for Jorgensen, Denmark			
13. Book for Goncalves, Portugal			
14. Book for Wilson, U.K.			
15. Book for Bratelli, Norway			
16. Book for Ortoli, EEC			
17. Book for Trudeau, Canada			

EVENT	Drafts Received from State Dept. and Others	Cover Memo Drafted	Forwarded to HAK
18. Book for Mrs. Ford, Belgium			
19. Departure Remarks			
C. SPAIN May 31–June 1			
20. Arrival and Departure Statements			
21. Toasts			
22. Book for Spanish Leaders			
23. Book for Mrs. Ford, Spain			
D. AUSTRIA June 1–2			
24. Arrival and Departure Statements			
25. Toasts			
26. Book for Chancellor Kreisky, Austria			
27. Book for President Sadat, Egypt			
28. Book for Mrs. Ford, Austria			
29. Arrival and Departure Statements			
E. ITALY Vatican June 3			
30. Toasts			
31. Book for Meetings with Moro and Leone			
32. Book for Meeting with Pope			
33. Book for Mrs. Ford, Italy and Vatican			
F. Draft of Report to Nation on European Trip			

In each instance, my reference to Cover Memo drafted involved the preparation by me and my staff of a succinct document, to be forwarded to the President by Secretary Kissinger in his NSC role. Stated therein was the President's purpose—or primary reason for holding the talks—the background information relating to each issue to be addressed, and recommended talking points. These statements, covered issue by issue, were couched in the language that the President might choose to draw on in his meetings with each of the other leaders to pursue the U.S. and Allied positions to the greatest advantage.

In accordance with directions contained in the trip bible, I was at the Andrews Air Force Base Distinguished Visitors Lounge at 6:45 a.m., on May 28. With luggage inspected and checked through by the Secret Service, I boarded Air Force One in advance of the President and Mrs. Ford, and the six members of his staff accompanying them by helicopter from the South Lawn of the White House.

I always made it a practice to learn the interior layout and the location of important equipment aboard each of the special mission Air Force jets I traveled on—the location of back-up supplies in the staff work area, idiosyncrasies of the telephones at various points in each aircraft, idiosyncrasies of the copier machines. Similarly I always made a point of introducing myself and getting to know the crew members in the passenger compartments and the communications center aboard each aircraft. White the flights can be extremely long, the drafting, revisions, and communications required during a Presidential flight often must be carried out under extreme time pressure. The staffer learns that if revisions are to be made to the text of the President's arrival statement, they must be anticipated. Even the best of seasoned summit secretaries can type only so quickly when the jet is banking for its final approach to the President's summit destination; and even the best of copier machines won't copy when the jet is climbing or descending at a certain angle.

The newest of the Presidential Air Force jets at the time—VC 137C Tail Number 27000—was a handsome machine, now halfway through its third decade of service. Its exterior was distinguished from those of commercial Boeing 707s by a distinguished paint scheme of white, royal and pastel blues bearing the Presidential seal in full color, the name UNITED STATES OF AMERICA in black against the white of the upper fuselage, the American flag and tail number on the vertical stabilizer, and the underbody and wings a gleaming, carefully polished metal—a paint scheme used by its 747 successors.

Air Force One 27000 flown by Ford, was 145-feet-9-inches wing-tip to wingtip, and 152-feet-11-inches for the nose radar forward to the tip of the tail. The interior layout was designed to be of maximum efficiency, comfort and service to the President, his party and support personnel. Moving aft from the cockpit, you passed the communications center on the left, a forward galley, bunks for the crew on the right, seat for the crew and members of the Secret Service detail. A somewhat narrow passageway then took you along the port side of the aircraft past three doors opening onto the President's Office, the President's and First Lady's Sitting Room, and a lounge and conference room. The jet's interior then opened out again to a senior staff room covering the full beam of the aircraft—two fabric covered conference tables with four first-class seats fore-and-aft, as well as telephones connecting to the communications center. Immediately behind these tables, the staff room had two L-shaped secretary's desks, each with its own aircraft seat, each fitted with typewriters and other support equipment. The jet's next compartment was the aft lounge, with eight first-class seats. Beyond this was the security compartment, providing for the balance of the onboard Secret Service detail. Through another door was the aft compartment, with more seats for staff and the traveling Press Pool, as well as the jet's highly capable galley.

On the flight to Brussels, I was at one staff table in the senior staff room with General Scowcroft. The President's Chief of Staff Donald Rumsfeld, Press Secretary Ron Nessen, Presidential Aide Terry O'Donnell, and Advanceman Red Cavaney were across the aisle. As the minutes ticked away on the seven-hour-ten-minute passage across the Atlantic, a steady flow of papers moved to and from the President's office, and from time to time he and Mrs. Ford would stroll through the jet to converse with staff and the traveling press. In my experience, long flights can be a time both of productive work and of unnecessary busy work. The latter on the part of a very few of the traveling parties with whom I have flown, who have sought to impress Presidents and Vice Presidents by recommending last-minute changes to already well-staffed documents. It is often an affliction borne of boredom aloft. Later in my career I would advise one distinguished airborne delegate that I planned to buy him a coloring book and crayons at the next stop to keep him occupied during the onward legs of our overseas travel.

President Ford encouraged an atmosphere aboard Air Force One that was at the same time professional and relaxed, and the busy-work problem was not pronounced en route to the NATO summit. Final changes to the President's summit address were made, and General Scowcroft entrusted me to oversee their incorporation and the safeguarding of the text—with no further offers of review or revision to be accepted.

From the moment of arrival at Zavantem Airport Brussels precisely at 8:00 p.m., the scheduled hour, the President began an extremely heavy schedule, with each event planned to contribute to his summit objectives. Following his remarks at the airport arrival ceremony, he traveled by motorcade to the Royal Palace for a courtesy call on the King and Queen of the Belgians and then the first of his NATO bilateral meetings with Prime Minister Tindemans and the Belgian Minister of Foreign Affairs.

Ambassador Firestone had turned over the American Ambassador's Residence in Brussels to the President and Mrs. Ford for the duration of their stay. From the residence, the President launched Thursday, May 29, with an hour's working breakfast from 8:15 to 9:15 a.m., with Prime Minister Thorn of Luxembourg, followed by back-to-back meetings more than an hour each with Prime Minister Caramanlis of Greece and Prime Minister Demirel of Turkey. He then hosted a working lunch for Helmut Schmidt, and had two additional back-to-back meetings with Prime Minister Jorgensen of Denmark and Gonclaves, the new Prime Minister of Portugal.

At 4:15 p.m., I was aboard the Presidential motorcade en route to NATO Headquarters for the first of two days of multilateral NATO summit sessions. Following the opening ceremony and the "family portrait" of the NATO leaders, our delegation proceeded to Conference Room Number One for the restricted session, not open to the press. There the President, flanked by Secretary Kissinger and U.S. Ambassador to NATO David Bruce, took his seat at the enormous, open-centered oval conference table, with the emblem of the NATO sword and shield on the conference room floor at its center. With the United States placed between the NATO Secretary-General and the U.K. Delegation, the principals of the 14 nations faced each other as Allies and peers. Behind them were their accompanying delegations seated in conference chairs fitted with translation headsets. I studied the reactions of the other participants to President Ford's address.

The summit staffer need not, and often should not be at various of the events that are scheduled during a President's overseas travel. I believe it was President Franklin Roosevelt who said that a good White House staff member should have a passion for anonymity. Similarly, a good staff member should have a dedication to discretion and to the exercise of good judgment on when and where his presence is required. It is then the staffer's responsibility to ensure that those in charge of the detailed scenario planning and scheduling for the summit travel reflect his participation in all appropriate events in the printed schedules and trip bibles that are prepared prior to departure. These schedules are coordinated by the advance teams with the host countries. The names of those who will participate in each event are forwarded to the protocol offices and those responsible for security in each host country. Invitations are prepared; identification passes and identification pins to be worn by each participant are readied by name in advance of the President's arrival. Once the summit is underway, all such arrangements are adhered to as much as possible.

At 6:30 p.m., the President returned to the Residence to change into black tie for the King's Dinner at the Royal Palace, and the accompanying informal tete-a-tete with Giscard d'Estaing. A long, productive day ended with his return once again to the Residence shortly after 11:00 that night. Some eight hours later he was again at the entrance of the Residence to greet Prime Minister Wilson, Foreign Secretary Callaghan and Cabinet Secretary Sir John Hunt who had joined him for a working breakfast. From 10:00 a.m., until 2:00 p.m., the President was again at NATO Headquarters, and at the conclusion of the second round of NATO deliberations he held his first press conference of the European trip.

In his summit address, President Ford has emphasized the enduring bonds and purpose of the NATO Alliance: "Together we continue to be greatest reservoir of the economic, military, and moral strength in the world. We must use that strength to safeguard our freedom and to address the grave problems that confront us. I am proud of America's role in NATO, and I am confident of the future of our Alliance....There have been strains and difficulties within the Alliance during the past year. Serious disagreements have marred relations among some members. The unity of the Alliance and our common resolve have come into question...we must maintain a strong and credible defense....A society that does not have the vigor and dedication to defend itself cannot survive—neither can an alliance...we must preserve the quality and integrity of this Alliance on the basis of unqualified participation, not on the basis of partial membership or special arrangements." And, looking to the future of detente, the President said that the NATO Allies must, "assure that the promises made in the Conference on Security and Cooperation in Europe are translated into action to advance freedom and human dignity for all Europeans. Only by such realistic steps can we keep CSCE in perspective, whatever euphoric or inflated emphasis the Soviet Union or other participants may try to give it."[2]

Speaking with his customary candor, the President told the press on May 30, how he had dealt with the most difficult of these problems in his private discussions with the Allied leaders. He said his discussions with Caramanlis of Greece and Demirel of Turkey gave him hope that progress might be realized on the problems of Cyprus in a meeting encouraged by the United States, to be held by the Greek and Turkish Foreign Ministers immediately after the NATO summit. He said he had advised Prime Minister Goncalves of Portugal of "the contradiction that would arise if Communist elements came to dominate the political life of Portugal, and it is my judgment that others among the allies had a similar concern. There is a general agreement that the situation must be watched with care and concern but, also, with deep sympathy and friendship of the people of Portugal."[3] Turning to another major political issue on which there was not yet Alliance unity, the President stressed the important future role to be played by Spain in the work of the Alliance and the West, and he said that the United States would continue to favor and work for a Spanish relationship with NATO.

The NATO summit's final communique emerging from the two days of consultations, while cast in the rounded language of diplomacy, captured the critical points the United States identified as essential for progress across the Alliance. The Allies as a result of the summit were agreed that, "the maintenance of the Allied defense effort at a satisfactory level encounters new difficulties arising from the world-wide economic situation. The Allies are resolved to face such challenges together and with determination....In a troubled world subject to rapid transformation the Allies reaffirm that the security of each is of vital concern to all. They owe it, not only to themselves but to the international community, to stand by the principles and the spirit of solidarity and mutual assistance which brought them together as Allies."[4] And, the communique reaffirmed that the Alliance's essential purpose remained the safeguarding of its members and creation of lasting peace.

The Communique was important as a point of formal Alliance agreement and reference. The many bilateral talks had been of even greater importance in developing frank, constructive understandings among the leaders of the member nations—in terms far more explicit and operationally oriented than either possible or desirable in a communique—to guide the work and the cooperation to be pursued by the individual nations's foreign policy and defense ministries following the departure of the summiteers from Brussels.

While most of the U.S. traveling party turned its attention to the flight to Madrid and the U.S.-Spanish summit scheduled for the following day, President Ford conducted two more sessions of bilateral talks, with Prime Minister Trygve Bratteli of Norway and President Ortoli of the European Economic Commission, to take maximum advantage of the valuable opportunities afforded by the summit visit to Brussels. Serving as notetaker during the President's talks with Bratteli, I was impressed by the depth of the ties of friendship and purpose—far greater than any transitory Alliance problems—that the United States enjoys with its partners among the Western democracies. As the two leaders' conversation ranged easily over the events of the summit, the white-haired Prime Minister told the President that most of the Bratteli family had emigrated from Norway to the United States, that he had many relatives in Staten Island, New York, with whom he stayed in touch, and that it was only through unpredictable twists of fate that he, himself, had not become an American.

The flight to Madrid, while only two hours, marked a passing from the present to both the past and the future. Ford, as Vice President, had visited Spain in 1973 for the funeral of assassinated Prime Minister Carrero Blanco. Now, as President he was seized by the importance of negotiating a new agreement governing U.S. use of Spanish military bases. Of even greater geopolitical importance, he saw Spain at a crossroads of tremendous significance for the Western democracies. With Generalissimo Franco nearing the end of his days, the President believed it essential that Spain receive credit for its contributions in fact to the security of the West, and that it be encouraged at the start of the final quarter to the 20th Century in the steps required for its transformation in fact into a democracy.

The President had pressed the case for Spain at the NATO Summit and had been rebuffed. "The Spaniards," he would write, "had a role to play in the defense of the West. They recognized that and were willing to join the Alliance. The problem was that some of our more liberal NATO Allies—the Dutch, Norwegians, and Danes—insisted on blocking Spain's membership as long as Generalissimo Franco was alive."[5]

The fact that the President chose to come to Madrid in the face of this continuing Allied opposition would underscore the boldness and the wisdom of his summit diplomacy. The welcome— colorful, enormous, at the highest level of protocol—reflected Spain's appreciation. The Generalissimo and Mrs. Franco, Prime Minister and Mrs. Arias, and the Foreign Minister and Mrs. Cortina were at the foot of the ramp when the front door of Air Force One swung open at 11:00 a.m., on May 31. Following the Generalissimo's warm words of welcome, the summit motorcade proceeded along routes lined with a military guard of honor, the sidewalks several people deep with spectators.

The limousines stopped at the Plaza Cibeles for a second ceremonial welcome and a presentation of the key of the City of Madrid by Mayor Garcia-Lomas. The Royal Palace Guard dressed the parade as the motorcade continued into the city. The guardsmen, mounted on tall, matched chestnut horses, rode majestically in golden spiked silver helmets, scarlet tunics, breeches and boots and flowing ivory capes extending to the riders's stirrups and lying across the horses' rumps.

From the heart of Madrid, the motorcade proceeded toward University City and Moncloa Palace, the Ford's residence for the visit. The President and his wife greeted the Palace staff, and in 15 minutes they were again on the move, embarked on an intensive afternoon and evening of summitry beginning with a formal call on the Spanish Chief of State, Generalissimo Franco at El Pardo Palace. Protocol and the interests of both nations had dictated the correctness of this first meeting. However, the heart of the visit began with the President's return to Moncloa Palace for a working luncheon with Prime Minister Arias. There were, perhaps, 20 of us at this single table setting. My impression remains of a tentativeness to the conversation—at least at my end of the table—with both sides eager to pursue the very positive goals we shared together, but with both sides still formal, still searching for the dialogue that would have to come from the growing meetings of the improving U.S.-Spanish relationship.

In his toast to the President, Prime Minister Arias was both eloquent and direct: "Spain believes that the hour has come for this direct, loyal, and disinterested contribution on her part to be acknowledged in specific and practical terms by the nations that formed the Western world, to which our country belongs, as well as for its geographical position, its history, and its culture and for its past and present contributions."[6]

Following the luncheon, the President and Prime Minister adjourned to a lounge to continue their conversations. At 4:00 p.m., the Prime Minister departed. At 5:00 p.m., Prince Juan Carlos and Princess Sophia arrived to call on the President and Mrs. Ford. The President and the Prince spoke alone for more than half an hour. This meeting, to me, remains of special importance to the contemporary history of the West. The Prince, who would be King following Franco's death, shared thoughts of the greatest importance with the President on the future of Spain, and on the identical purposes on so many fronts of the United States and Spain. And the President again reaffirmed the importance the United States attached to Spain's contributions to the West and to Spain's role in the years ahead as a Western democracy.

Shortly after 6:00 p.m., I departed the staff offices at Moncloa Palace to pay a brief call at the hotel room, wherever it might be, that the advance team had designated for me, that held my baggage and the black tie outfit I required for the evening's State Dinner. The room, as always, could not have been much better. The suitcase was there together with the WHCA sheet reminding me of communications services and and advance team note; "ELEVATORS IN THIS HOTEL DO NOT LEVEL OUT AT EACH FLOOR BEFORE DOORS OPEN. PLEASE WATCH YOUR STEP!" This was my first visit to Madrid, and my mind traveled back through the decades, through the history of literature:

> The window of the hotel is open and, as you lie in bed you hear the firing in the front line seventeen blocks away. There is a rifle fire all night long. The rifles go tacrong, carong, craang, tacrong, and then a machine gun opens up. It has a bigger calibre and is much louder, rong, cararong, rong, rong. Then there is the incoming boom of a trench mortar shell and a burst of machine gun fire. You lie and listen to it and it is a great thing to be in a bed with your feet stretched out gradually warming the cold foot of the bed and not out there in University City or Carabanchel. A man is singing hard-voiced in the street below and three drunks are arguing when you fall asleep.[7]

At 7:30 p.m., our delegation departed for the State Dinner at the Royal Palace, and there in the midst of incredible opulence we were transported three centuries earlier into the rich history of Spain. At 9:00 p.m., we were escorted through halls and drawing rooms all heavy in gold, in tapestries, statuary and oils to the palace's ceremonial dining room where 150 of us took our seats at a single table beneath 16 chandeliers. The waiters and attending staff were in livery of deep blue and orange. The courses of the banquet came in profusion, but to my growing amazement each course was removed little more than three to four minutes after it had been served. I discreetly checked to my left and right and saw that others of my American colleagues, and of my Spanish hosts were also starting to eat faster. The food was spectacular, but it was being whisked away. Finally, a newly created grapevine began to carry the explanation. The head of the Grand Palace's dining staff was timing each course to the pace of the Generalissimo's eating, and given Franco's physical condition he cared for very little food. This challenge during the course of the banquet was more than matched by the warmth and the generosity of Spanish hospitality. A sparkling Spanish white wine produced for the banquet in bottles dressed with a label bearing President Ford's signature accompanied the toasts.

The Generalissimo and Mrs. Franco then guided the President and Mrs. Ford, and our party first to the Salon de Gasparini for coffee, and then to the Salon de Conciertos for an after-dinner concert. Selections from Borodine and Joaquin Curina were performed on an ornamented quartet set of two violins, one viola, and one cello made for the Spanish Court at the end of the 17th Century by the Italian master Stradivarius.

The following morning, the President and Mrs. Ford paid a farewell call on the Generalissimo and Mrs. Franco. At 9:25 a.m., we were again airborne aboard Air Force One en route to Salzburg, Austria. The U.S.-Spanish summit had involved less than 24 hours. During that brief time, the President had laid the groundwork for the successful renewal of U.S.-Spanish defense cooperation He had dramatically emphasized America's friendship for Spain and America's respect for Spain's contributions to the West, and he had begun a candid, forward-looking process of consultation with the emerging leadership of Spain, a process that would contribute significantly during the transition from the Franco era to the present era of restored Spanish democracy.

The flight from Madrid to Salzburg, Austria was two hours and ten minutes. It was Sunday; we had now been on the road since Wednesday. Days of the week were not important; my orientation came from the trip bible, the summit location and the summit event. The bible included its usual detailed diagram of the arrangements for each arrival ceremony—a black and white sketch with typed annotations showing the Salzburg Airport terminal building on the left, with areas of the welcoming band and Austrian crowd indicated to the front of the terminal building. In the center of the diagram, running from top to bottom, the vehicles of the motorcade were shown and identified—U.S. pilot, Austrian pilot, U.S. security, lead Presidential, Austrian follow-up, U.S. follow-up, Mrs. Ford's car, follow-up, Secretary's car, Austrian follow-up, U.S. follow-up, control, camera #1, wire #1, wire #2, camera #2, camera #3, VIP bus (as a staffer you scan the diagram for that key euphemism VIP bus—your ride—prior to arrival), WHCA, spare, and tail. Further to the right, again from top to bottom, the diagram indicated the positions that would be occupied by the Austrian Honor Guard and the Official Party greeting the Fords, as well as the area designated for the press and the location for the staff upon debarkation for the arrival ceremony. The diagram showed the location of the microphone, the positioning of Air Force One, and the President and Mrs. Ford's debarkation stairs—ah, the stairs.

It was drizzling when we arrived. Two-thirds of the way down the stairs, the President caught a heel and fell, hands first onto the wet tarmac. Chancellor Kreisky jumped forward to assist as did the President's military aide. Ford took the mishap in good humor. No physical damage had been done and, extemporizing at the beginning of his arrival statement, he sought to put his hosts at ease: "Mr. Chancellor, Mrs. Kreisky, ladies and gentlemen. Thank you for your gracious welcome to Salzburg, and I am sorry that I tumbled in."[8] The President was scheduled to have a 30-minute conversation with the Austrian Chancellor immediately following the arrival ceremony and the motorcade to Schloss Klessheim, an enormous mansion and estate that would serve as the Fords' residence for the visit. Thereafter, the President's purpose for being in Salzburg was to meet for the first time with President Anwar Sadat of Egypt to establish face-to-face contact and to develop a summit-level dialogue essential for further progress in the Middle East. The substance of staffing the U.S.-Egyptian talks fell to my Middle East colleagues on the NSC Staff and State. During the first round of the Ford-Sadat talks on June 1, I found a vacant desk in the staff office at Schloss Klessheim, and drafted a lengthy message from the President to Vice President Rockefeller on the substantive highlights of the NATO Summit and the visit to Madrid. This message, which would be reviewed by General Scowcroft and transmitted later in the afternoon, marked another noteworthy part of the business of summitry. There is always intense interest in Washington in both the Executive and Legislative

Branches when a President is engaged in summitry. While the international press necessarily provides much of the day-to-day report, a message such as this would permit the Vice President to stay well-informed and to provide more authoritative status reports to members of the Congress and the Cabinet.

As Ford and Sadat pursued their preliminary exploration of the Middle East situation with their foreign ministers, exchanging respective analyses of developments and respective thoughts on the best diplomatic options for progress, I made my way from Scholss Klessheim to downtown Salzburg to the Oesterreichischer Hof hotel, once again to change for dinner. Moving from country to country, there continued to be a very special reward in terms of the mix of hard work and summit adventure. The Oesterreichischer Hof was a truly refined establishment, with an indoor, multi-storied inner courtyard bedecked with palms and ringed with balconies, one of which led to my room. Here, the windows opened on the Salzach River flowing swiftly, swollen by rains, and beyond on the left bank the public squares, spires, monuments, and distinctive architecture of Salzburg, "the German Rome."

At 9:00 p.m., Chancellor Kreisky again greeted his Egyptian and American guests on the occasion of his official state dinner in their honor at the Residenz palace. Earlier in the day, during his first meeting over luncheon with President Ford, Sadat had spoken with polish and confidence, choosing words that on the surface were optimistic but that served, in fact, to remind how wide and intractable the difference were among those with strategic interests in the Middle East. "In my opinion'" he had said, "and in all candor, I believe that there is no other problem which is easier to solve than the Middle East problem. It is a simple question as long as the parties concerned, including the superpowers who are, in one form or the other wittingly or unwittingly involved in the problem, adhere to the basic an undisputed principle; namely, the recognition of independence and territorial integrity of States, the inadmissibility of acquisition of territory by force, the acceptance and respect of the basic kind of self-determination by the Palestinian people, and their right to live in a national home."[9] Now, during the state dinner, Sadat chose similar words. However, as a gesture of respect for his Austrian host and as a demonstration of his own accomplishments as a statesman, the Egyptian President delivered his entire toast in German, a tongue he had learned during the era of his opposition to British rule of his country.

Ford and Sadat met again the following morning and continued their talks into the late afternoon of June 2. That evening, the President and Mrs. Ford invited a very few of us on the traveling staff to join them for a private dinner at Schloss Klessheim. The following morning we would again be airborne for Italy, Rome, and the Vatican. Over dinner the conversation dwelt primarily with different impressions of the European trip, and thoughts about the day ahead. A trio of Salzburg musicians provided background music and, after dinner after the Fords had retired for the evening, I borrowed one of the player's guitars. We played and sang well into the night, with the sound carrying most impressively in the high-ceiling chamber of the Schloss.

During my visit to Rome with Secretary Kissinger in October 1974, I learned that there were two routes to the Italian Prime Minister's office in the Villa Madama, a 16th Century architectural masterpiece of vaulted ceilings, framed in gardens and surrounding parks, and rich in frescoes and stucco work. One route is via a small elevator that ascends through the middle of a steep corkscrew staircase; the other—the staff route—is via the steep corkscrew staircase. The summit staffer is always expected to be where he or she should be at the appointed time.

I reflected on that earlier dash up those stairs during the June 3 flight aboard Air Force One to Rome. There were full ceremonies once again for the President at Ciampino Airport upon our arrival at 10:00 a.m., following which the President and a few aides departed by helicopter for Quirinale Palace, while the rest of the delegation tore along beneath and behind them by motorcade to the same destination. A full summit's work had been packed into a very few hours: head-to-head talks with President Leone at the Quirinale, followed by an expanded U.S.-Italian session, followed by a lavish banquet at the palace that ended at 3:30 p.m.. Another motorcade than took us to the Villa Madama for the President's talks with Prime Minister Aldo Moro and ministers of his government. Throughout the day, the themes, public and private, where much the same as those of the NATO summit, with the President repeatedly emphasizing the importance of Italy's contributions as a NATO ally, and the importance of our shared belief in democratic government, freedom, and liberty. While taking care not to interfere with Italy's internal political processes, the President minced few words in indicating his preference for the future political coloration of America's important Mediterranean ally.

As we were leaving the Villa Madama, General Scowcroft asked me if I had drafted suggested remarks that the President might draw upon following his meeting with His Holiness, Pope Paul VI. This hasty discussion next found me in the back seat of a limousine, briefcase on my knees, drafting the necessary sentences. As the motorcade raced through twisting streets toward Vatican City, I braced myself against sways and lurches, concentrating on both the sense of the words and their legibility—there would be no typewriter between us and this next summit event.

Having been with the NSC staff since 1971, I had a very keen awareness of the major humanitarian and other international issues that shaped the U.S.-Vatican agenda. President Nixon had attached great importance to his correspondence with Paul VI, and I had had a hand in many drafts of that correspondence. Now, toward the end of his intensive day, President Ford met privately for almost an hour with Paul VI. Following which our Official Party was ushered into the Pope's Library to be introduced to His Holiness and, having taken seats in a large U of chairs, to receive his words as well as those of the President.

At 7:25 p.m., another motorcade sped us from the Courtyard of St. Damassus to an improvised helicopter pad at Oratorio di Sa Pietro, where three helicopters were awaiting our Presidential party for the return to Ciampino. As we boarded our assigned craft, the main rotors of each started to turn, until each was ready amidst the whine, the din and the downwash of helo operations to lift-off. One of my colleagues, one of the President's most important immediate aides, was among the last to leave the motorcade. While dashing across the lawn to his helicopter, his attache case fell open and its contents took flight like the feathers of a burst pillow. Strapped in inside our own craft, there was nothing we could do to help. The flight waited while as many of the papers as could be found were recovered. Even the choice of briefcases has a place in the life of the summit sherpa. I have long since come to prefer the academic style of soft leather case with expanding sides that 'feeds' from the top with a leather band and clasp across the top, rather than a rigid case that opens in the middle.

At 8:00 p.m., we departed Ciampino on a ten-hour flight, with a time change of six hours, that brought us back to Andrews Air Force Base precisely at midnight. Within a very few hours the President was again airborne to deliver the June 4 commencement address at the

United States Military Academy, and I was again in the Old Executive Office Building preparing for the next round of summitry.

From the most frigid times of the Cold War in the mid-1950's, the USSR had advanced the notion of a conference to address over-all European security, and because of Soviet policy and behavior, the West had brushed the suggestion aside as unrealistic. However, the subject remained on the East-West agenda, and with the turn of the decade from the 1960s to the 1970s, progress in the early years of detente again brought the proposal for a European security conference to the fore. As East-West negotiations expanded and began to take root, the United States and its NATO partners set important preconditions for such a conference. We insisted on a new Berlin Agreement among the U.S., U.K, France, and the USSR, ending the USSR's blantantly unacceptable actions harassing West Berliners and challenging clearly established Western rights relating to the divided city. In June 1972, a new Berlin Accord, signed the preceding September, took effect—the Soviets had formally agreed to a greatly improved status for West Berlin and its total relations with the Federal Republic of Germany. At the same time, the Soviet Union and its Warsaw Pact allies agreed to talks on force reductions in Eastern and Western Europe—the Mutual and Balanced Force Reduction (MBFR) talks.

Procedurally, the conference had involved a Stage I round of negotiations in Helsinki that had established the agenda, rules of procedure and instructions to the working bodies and the publication in 1973 of the Final Recommendations of the Helsinki consultations. This was followed by Stage II negotiations—with a shift of the 35 nations' delegations to Geneva—for lengthy substantive negotiations on each agenda item that would not draw to a close until the late Spring of 1975.

During the preliminary wrangling over the agenda in Stage I, with the Eastern and Western delegations vying to place the greatest emphasis, unacceptable to one bloc or the other, on competing issues, one enlightened delegate had suggested sorting the issues into different categories—he had used the term 'placing them in separate baskets'—permitting them to receive co-equal attention category by category, or basket by basket. Such is the stuff of diplomatic progress. As the Stage II negotiations proceeded, the political and security issues to come before the conference were placed in Basket I. Economic, scientific and technological cooperation went into Basket II. Basket III addressed the cultural and educational issues, the

exchange of information among the nations involved, and cooperation in strengthening human contacts. Basket IV addressed the
follow-up arrangements to be made to permit monitoring of the
CSCE results.

The key issues lay in Basket I and Basket III. In testimony before
the Congress in May 1975, Assistant Secretary of State Arthur
Hartman placed them in the following context: "The Soviets have
been especially anxious to gain Western acceptance of an unambiguous principle on inviolability of frontiers. Western participants have
made clear, however, that their agreement to this precept would in no
sense constitute formal recognition of existing European frontiers or
imply that present borders are immutable....We and our Allies also
attach special importance to the principles concerned with respect for
human rights (Basket III) and fundamental freedoms, peaceful
settlement of disputes, self-determination and non-intervention of
human affairs....The seventh principle, dealing with human rights, is
the longest and most detailed principle and is a remarkably strong
reaffirmation of human rights considering the character of the participating states and the circumstance under which the principle was
negotiated."[10]

With the important work of the June 1975 NATO summit and
the consultations in Spain, Austria, and Italy accomplished, President
Ford's agenda for the second half of 1975 called for three additional
overseas sets of summit travel. First to The People's Republic of
China to build on the Nixon break-through, with side visits to the
Philippines and Indonesia in December; to Ramouillet, France in
mid-November for the first of what would become annual economic
summits among the leaders of the major Western democracies; and to
Finland in late-July/early-August for the Conference on Security and
Cooperation in Europe, with preceding visits to the Federal Republic
of Germany and Poland, and with follow-on visits to Romania and
Yugoslavia. This second major summit swing through Eastern and
Western Europe would permit the President to reaffirm America's
defense commitment to the FRG, to continue the process of broad-
ening ties with Warsaw Pact nations other than the USSR, to reaffirm
America's support for the independence and territorial integrity of
Yugoslavia, and in the broadest context to continue the process of
detente with the signing of the CSCE document. "Yet," Ford would
write, "no trip I made during my Presidency was so widely misunder-
stood. 'Jerry, don't go,' the *Wall Street Journal* implored, and *The New
York Times* called the trip 'misguided and empty....A sampling of

White House mail showed 558 letters against the Helsinki agreement and only 32 in favor of it. Lithuanian, Latvian and Estonian groups scheduled a vigil in front of the White House to protest Administration policy."[11] Divided opinion over the pros and cons of the CSCE Conference went far beyond the views of Americans of Eastern European origin. Once again, a fresh reminder was being offered to an American President that in the U.S. democracy for summitry to be successful, it must have the support of domestic public opinion.

Throughout June and July 1975, we worked intensively not only preparing for each summit event scheduled for this major trip to Europe, but also supporting the White House staff with the development of substantive statements and background papers for the President's meetings prior to departure with members of the House and Senate, and the various groups of concerned Americans. In these meetings, the President emphasized the opportunities for progress in America's best interests, stating the U.S. now had the chance formally to commit the Warsaw Pact nations to CSCE undertakings that would require a greater respect for human rights and greater freedom of travel for the people of the USSR and other Pact nations. He stressed that his participation at Helsinki contributed to America's policy of encouraging greater freedom for Eastern Europe, and that it in no way involved recognition of the USSR's incorporation of the Baltic States. In those meetings that I attended, his guests were polite but often not persuaded.

On Saturday July 26, 1975, we lifted off from Andrews Air Force Base in Air Force One at 8:30 a.m., for the trans-Atlantic flight across five time zones for the 8:45 p.m., landing at Bonn/Cologne Airport. Schmidt and Ford were by now the best of friends. Having just met on the fringe of the NATO summit, they continued with consultations on the mornings of the 27th and 28th, both aware that one of the most important purposes of their meeting would be a clear public demonstration of firm allied agreement and unity of the eve of Helsinki. This, they did. Additionally, to underscore the firm American commitment to the defense of Europe, the President traveled by Army One helicopter to the Ayers Kaserne for a picnic with American and German troops and their families, and for an inspection of tanks, artillery and infantry equipment of the U.S. 3rd Armored Division.

While the picnic was in progress, I remained in Bonn working on additional papers for the days ahead. On Tuesday the 29th, the President would be on the second day of his visit to Poland and would honor the Polish nation by laying a wreath at the Oswiecim International Monument, at Auschwitz, the former Nazi death camp. A careful look at the trip bible revealed that the President would be invited to sign the Special Visitors Book at the monument. Accordingly, one of the White House speechwriters and I collaborated on a recommended inscription for the occasion that would be in the President's pocket on a 3" x 5" card, available for him to draw on should he choose to do so during his visit to the monument. Additionally, the days in Helsinki would involve several important bilateral meetings built around the schedule of the CSCE Conference. Other papers were still required for these events—a cover paper, for example, on the over-all status of U.S.-Soviet trade relations for the meeting with Brezhnev. That evening I was honored to be among the party joining the President and Mrs. Ford as the guest of FRG President Walter Scheel for a black-tie State Dinner cruise on the Rhine River on the *M.S. Drachenfels*, a handsome white multi-decked Rhine riverboat. With the coming of night, castles high above the Rhine were illuminated in floodlight, dressing the dinner route. The *Drachenfels'* interior decks were dressed in flowers; there was music and dancing following the dinner; and, in this festive atmosphere, a brief hoving-to at a pier on the Rhine to permit a ceremonial exchange of greeting between the President and the Burgermeister of Linz. At 10:00 the following morning we were airborne for Warsaw, Poland.

Poland's First Secretary Edward Gierek had been honored by the warm reception President Ford had given him at the White House in autumn of 1974, and the red carpet of Poland was extended to its fullest on our arrival at Okecie International Airport. The motorcade route was dressed with U.S. and Polish flags. Large crowds cheered lustily as the President, standing with the First Secretary in an open car, made his way into the capital city. At 1:40 p.m., the President laid a wreath at the Tomb of Unknown Soldiers. At 2:00 p.m., the first Secretary and Mrs. Gierek offered a luncheon banquet and concert at the Palace of Council of Ministers. The Fords then went on a walking tour to view the Old Town's buildings, reconstructed following total destruction during World War II. Monday, July 28, was a day of non-stop activity. As recorded in the Joint Communique, issued on the following day:

> Plenary talks were also held with the participation of: From the American side: The President of the United States of America, Gerald R. Ford; the Secretary of State and Assistant to the President for National Security Affairs, Henry A. Kissinger; Ambassador of the United States of America in Warsaw, Richard

T. Davies; Deputy Assistant to the President, Lt. General Brent Scowcroft; Counselor of the Department of State, Helmut Sonnefeldt; Assistant Secretary of State for European Affairs, Arthur A. Hartman; Senior Member of the National Security Council, A. Denis Clift; and Director Nicholas G. Andrews of the Office of Eastern European Affairs of the Department of State."[12]

These talks, in the late afternoon of the 28th, with Gierek and his Ministers of Government focused on the status of the network of bilateral agreements signed the preceding fall, and on the importance of the upcoming conference in Helsinki. With the Joint Communique signed, the President returned to Wilanow Palace, the Fords's residence for the visit, and prepared to return the day's hospitality with a formal reciprocal dinner for the Giereks and other Polish dignitaries.

There is a very special, almost mystical art, to the business of giving a formal White House dinner—with gilt-edged White House invitations and White House china—on little notice anywhere the President may be in the world. It is, of course, not so much a mystical art as it is an extremely professional skill based on extremely hard work and precision planning by the Director of the White House Mess and his staff. I had first witnessed this dimension of the all-inclusive traveling Presidency at Spaso House, the U.S. Ambassador's residence in Moscow, at the dinner given by President Nixon for General Secretary Brezhnev in 1974, and again at Martinique, at Ford's return dinner in honor of the Giscard d'Estaings. On Monday evening, July 28, 1975, the menu card at each place bore the President's seal in gold and announced:

DINNER

Consomme with Sherry

Robert Mondavi	Cornish Hen
Pinot Chardonnay	Wild Rice
1972	Bouquet of Vegetables

Hearts of Palm Salad Vinaigrette
Port-Salut Cheese

Mirassou au Naturel	
1971	Chestnut Souffle
	Petits Fours

Demitasse

WILANOW PALACE
Warsaw Poland
Monday, July 28, 1975

This delightful fare led during the course of the dinner to a memorable exchange between one of the President's Polish guests and one of my colleagues:

"The rice is tough," the guest said.

"Oh, you see, it's wild rice. It's very chewy, meant to be served that way."

The explanation was greeted with silence. The entree was in due course removed, and the finger bowls, with a floating flower, placed before each of the dinner's company. Whereupon, the same guest picked up his bowl, sipped, then drank it down and pronounced; "Thin soup...thin soup," and turning to my colleague, "I suppose you call this wildflower soup."

The second day of the visit to Poland was marked by solemnity, ceremony and more large, enthusiastic crowds. Following the flight south to the city of Krakow, the President helicoptered to Auschwitz where guides escorted him through the ruins of the concentration camp. Following the laying of a wreath, the President proceeded to sign the visitor's book, writing: "This monument and the memory of those it honors inspire us further to the dedicated pursuit of peace, cooperation and security for all peoples."[13] The President then proceeded to Krakow for a tour of the Pediatrics Institute of the Medical Academy of Krakow, then a motorcade to the city square where upwards of 100,00 people had assembled to hear him praise the long ties of U.S.-Polish friendship and the important progress in bilateral relations. Then, following another elaborate luncheon at Wawel Castle, we were back aboard Air Force One bound for Helsinki, Finland.

Helsinki was at its summer best for the incredible gathering of 35 Chiefs of State and Heads of Government. Various streets had been cordoned off for security and to assist in the intricately timed movements of official delegation motorcades to and from Finlandia Hall, the site of the Conference on Security and Cooperation in Europe, and elsewhere around the city. The many papers we had prepared for the President's use quickly came into play as he launched into an intensive program of formal CSCE meetings and associated bilateral talks. The flow of meetings began at 8:00 a.m., on Wednesday, July 30, with the President's working breakfast with Harold Wilson. At 9:30 a.m., the President proceeded to the first of two bilateral meetings with General Secretary Brezhnev. At noon, he entered Finlandia Hall for the cremonial opening of the CSCE Conference, followed by talks with Prime Minister Caramanlis, then for the balance of the afternoon the first CSCE Plenary Session, with the first of 35 formal addresses. That evening, president Kekkonen gave a formal dinner for the CSCE Heads of Delegation.

Prime Minister Demirel of Turkey joined the President at the U.S. Ambassador's residence for a working breakfast on Thursday, July 31, with the President continuing to search for a breakthrough in the Cyprus crisis, now in its second year. The day's morning and afternoon conference sessions ran from 9:30 a.m., until 5:00 p.m.. During the midday break, Ford, Giscard d'Estaing, Schmidt, and Wilson gathered with their Foreign Ministers for lunch at the British Embassy. The day's official events ended with a lakeside lawn reception, with the sun still high in the evening sky, for all members of the CSCE Delegations.

After a breakfast meeting with Italian Prime Minister Moro on August 1, the President again boarded a motorcade for Finlandia Hall to deliver the U.S. address to the conference, a statement almost a half-hour in length, with the President's words focused as much on the American public as on the standing-room only audience at the conference:

> These documents, which we will sign, represent another step—how long or short a step only time will tell—in the process of detente and reconciliation in Europe. Our peoples will be watching and measuring our progress....
>
> They affirm the most fundamental human rights: liberty of thought, conscience and faith, the exercise of civil and political rights, the rights of minorities.
>
> They call for a freer flow of information, ideas and people, greater scope for the press, cultural and educational exchange, family reunification, the right to travel and to marriage between nationals of different States, and for the protection of the priceless heritage of our diverse cultures....
>
> They reaffirm the basic principles of relations between States: non intervention, sovereign equality, self-determination, territorial integrity, inviolability of frontiers and the possibility of change by peaceful means....
>
> History will judge this Conference not by what we say here today, but what we do tomorrow; not by the promises we make, but by the promises we keep."[14]

Ford and Giscard d'Estaing met again for lunch before the afternoon's concluding Plenary Session. And, on Saturday morning, August 2, the President held his second round of talks with Brezhnev before our departure for Bucharest, Romania.

As one of America's official delegates to the conference I spent many hours in Finlandia Hall, listening to the addresses and following up on a succession of staffing requirements. The hall, a creation of Finland's Sarininen, had rich use of blues and natural wood, contrasting with the white ceiling, the silver organ pipes on either side of the the stage, and a dramatic U-shaped balcony, stepped downward in bold white facing toward the stage. The world's media vied for accreditation to the conference, and those with the essential passes were admitted through extremely tight security to take their place in the press ranks packing the balcony. The CSCE conference offered another reminder that all who participate in any summit must anticipate the presence of the press wherever you are, whatever the hour, whenever you are on the road. Secretary of State Kissinger took the occasion of his presence in the Hall not only to listen to the speeches but also to act on other foreign policy matters requiring his attention, with members of his staff discreetly appearing with papers for his reading and departing from the hall with his instructions for further action. The system worked well until portions of a classified U.S. paper on the Middle East appeared one morning in the press. An enterprising photographer in the balcony above us had kept his telephoto lens trained on the Secretary's reading until he had captured one of the documents.

My friendship with the U.K.'s Foreign Minister Jim Callaghan grew during the days at Helsinki. During the reception on the evening of the 31st, he hailed me: "Well, what was the score?" I smiled, having no idea what he was talking about, and he laughed: "That's the London Cricket Club's tie you're wearing; I thought you'd know the score!"

President Ford's speech to the CSCE Conference had received good press coverage, and with the signing of the CSCE Final Act, the follow-on process of monitoring implementation of the provisions of each CSCE basket began, continued in the 1980s with the deliberations of the Conference on Disarmament in Europe held in Stockholm, and into the 1990s. However, the President's talks with Brezhnev were difficult. The SALT process was stalling over such difficult strategic arms issues as the USSR's deployment of a new supersonic BACKFIRE bomber, and the United States's development of new cruise missiles. The heavy sledding was reflected in an exchange between the President and a reporter aboard Air Force One during the flight from Helsinki to Bucharest:

QUESTION: We have been told in the past of three basic areas of disagreement. One was verification, one was cruise missiles and one was the BACKFIRE bomber. Can you give us a run-down on where now you're making progress and where you still don't have agreement?

THE PRESIDENT: Those are very important areas, but I think it would be unwise for me to try to identify the particular areas of dispute in those instances. They are very precarious and are crucial points, and this is where Mr. Gromyko and Dr. Kissinger will try to more fully identify the differing positions and give us an opportunity, Mr. Brezhnev and myself, to achieve some kind of an honorable settlement.[15]

Trade, not SALT, was foremost on President Nicolae Ceausescu's agenda upon our arrival in Bucharest. Thirty-six hours later, a reaffirmation of the U.S.-Yugoslav joint statement of principles first enunciated by President Nixon and President Tito in 1971, was the centerpiece of President Ford's 25-hour visit to Belgrade, Yugoslavia. The visits underlined America's respect and support for Romania's determination to develop at least a minimal amount of flexibility and quasi-independence in its dealings with Western Europe and the United States, the vice-like grip of the Warsaw Pact notwithstanding—and America's respect and support for Yugoslavia's policy of non-alignment, outside the Warsaw Pact.

The Advance Team and hosts had scheduled the maximum of substance and ceremony into each brief stopover. Having returned from Helsinki on the night of the 1st, President Ceausescu was at Otopeni Airport to greet the Fords and 3:30 p.m., on August 2. The flags, the bannered slogans, the marshaled crowds of the socialist state were all in place as expected, and the afternoon and evening moved from the arrival of the motorcade, to first round of talks, and formal state banquet in the Palace of the Republic's Marble Dining Hall. This was an event memorable for the August heat of the chamber and sweat running freely from the American TV camera crews on hand with their cameras and lights powered by bodypack of batteries to record the marathon toast by the Romanian President. Early in the morning of August 3—a full week had already passed from the Rhine cruise on the *M.S. Drachenfels*—we were rolling north through Romania on a Presidential train, climbing into the Transylvanian Mountains, the celebrated land of Vlad the Impaler. Our destination was Peles Castle, in the mountain village of Sinaia at 5,000 feet elevation, where Ford and Ceausescu resumed their formal talks and put their signatures to a document confirming U.S. agreement to Most

Favored Nation Treatment for Romania, in accordance with the U.S. Trade Act of 1974. To reach this moment of such importance to Romania's economy and political prestige, Ceausescu's government had been forced to bend to U.S. Congressional pressure requiring unambiguous evidence of the right of emigration from Romania, a policy issue that had required many hours of staff work in Washington and Bucharest prior to the summit.

Following the descent by train from the mountains, motorcade, departure ceremony, flight, arrival ceremony, and motorcade, President Ford entered the Federal Executive Council Building in Belgrade, Yugoslavia at 7:00 p.m., for talks with President Tito. Ford was still going strong, commenting during the photo session, "I think we're wearing out our American press. At least the groups are getting smaller." Filing his pool report of the event, Kessler of the *Wall Street Journal* commended the President for "Good reporting, the pool was a little undermanned."[16] The talks ranged across international political issues of East and West, the Middle East and North and South, the possibilities for further trade, including the issue of American military sales to Yugoslavia. At 8:15 p.m., the two Chiefs of State joined their respective delegations for a banquet that concluded with a program by the Abrasevic Company of Folk Dancer and Singers—dances from the Island of Susak, dances from Serbia, women's dances from Macedonia, dances from Croatia, and dances from Vojvodina—a program that both celebrated the richness of Yugoslav culture and reminded of Tito's extraordinary success in confining and harnessing the centrifugal pull of Yugoslavia's competing nationalities. At 8:30 a.m., Monday August 4, the President and Yugoslav Prime Minister Bijedic bore in greater detail on the prospects for further advances in U.S.-Yugoslav relations over a working breakfast at the Old Palace. A motorcade then sped the President to a tree planting ceremony at the Park of Friendship in front of the Federal Executive Council building. In the blazing passage from country to country in the era of jet age summitry, the summit sherpa must remember, must keep in perspective, the importance attached to each such event at the earliest stage of the pre-travel planning process. As much as one's thoughts might turn to the flight back to the United States during the ceremonial spading of earth at the end of the multi-country passage through the time zones, the ceremony in whatever country is of great significance, fully covered in the national media and officially recorded in the history of the relations between the two nations. International formality and American casualness are the voices of good and evil forever vying for the sherpa's attention.

Following a second round of talks with Tito, a working lunch, and another ceremonial event—receipt of the Golden Plaque of Belgrade, Tito gave the President a formal farewell at Surcin Airport and at 6:00 p.m., Air Force One was racing for the barn, with a brief refueling stop at Mildenhall Air Force Base, England. The U.S. Press corps was in attendance in the early hours of August 5th, to hear the President report during the course of his statement upon arrival:

> The reception I received from the people of the five countries I visited—West Germany, Poland, Finland, Romania, and Yugoslavia—was not a tribute to me so much as to the ideals and the continuing leadership of the United States in the worldwide effort for peace, progress and prosperity for all nations.[17]

The facts and the results of President Ford's intensive European summitry gave credibility to these words. In the few months of his Presidency he had proceeded from the bonding of relations among key Allies to progress on a far broader agenda. With the turn of the calendar from 1975 to 1976, President Ford prepared for the role of summit host, not visitor, as the American democracy entered its 200th year.

End Notes

1. While France's precise interpretation of its NATO role would not permit the French President to meet with the North Atlantic Council, he would fly to Brussels for talks with Ford on the fringe on the King of the Belgians' dinner honoring the summit.
2. President's Address at the Ordinary Session of the Council of the North Atlantic Treaty Organization in Brussels, Belgium, May 29, 1975, *Presidential Documents*, Vol. II, Number 23, Pages 576–78.
3. Press Conference No. 14, of the President of the United States, *Office of the White House Press Secretary*, May 30, 1975, Brussels, Belgium.
4. Final Communique of NATO Summit, NATO Press Communique M1 (75) 12, *NATO Press Service*, Brussels, Belgium, May 30, 1975.
5. Ford, Gerald R., *A Time to Heal*, Harper and Row Publishers, New York, 1979, page 285.
6. Exchange of Toasts between the President and Prime Minister Arias Luncheon at Moncloa Palace, Madrid, Spain, May 31, 1975.
7. Hemingway, Ernest, *By-Line: Ernest Hemingway*, Charles Scribner's Sons, New York, 1967, p. 262.
8. Remarks of the President upon arrival at Salzburg Airport, *Office of the White House Press Secretary*, Salzburg, Austria, June 1, 1975.

9. Exchange of Toasts between the President and Anwar Sadat, President of Egypt, *Office of the White House Press Secretary*, Schloss Fuschl, Salzburg, Austria, June 1, 1975.

10. Statement by Arthur A. Hartman, Assistant Secretary of State for European Affairs, before the Subcommittee on International Political and Military Affairs of the House Committee on Foreign Affairs, May 6, 1975.

11. Ford, Gerald, *A Time to Heal*, pages 300-01.

12. Joint Communique of the United States Government and the Polish People's Republic, *Office of the White House Press Secretary*, Krakow, Poland, July 29, 1975.

13. White House Press Pool Report, Krakow, Poland, July 29, 1975.

14. Remarks of the President to the Conference on Security and Cooperation in Europe, Helsinki, Finland, August 1, 1975.

15. The Air Force One Press Pool, Aboard Air Force One, August 2, 1975.

16. Pool Report No. 2, *Office of the White House Press Secretary*, Belgrade, Yugoslavia, August 3, 1975.

17. Statement by the President, *Office of the White House Press Secretary*, Andrews Air Force Base, August 5, 1975.

CHAPTER SIX
The Bicentennial — 1976

Yonder, Citizen blood for Citizen runs
On Boston beach midst Scream and Thrust;
And which of Them the Victory wins,
That decides just One—the Great God—
An advantage they have, though, who
    for their Freedom fight,
That virtue seems mostly to lie in their cause.

Paketbaaden No. 6, April 1777
Pastor Soren Moller

Preparations for the celebration of the 200th Anniversary of Declaration of Independence of the United States began long before 1976, both in the United States and in scores of foreign countries. In capitals abroad, commissions were formed to shape each nation's role, commemorative medals were designed and struck, books commissioned, and schedules drawn for visits by warships, tall-masted training ships and royal yachts. Gifts—nation to nation and people to people—were proposed and selected, to be presented to the President, the Congress and the American nation during elaborate State Visits by Kings, Queen, Presidents, and heads of government that would grace the Bicentennial Year.

America's celebration was more, far more, than a diplomatic event correctly to be observed in accordance with the dictates of diplomatic protocol; it was a celebration for all concerned. America, the nation of immigrants, the melting pot, was in so many ways a 'second national home' for peoples around the world. Not only the weak and the poor, but also the finest seed and seedlings that had germinated and taken root had created the American Nation. In turn, the United States had repaid the Old World handsomely in both peace and war, beginning with the inspiration and the precedent of democracy, justice and high principle embodied in the American Revolution—of profound importance to the history of Europe.

"The American Declaration of Independence, which was signed in Philadelphia on July 4, 1776, marked the advent of momentous political developments on the North American continent and in Europe. The Declaration did not only lay the foundation of a democratic constitution for the United States; it also became the source of inspiration for the political upheavals in the Old World from which emerged, in the eighteenth and nineteenth centuries, the dedication of the countries of Western Europe to democratic rule, human rights and fundamental freedoms. The ideology of the Declaration was deeply rooted in European thought, and outmoded authoritarian forms of government ripened Europe for responsiveness to the message from Philadelphia."[1]

With the coming of 1976, the steady, heavy flow of 'routine' NSC work continued through my office: the monitoring of the NATO consortium of nations implementing the Alliance's F-16 fighter production program; the staffing of Canadian, West European, East European, and Soviet issues; the sheparding of NSC-system interagency policy deliberations on such issues as the U.N. law of the sea negotiations—with upwards of 14 U.S. departmental, agency and Executive-Office-entities engaged in continuing debate over the recommended positions to be taken on two-score issues in the negotiations—the monitoring of daily message traffic; and the staffing of the Information Memoranda and Action Memoranda to General Scowcroft and the President. This said, 1976 also brought a geometric increase in staffing requirements for the Bicentennial.

On June 27, 1975, the White House announced that the President had invited Queen Elizabeth II and the Duke of Edinburgh to pay a State Visit to the United States from July 6–11, 1976, and the fact that the invitation had been accepted with pleasure. On September 10, 1975, the White House announced that President Giscard d'Estaing would pay a State Visit during May 17–20, 1976. The Press Release attached the following exchange of correspondence between Ford and Giscard d'Estaing underlining the ceremonial importance both nations attached to the visit:

The White House
July 25, 1975

Dear Mr. President:

On behalf of the people of the United States of America, I cordially invite you and Madame Giscard d'Estaing to make a State Visit to the United States from May 17-20, 1976, during the celebration of our 200th anniversary as a Nation.

France is America's oldest friend and its first ally. Your visit would underscore the long-standing and very close ties between our peoples. There could be no more fitting observance on this important occasion in our nation's history than a visit by the President of France. We would be honored by your acceptance.

Sincerely,

/s/ Gerald R. Ford

His Excellency
Valery Giscard d'Estaing
President of the French Republic
Paris

Paris
August 6, 1975

Dear Mr. President:

Thank you for your letter of July 25, inviting me to make an official visit to the United States during May 17-20, 1976, on the occasion of the celebration of the two hundredth anniversary of the American nation.

It is with the greatest pleasure that I accept your invitation. Mrs. Giscard d'Estaing and I will be happy to come to your country on the date you propose, marking the beginning of your country's history.

As President of the French Republic I can also bear witness of the friendship which for two centuries has united our two peoples and which has shown forth on the battlefields of your country and ours, as well as in our countries' efforts on behalf of freedom and peace.

I ask you to accept, dear Mr. President, the assurance of my high consideration and my very friendly wishes.

/s/ V. Giscard d'Estaing

His Excellence
Mr. Gerald R. Ford
President of the United States of America
Washington, D.C.[2]

With the issuance of each new announcement, interest intensified across the nation, and through phone calls and letters, as well as
personal contact, the White House received a mounting flood of
inquires from individuals, organizations, societies, schools, universi-
ties, state and local governments, and Mayors of the nation's cities
eager to participate in one or more of the State Visits. The year 1976,
of course, would also be an election year for President Ford, making
extremely heavy demands on the entire First Family's calendar.
Accordingly, very early in the Bicentennial planning, Mrs. Ford
turned to General Scowcroft, who had now taken the position of
Assistant to the President for National Security Affairs with Secretary
Kissinger continuing as Secretary of State, with the request that he
take charge of the arrangements being made for each of the State
Visitors from abroad. In turn, Brent Scowcroft looked to me to help
assure that the planning and implementation of each European visit
proceeded smoothly.

We set in motion a program of planning sessions for each visit
involving State Protocol, the White House Advance Office, the
White House Social Secretary, the NSC staff, and the Ambassadors,
Embassy representatives, and pre-advance teams from each leader's
nation. The bilateral planning sessions, held in the refined atmosphere of fine china, polished mahogany and original oils of the President's Blair House guest quarters, were designed to produce the
event-by-event detailed schedule for each visit. Before entering these
sessions we held our own internal U.S. consultations, sorting out the
nationwide proposals being suggested for each visit, confirming the
President and Mrs. Ford's scheduling preferences, and establishing
the network of working-level contacts to assist the foreign
pre-advance teams in every aspect of each visit from arrival to departure—protocol, travel inside the USA, communications, security, the
details of every event in the visit.

St. Patrick's Day launched the European procession to the
White House with the visit of Prime Minister and Mr. Liam Cosgrave
of Ireland. Traditionally, the Government of Ireland had marked
each March 17th with a presentation of shamrocks flown from Ireland
with Irish crystal to the President and First Lady. During the Nixon
years, this ceremony had taken on on even more special significance
with March 17th being Mrs. Nixon's birthday. From 1971 on, I had
staffed these events, and in 1976, the celebration captured the richness of shared history and of past and present friendship in words

exchanged beneath the crystal chandeliers of the White House State Dining Room fully dressed in green.

"As I observed this morning, Mr. Prime Minister," President Ford said turning to his Irish guest, "eleven signers of the Declaration of Independence were Irish Americans, and the White House itself, where we are dining tonight, was designed by a native of Kilkenny, James Hoban, in 1792....Today, some 20 million Irish-Americans are building energetically on the great legacy of their ancestors....but, nowhere have Americans of Irish descent been more prominent than in Government and in politics. We have some good evidences of that here tonight. The Irish have the love of people, gift of language, warmth of heart and capacity of courage that makes them grand and great competition."

"As you remarked, Mr. President," Prime Minister Cosgrave replied, "we do claim that Saint Brendan the Navigator reached America. Sometimes we think, or like to think, that he got here before Columbus....In the past, as you remarked, Mr. President, many of our countrymen came to America, came to America because it provided not merely freedom from oppression, but freedom to work and freedom to develop. Indeed, I recall the words of a well-known Irish politician 100 years ago in which he said, when he came to America, "I have found a greater Ireland here than I have left behind."[3]

The White House Bicentennial Foreign visitor calendar continued to fill. By late March, my checklist showed:

Visitor	Dates/ Press Release	Background Books, President, Mrs. Ford Vice President	Arrival Communique/ Toasts Press Remarks	Guest Gifts List
Prime Minister Cosgrave, Ireland	March 17			
King Carl XVI Gustav, Sweden	April 5			
Queen Margrethe II, Denmark	May 11			
Giscard d'Estaing, France	May 17			

Visitor	Dates/ Press Release	Background Books, President, Mrs. Ford Vice President	Arrival Communique/ Toasts Press Remarks	Guest Gifts List
Prime Minister Trudeau, Canada	June 16			
King Juan Carlos I, Spain	June 2			
Queen Elizabeth II, U.K.	July 7			
Chancellor Helmut Schmidt, FRG	July 15			
President Kekkonen, Finland	August 3			

Each new visit raised to prominence another feature of the American profile. With the the arrival of Queen Margrethe II—"Daisy"—and her French-born husband His Royal Highness Prince Henrik, the Danes would remind us that 22 towns and cities in the United States are named Denmark. Daisy was accompanied by her stately white-hulled Royal Yacht *Dannebrog*, and it was aboard the *Dannebrog* the the Royal couple received my wife Gretchen and myself for a reception and black-tie buffet dinner in honor of Mrs. Ford prior to the opening performance of the Royal Danish Ballet at the Kennedy Center on May 11. Hour after hour of detailed planning among the Department of State's Office of Protocol, the Danish Embassy, and the NSC staff and White House were devoted to such events as: the scenario for entertainment aboard the *Dannebrog*, the motorcade to the Kennedy Center, the arrangements for Her Majesty's arrival, the seating plan, the arrangements for the first intermission, the arrangements for the second intermission, and for the reception following the performance. Such precise attention to detail permitted the largest number of Americans to meet the Danish Queen. While Denmark would commission the book *Denmark Gets the News of '76*, and while Royal Copenhagen would produce a special edition blue and gold porcelain plate honoring the Bicentennial, the Danes had shaped their salute to America in the form of people to people gifts. Both the Royal Danish Ballet and the Copenhagen Boys Choir would make extensive tours of the United States as part of the Danish gift of a Bicentennial program of performances and exhibits embracing music, history, and the arts.

With the arrival of President Giscard d'Estaing at the the White House less than a week later, France—the nation that had contributed so vitally to America's independence, and that had made the gift of the Statue of Liberty 100 years before, again opened her heart to America, with the day-to-day reserve and frictions of U.S.-French political life swept aside by an outpouring of friendship.

The French Ministry of Tourism published a delightful booklet, with Washington and LaFayette at Yorktown in full color on the cover, ladened with choice snippets of history, to wit: Paul Revere was the son of Apollos Rivoire, a French Bostonian who still called Bunker Hill, Bon Coeur Hill. At the British surrender at Yorktown, Cornwallis' second in command, General Charles O'Hara attempted to snub George Washington by offering his sword to Rochambeau, only to be told; "You are making a mistake, Monsieur, the commander of our army is on your right." And, between World Wars I and II, France was a haven for avant-garde Americans escaping the restraints of prohibition and censorship. "Harry and Caresse Crosby founded the Black Sun Press, which published rare works of Joyce, Ezra Pound, T.S. Eliot, and Hart Crane....Caresse, a descendent of Robert Fulton, invented the brassiere by tying two handkerchiefs together with a ribbon."[4]

On January 12, 1976, France's Ambassador to the United States, Jacques Kosciusko-Morizet, reviewed the plans for France's Bicentennial participation, noting that the focus would be in keeping with America's plans, with events to be scheduled at the local level across the United States rather than 'grand events at the national level.' The official French gift was to be a Sound and Light Spectacle for Mount Vernon, consisting of "an art form...developed and perfected for [French] cathedrals and chateaus. These spectacles aimed to bring to life a period in the past through the skillful interplay of light and sound....Each evening at nightfall, thousands of visitors [would] watch as Mount Vernon [came] alive with the voices of great American and French actors, with the sounds, music and lights of the Son et Lumiere."[5]

To commemorate the Battle of Yorktown, France announced that it would contribute exact replicas in silk of the flags of the 20 French regiments that fought in the War of Independence, and that in October 1976, the guided-missile cruiser *Colbert* and frigate *DeGrasse* would lead the French Navy units sailing to Yorktown for the anniversary of the battle.

To the city of Philadelphia, France would give exact replicas of oil portraits of Louis XVI and Marie Antoinette, originally presented by the French Emperor to the American Congress in 1784, then destroyed in the burning of Washington in 1814.

France would participate in commemorative celebrations in the towns and cities where French forces had played a decisive role—Virginia Beach, Annapolis, Hartsdale, Hartford, Valley Forge, Hull, Savannah, Newport—and a total of 10,00 French sailors would be aboard the French warships calling at 40 American ports.

The French Committee for the Bicentennial would sponsor an American academic expedition retracing the explorations in the 17th century of LaSalle from Montreal to New Orleans, and would contribute to a museum devoted to LaSalle at the site of his death, Navasota, Texas. Eight times as many cultural events as in other years would be organized by France to tour the United States—art exhibits, musical performances, joint preparation of historical publications, as well as film, stage, and opera productions, and benefit balls. French Parliamentarians would present a specially bound edition of *L'Histoire de la Participation de la France a l'Establissement des Etats Unis d'Amerique* to the Congress. French and American sister cities— Bar-sur-Loup and Yorktown, Nice and Houston, Lyons and St. Louis, Grasse and Savannah—would host special celebrations. And, the Ambassador announced, the President of the French Republic would formally present the Son et Lumiere Spectacle at Mount Vernon during his May 17–20 State Visit to the United States.

Giscard d'Estaing's Bicentennial itinerary would take him to Washington, D.C., Yorktown, Philadelphia, Houston, and New Orleans. The Department of State's detailed schedule for this journey so rich in commemorative events ran to more than 100 pages. The events of May 19, offer the flavor:

Wednesday
May 19, 1976

> *8:15 a.m.* Official Party departs Statler Hilton Hotel en route Blair House. (Cars will be waiting in front of hotel.)

8:30 a.m.   Depart Blair House via motorcade en route Andrews Air Force Base.

Lead Car USSR/Mr. Codus

President's Car:	President Giscard d'Estaing
	Vice President Rockefeller
	Lt.Col. Arnold
Car Two	Mrs. Giscard d'Estaing
	Mrs. Rockefeller
Car Three	Mr. Barre Amb. Catto
	Amb. Rush
Car Four	Mr. Pierre-Brossolette
	Amb. Kosciusko-Morizet
Car Five	Mrs. Kosciusko-Morizet
	Mrs. Rush
	Amb. Angles
Car Six	Gen. Vanbremeersch
	Mrs. Gouyou-Beauchamps
	Amb. Vaurs
	Mr. Kabler
Car Seven	Mr. Montarras
	Mr. Larche
	Mr. Baudelot
	Mr. Thierry
Car Eight	Mr. de Menthon
	Dr. Van Haecke
	Mr. Luttringer
	Mr. Morizot

8:55 a.m.   Arrive Andrews Air Force Base

9:00 a.m.   Depart Andrews Air Force Base via USAF VC-9 aircraft en route Patrick Henry International Airport, Newport News, Virginia.

Flying time: 40 minutes

Manifest:

Pres. Giscard d'Estaing
Mrs. Giscard d'Estaing
Mr. Barre
Mr. Pierre Brossolette
Ambassador Kosciusko-Morizet
Mrs. Kosciusko-Morizet
General Vanbremeersch
Amb. Vaurs
Amb. Angles

Mr. Montarras
Mr. Gouyou-Beauchamps
Mr. Larche
Mr. Baudelot
Mr. Thierry
Mr. Menthon
Dr. Van Haecke
Mr. Morizot
French Security-3
Amb. Catto
Amb. Rush
Mrs. Rush
Mr. Codus
Mr. Kabler
Mr. Pinto
USSS-5
SY-2
VP Rockefeller
Mrs. Rockefeller

Captain Howe	Ms. Herter
Mr. Morrow	Mr. Dixon
USSS-2	(on VP plane)

9:40 a.m.   Arrive Patrick Henry International Airport,
Newport News, Virginia

Welcoming Committee

The Honorable Mills B. Godwin
Governor of the Commonwealth of Virginia
Mrs. Godwin
The Honorable Harry E. Atkinson
Mayor of Newport News
Mrs. Atkinson

9:45 a.m.   Depart airfield via motorcade en route Yorktown, Virginia
(listing of motorcade assignments)

10:00 a.m.   Arrive Yorktown Victory Center.
The following party mounts the platform:
President Giscard d'Estaing
Mrs. Giscard d'Estaing
Vice President Rockefeller
Mrs. Rockefeller
Governor Godwin
Mrs. Godwin
Mr. McMurran
Mrs. McMurran

Scenario For Bicentennial Ceremony

National Anthems of France and the United States

10:15 a.m.   Governor Godwin welcomes
President and Mrs. Giscard d'Estaing

10:20 a.m.   Vice President Rockefeller makes brief remarks.

10:25 a.m.   President Giscard d'Estaing makes remarks and directs unveiling of final kiosk.

Governor thanks him and presents gift.

Official Party proceeds into Center.

10:35 a.m.
(approx.)

President Giscard d'Estaing,
Vice President Rockefeller
Governor Godwin and Mr. McMurran proceed to riser in lobby.

Mr. McMurran introduces Dr. Thomas Graves, President of College of William and Mary, who will present a book to President Giscard d'Estaing.

Mr. McMurran introduces other distinguished guests.
(Dr. Pierre, President, French Association of Veterans)

Mr. McMurran escorts group through Center to Museum for departure.

11:00 a.m.
(approx.)

Depart via motorcade en route Yorktown Victory Monument
Motorcade—same as on arrival

Visit Yorktown Victory Monument.
President Giscard d'Estaing will be greeted by Mr. James Sullivan, Superintendent of National Colonial Historical Parks, and presented a commemorative plaque.

11:15 a.m.

Depart Yorktown via motorcade en route Newport News
Motorcade same as on arrival

11:30 a.m.

Arrive Patrick Henry International Airport.

NOTE: Vice President and Mrs. Rockefeller will take leave.

11:35 a.m.

Depart via VC-9 aircraft en route Philadelphia.
Flying time 40 minutes

Manifest: Same, less Vice President and Mrs. Rockefeller and his staff.

12:15 a.m.

Arrive Philadelphia International Airport, Annenberg Hanger (satellite area).

Welcoming Committee

The Honorable Milton J. Shapp
Governor of Pennsylvania
Mrs. Shapp
The Honorable Frank L. Rizzo
Mayor of Philadelphia
Mr. Albert Gaudiosi
City Representative and Director of Commerce
The Honorable Garard Gaussen
Consul General of France in New York
Mrs. Gaussen
Mr. Yves Rodrigues
Mr. John V. Fawcett III
Honorary Consul of France
Mrs. Fawcett

21-gun salute

12:20 p.m.

Depart airfield via motorcade en route
Bellevue Stratford Hotel
(Detailed motorcade assignments).

12:40 p.m.   Arrive Bellevue Stratford Hotel
               Greeting will be Mr. William Chadwick,
               Vice President of Hotel
               (Mayor Rizzo will take leave at the Hotel).

               President and Mrs. Giscard d'Estaing proceed to Presidential
               Suite on the 15th floor. (Remainder of party proceed to Crystal
               Room, second floor).

12:50 p.m.   President and Mrs. Giscard d'Estaing depart suite and proceed
               to Crystal Room and are greeted by:
                   Mr. Frederick Heldring, President of the Philadelphia
                   National Bank and General Chairman of the World Affairs
                   Council.
                   Mrs. Heldring.
                   Mr. and Mrs. Jan MacGregor.
                   Mr. Harvey Williams, President of the United States
                   Council of the International Chamber of Commerce.
                   Mrs. Williams.
                   Mr. Addison Roberts, President of Reliance Insurance
                   Company and President of World Affairs Council of Phila-
                   delphia.
                   Mrs. Roberts.
                   Mr. William Bodine, President of World Affairs Council.
                   Mrs. Bodine.

                   Head table guests are presented to President and
                   Mrs. Giscard d'Estaing in the Crystal Room.
                   Cocktails served in the Crystal Room.

                   Following cocktails, entire party proceeds to Grand
                   Ballroom for luncheon.

1:00 p.m.   Luncheon Scenario
                   National Anthems
                   Invocation
                   Welcoming introduction by Mr. Heldring
                   Introduction of President Giscard d'Estaing by
                   Mr. MacGregor
                   Presentation of International Statesman Award
                   Remarks by the President

2:40 p.m.   Depart Hotel via motorcade en route Independence Hall
               Motorcade—same as on arrival.

2:50 p.m.   Arrive Independence Hall for brief visit to Signers Room where
               Congress of 1776 met and to old Supreme Court Chamber for
               the presentation.

               President Giscard d'Estaing presents paintings of Louis XVI
               and Marie Antoinette to Mayor Rizzo and Secretary Kleppe,
               followed by presentation of gifts to President by Mayor Rizzo.

3:10 p.m.   Depart Independence Hall en route Liberty Bell Pavilion for
               brief tour and photo opportunity.

3:25 p.m.   Depart Liberty Bell Pavilion en route Lewis Quadrangle.

3:30 p.m.	Arrive Lewis Quadrangle to attend special session of General Assembly of Pennsylvania. Greeted at curbside by Mr. Fineman, Speaker of the House of Representatives of Pennsylvania.

National Anthem
Welcoming remarks by Mr. Fineman
Remarks by Mayor Rizzo and Governor Shapp

Presentation of Honorary Degree from
University of Pennsylvania by Mr. Martin Meyerson, President of the University

Introduction of the President by Mr. Fineman

Response by President Giscard d'Estaing

Mr. Fineman presents gifts to President and Mrs. Giscard d'Estaing

4:15 p.m.	Depart Lewis Quadrangle via motorcade en route Philadelphia International Airport (Motorcade—same as on arrival).
4:35 p.m.	Arrive Airport
4:40 p.m.	Depart Philadelphia via USAF VC-9 aircraft en route Washington, D.C.
5:20 p.m.	Arrive Andrews Air Force Base
5:25 p.m.	Depart via motorcade en route Blair House (Details of motorcade assignments)
5:45 p.m.	Arrive Blair House

Private Dinner at Blair House

8:15 p.m.	Official Party departs Blair House en route Mount Vernon
8:30 p.m.	President and Mrs. Ford arrive Blair House to accompany President and Mrs. Giscard d'Estaing to Mount Vernon
8:35 p.m.	Depart via Motorcade en route Mount Vernon (Details of motorcade assignments)
8:55 p.m.	Arrive Mount Vernon

Greeted by Ambassador Catto who will introduce Mrs. Thomas Turner Cook, Regent of Mount Vernon Ladies Association, and Mr. Charles C. Wall, Resident Director, to the Presidents and First Ladies.

9:00 – 10:00 p.m.	Reception, Presentation and Premiere of "The Father of Liberty," the Bicentennial Gift of the French Nation to the United States.

At the conclusion of the program, return to Blair House

Overnight: Blair House

*Note: Baggage call will be at 7:30 a.m.
tomorrow.*

The anatomy of Giscard d'Estaing's Bicentennial summit visit included two substantive rounds of Oval Office discussions with President Ford requiring careful NSC staffing, permitting the two Presidents to continue with important progress they had realized with other key members of the Atlantic Alliance since 1974. Central to this process was the progress they had realized on economic, trade and monetary issues at the first of the international economic summits in November 1975, and their desire to continue to sustain the Western World's economic recovery, working with their colleagues the leaders of the Federal Republic of Germany, Canada, Italy, Japan, and the United Kingdom at the second economic summit, to be held in only a few weeks at Dorado Beach, Puerto Rico on June 27 and 28.

The satisfaction of staffing these talks during Giscard d'Estaing's visit was further enhanced by the opportunity I had to work increasingly with the President and Mrs. Ford's Social Secretary, Maria Downs, a charming, unflappable expert in her field, on the details of each of the European leader's Bicentennial visits to the White House. During the American Revolution, Count Charles d'Estaing had commanded the first French naval expedition sailing in support of the American Colonies. During my years in the White House as a member of the NSC staff, I had come to know a marble bust of the Count that was on display, amidst paintings of former First Ladies, in the main hallway of the ground floor of the White House Residence, one floor below the State Dining Room. While a distant relative, he was a d'Estaing.

At my suggestion, Maria included the marble Count among the guests at the White House State Dinner on May 17, and in his champagne toast, President Ford paid tribute: "Count d'Estaing's arrival on July 3, 1778, was stunning news to our opposition at that time and was a great blessing to the hard-pressed Continentals. Unfortunately General Washington never met Admiral d'Estaing. I count it a special privilege as the 38th President that I can welcome one of his descendants to this house and personally express our long overdue thanks for the distinguished contribution that was made by one of your predecessors in our struggle for our independence. In his honor we have displayed in this room tonight a bust of the Admiral, which has long resided at the White House, and I am certain that all of you will agree that it is a distinct pleasure to have the Admiral with us on this occasion, as well as one of his family."

Giscard d'Estaing thanked the President and, in two sentences of his eloquent return toast, captured the sense of his visit: "We are here for a warm, joyful celebration of a living idea, one of the great ideas of which it has been said that its spark is only to be alive in a single mind to set the world afire. I mean, of course, the liberty of men."[6]

With the end of May, the White House was readied for the next White Tie banquet, in honor of the State Visit of King Juan Carlos I of Spain and Queen Sophia. The months since the President's visit to Madrid had witnessed events of historic importance to the history of Spain and the relationship between the United States and Spain. The U.S.-Spanish Treaty of Friendship and cooperation had been signed in January 1976; Juan Carlos had ascended as the new leader of the Spanish nation. The arrival of His Majesty Juan Carlos I in Washington on June 2 marked the first visit by a King of Spain to the United States.

Spain's re-entry into the mainstream of international political life, denied almost absolutely until the early 1950s because of World War II associations with Germany and Italy, crested with the young Spanish Monarch's tour of the United States. Beneath him, a new Spanish Government represented Spain to the world; in him, Spain offered a voice of optimism and confidence.

The Bicentennial celebration included King Juan Carlos I's address to a Joint Session of the Congress on June 2, 1976. Other foreign visitors would address the House and Senate. The King of Spain's address would carry the message of Spain's renaissance. At 12:00 noon, June 2, the United States Senate and the United States House of Representatives assembled in Joint Session. As prescribed by Congressional protocol, the Speaker of the House and the Acting President *Pro Tempore* of the Senate named members from each body to escort the Royal visitor into the Hall of the House of Representatives. At 12:35 p.m., with the members of the Senate and House, the Diplomatic Corps and the President's Cabinet in their places, the Doorkeeper of the House announced His Majesty Juan Carlos I, King of Spain. The King was escorted down through the hall to the Clerk's Desk where he received the standing, prolonged applause of all assembled.

"Members of Congress," the speaker announced, "it is my great privilege and I deem it a high honor to present to you the sovereign leader of a great and friendly nation, His Majesty, Juan Carlos I, the King of Spain." The warmth and cordiality of this formal reception by the representatives of the entire American nation—a reception that would have not been possible even on year before—once again emphasized the tremendous change that had taken place in Spain, and the strong, wholehearted endorsement of that change by the United States.

In his address, Juan Carlos retraced highlights of the Spanish exploration of North America, and of Spanish settlement: "In 1776, the Spanish Monarchy extended over immense territories of the American continent, yet still maintained the rhythm of expansion. In the same year of the Declaration of Independence, Spaniards founded the city of San Francisco....In this year of the Bicentennial it is with pleasure that I recall the role that Spaniards, and Spain, with her diplomatic, political, financial, naval, and military resources played in the global struggle whose victory secured the recognition of the independence of the United States. And, he quoted from an issue of *El Mecurio Universal* of January 1776, reporting on the Congress of Philadelphia: "The striking description of their complaints and grievances, the spirit of concord and maturity reigning in their Congress, the forceful determination with which they universally manifest their resolution in the face of all danger...all this makes respectable their resistance and their just claims."[7]

However, Juan Carlos' most important message—the message shaping the bond between 1776 and 1976 in the relationship between Spain the the United States—lay in his description of the 'bill of rights' he had designed to guide his Monarchy in the Spain of the latter half of the 20th century. "The Spanish Monarchy has committed itself from the very first day to be an open institution, one in which every citizen has full scope for political participation without discrimination of any kind, and without undue sectarian or extremist pressures. The Crown protects the whole people and each and everyone of its citizens guaranteeing through the laws and by the exercise of civil liberties the rule of justice.

"The Monarch will ensure under the principles of democracy that social peace and political stability are maintained in Spain. At the same time, the Monarchy will ensure the orderly access to power of distinct political alternatives, in accordance with the freely expressed will of the people."[8]

As Americans prepared throughout the month of June for the many thousands, indeed millions, of community and family 4th of July celebrations, the flow of official foreign visitors continued. On June 16, Canada's Prime Minister Pierre Trudeau dropped down from Ottawa to Washington to pay Canada's respects. From July 1 through July 5, President Ford delivered a set of six Bicentennial speeches at the Smithsonian Air and Space Museum, the Kennedy Center, the National Archives, Valley Forge State Park, Independence Hall, Philadelphia, and Monticello, each capturing different dimensions of the American celebration: "So break out the flags, strike up the band, light up the sky and let the whole wide world know that the United States of America is about to have another happy birthday, still going strong at 200, and in the words of the great Al Jolson—You ain't seen nothin' yet!"[9]

Most certainly, America and the whole wide world hadn't seen nothin' like the year-long preparations for the State Visit of Her Majesty Queen Elizabeth II and His Royal Highness Prince Philip of Edinburgh to the United States from July 6–11, 1976. No Bicentennial visit demanded more attention; none was accompanied by more pomp and circumstance. Well before the June 1975 announcement of the Royal Couple's plans, both sides of the Atlantic were buzzing with preparations for the U.K.'s observance of the 200th anniversary of its former colonies' successful revolution.

In keeping with the French example, British participation would include months of exhibits, touring performances and other programs both in the United States and the U.K.. Early on it was decided that one of the principal gifts would be a Bicentennial Bell, to be cast at Whitechapel Foundry, London, where the Liberty Bell had been cast in 1752, a bell seven and one-half tons in weight, almost seven feet across the base, to bear the inscription "Let Freedom Ring", to be presented to the people of the United States during the Queen's visit to Philadelphia.

The British Parliament would loan the United States Congress one of two original copies of the Magna Carta dated 1215, to be on display for a year in a large gift case, and then to be replaced by the permanent gift of a gold and silver replica of the document. Here again, the Bicentennial provided the splendid opportunity for Americans to gain a fuller understanding of the roots of their nation. The influence of this historic document on the birth of democracies and the shaping of the rights of men could be found, for example, in its 39th clause:

> No freeman shall be arrested or imprisoned or deprived of his free-hold or outlawed or banished or in anyway ruined, nor we (the King) take or offer action against him except by the lawful judg-ment of his equals and according to the law of the land. [And the 40th clause:] To no one will we sell, to no one will we refuse or delay right or justice.[10]

In May 1976, a U.S. Congressional delegation led by Speaker of the House Carl Albert traveled to London to accept the gold and silver replica, and in early June, a British Parliamentary delegation accompanied the original copy of the Magna Carta to Washington.

For months I was in close and continuing touch with the Honorable John O. Moreton, CMG MC, Minister of the British Embassy, maintaining a working channel, in addition to that established between the Sate Department Office of Protocol and the Embassy, to permit proposals and issues requiring attention to move directly to the White House and the Buckingham Palace for consideration and guidance.

Her Majesty's Royal Yacht *Britannia* would provide a principal focal point for the Queen's visit. The *Britannia*, built at the John Brown & Company Shipyard in Clydebank, Scotland and commissioned in 1954, is a handsome ship with dark hull and white superstructure. Staffed with some 275 officers and men, the ship is 400 feet long with 5,000 tons displacement, and has three masts towering above the single smokestack to fly the flags of Royalty. The yacht's presence at the Queen's several ports of call on the U.S. East Coast would permit the Royal Couple to offer lavish entertainment to their many American hosts during the course of the visit. The schedule called the Queen to arrive at Penn's Landing, Philadelphia on the morning of July 6, with events in Philadelphia throughout the day and evening. On the morning of July 7, a Royal Air Force VC-10 of the Queen's Flight was pre-positioned to fly the Royal Couple to Washington D.C., with the official arrival ceremony on the South Lawn of the White House scheduled for 11:45 a.m.. The President and Mrs. Ford would give a luncheon and State Dinner in honor of their British visitors on the 7th. On the 8th, the Queen's schedule continued with events in Washington, the laying of the foundation stone for the new Chancery of the New Zealand Embassy, visits to the Capitol to view the Magna Carta, and to the Smithsonian, with dinner in honor of the Fords, followed by a large reception at the British Embassy that evening.

On July 9, the RAF VC-10 would fly the Royal Couple to Newark, New Jersey, for an eight-mile motorcade to Bayonne where they would reboard the *Britannia* for a Royal arrival off the southern tip of Manhattan, New York, at noon, with events in New York City throughout the remainder of the day and a dinner aboard the *Britannia* that evening. On July 10, the *Britannia* would proceed early in the morning to New Haven, Connecticut, where the Queen and the

Duke of Edinburgh would visit briefly and then reboard their RAF flight for a day of ceremonial events at Charlottesville and Monticello, Virginia. From there a return flight to Providence, Rhode Island, to reboard the *Britannia* at Newport, and to offer a dinner in honor of the President and Mrs. Ford aboard the Royal Yacht that evening. On July 11, the *Britannia* would proceed to Boston for the final, full day of Queen Elizabeth's Bicentennial visit, with the yacht scheduled to sail from Boston to Halifax, Nova Scotia at 7:30 p.m., on the 11th.

So much time and effort had gone into the shaping and refining of the schedule that I arrived at my NSC office on the morning of July 7, in high spirits, looking forward to participating in the White House Arrival Ceremony and the State Dinner that evening. At about 9:00 a.m., I received a call from the White House Social Secretary Maria Downs. With all the planning, with all the arrangements, the U.S. side had a gift for the Fords to present to the Royal Couple, but no gifts for Princess Anne, Prince Charles, and Prince Andrew. With the arrival now less than three hours away, and with all of the social details required for the White House luncheon and dinner, Maria's message was brief, "Denis, help!" Mrs. Ford did not want to select from the normal range of gifts that might be available from Protocol. She wanted distinctive gifts worthy of the occasion. Did I have any ideas?

I told Maria that I had long admired the turquoise and silver jewelry on display at the Indian Gift Shop at the Department of the Interior. The earrings, necklaces, belt buckles, and rings were beautiful, and they were distinctively, uniquely American. I volunteered to go over to the shop and to confirm what might be available. It was, of course, early July, and already hot as I dog-trotted the four blocks from the Old Executive Office Building to Interior. The shop had just opened and the two clerks watched as I moved swiftly from display case to display case and then asked to use their telephone. I told Maria that I knew the Fords would be very pleased with the Indian jewelry. I asked her to give Richard Cheney, the White House Chief of Staff a call, and to ask him, in turn, to give Secretary of the Interior Hathaway a call to have the necessary instructions passed down to the gift shop permitting me to borrow several pieces of the not-inexpensive turquoise and silver. All of this happened; I made my selection; and just as I was about to leave with a dozen different pieces, I turned and borrowed two of the black velvet display boards.

With this treasure in hand, I dog-trotted back to the West Wing of the White House and made my way along the ground floor, through the Residence to the East Wing and Maria's office. On July 8, the press duly reported that the exchange of gifts had included presents of Indian turquoise and silver for the Royal Couple's children. On August 6, the First Lady sent me a personal note of thanks:

> Dear Denis, Please know how very much I appreciated your kind assistance in obtaining gifts for the Royal Family. This was a most thoughtful gesture on your part. With warm best wishes, Sincerely, Betty Ford.

This personal exercise in summit gift selection would serve me well in the years to come. The quality and the character of a gift, what it symbolizes in terms of the United States and what it means to the recipient are another important ingredient of summit diplomacy.

On the evening of July 7, Gretchen and I were fortunate to be among the select company invited to the white tie banquet at the White House in honor of the Royal Couple. Cocktails were served in the Residence while a thunderstorm tore through the nation's capital. We then moved to the South Grounds to form a receiving line, and friends would call the following day to tell Gretchen that they had seen her in her long, hand-sewn ivory silk gown as we passed through the line preceded by former Secretary of the Treasury and Mrs. Connally, and followed by Telly Savalas. A white tent covered the entire Rose Garden, and within 24 circular tables decorated with elegant arrangements of at least a dozen different flowers awaited our presence.

On the afternoon of July 8, the Royal Couple's schedule indicated that they would be at Blair House at 5:30 p.m., for presentation of photographs and presents. Having received an invitation, I crossed Pennsylvania Avenue to Blair House and was shown into a drawing room where the Queen and Prince Philip were standing by a table. They greeted me, thanked me for my contributions to the success of their visit and after a few moments of conversation presented me with a photographic portrait, framed in blue morocco leather, of the Royal Couple in formal attire in Buckingham Palace, inscribed:

Elizabeth R   Philip
1976

Queen Elizabeth then turned again to the table and selected a Battersea enamel pill box, royal blue with a full-color portrait of the *Britannia* on the lid, the inscription "Bicenntenial Visit to the USA of the Queen and The Duke of Edinburgh, July 1976" and Her Majesty's crest inside the lid and at the base of the box, which she also presented to me.

I thanked them and told the Queen that I would like to present her with a gift—which, of course, had not been shown on their schedule and produced a look of curiosity on both their faces. From my pocket I drew a handsome blue-and-gold jacketed reprint of an article I had had published in 1968 of the building of, and the prospects for, the Cunard ocean liner *Queen Elizabeth 2*, which included a profile of the great ship and a cameo portrait of Her Majesty on its opening pages. During my year of graduate study in London, I had written the John Brown Yard at Clydebank with the proposal that I do an article on the liner. The Yard kindly paid my air fare to Glasgow, and permitted me to walk the decks of the *QE2* while she was still under construction on the building ways, and to conduct a number of interviews. I gave Her Majesty this article; Philip asked if he might take a look, thumbed the pages and said, "I say! I say!"

My British counterpart for the visit, John Moreton, was knighted by the Queen aboard the *Britannia* in Boston harbor. My brief encounter with Royalty now history, I turned my attention to the Bicentennial visit of the Federal Republic of Germany's Chancellor Helmut Schmidt. President Ford's words of welcome for Helmut Schmidt at the White House Arrival Ceremony fully captured his high esteem for his German friend and colleague, and for what they had already achieved together: "Mr. Chancellor, your arrival today marks our eighth meeting over the past two years, underscoring the continuity of our consultations on both sides of the Atlantic. Since you first visit as Chancellor in 1974, the countries of the West have been working more closely than ever between ourselves. At the NATO summit in Brussels, at the Helsinki summit last August and in our conferences at Rambouillet and Puerto Rico we have demonstrated new unity among the industrialized democracies, a new determination to achieve the objectives of peace and prosperity for all our people and a new confidence that we will achieve these objectives. The progress over the past two years clearly indicates that we will succeed."[11]

In keeping with their highly successful bilateral 'work ethic', Ford and Schmidt not only celebrated Germany's vital role in the War for Independence, but forged ahead together issuing a joint statement on mutual defense issues at the conclusion of two rounds of Oval Office talks in which the Federal Republic of Germany agreed to pay almost $70 million to help defray the expenses of relocating a U.S.

Combat Brigade into the northern area of FRG near Bremen—an act of considerable importance underlining the shared Allied contribution to NATO's defenses.

Germany was generous in her Bicentennial gifts, as well. On the afternoon of July 16, Schmidt was present at the Smithsonian Air and Space Museum for the inauguration of the official FRG gift, a multi-million dollar masterpiece of German optics entitled the Einstein Spacearium for the museum. The following evening, the Bicentennial's nautical dimension again came to the fore, as the President and Chancellor drove through a violent thunderstorm to Baltimore for a reception hosted by Schmidt aboard the German tall-masted sail training ship, the *Gorch Fock*.

A three-masted bark, 257 feet in length, with a crew of 206, the *Gorch Fock* had been one of more than 50 U.S. and foreign warships and sail training ships to participate in the 4th of July international naval review in New York harbor. Sails had been rigged as awning to protect against the rain when we boarded her in Baltimore's inner harbor. Fine beers and food were available in abundance. Ford saluted her Master, Captain von Stackelberg, and the ship's company on the *Gorch Fock's* victory in the tall ships' race from Burmuda to Newport. And, the President and the Chancellor again chose warm words to reaffirm bonds first forged between George Washington and General von Steuben 200 years before.

In August, the final Bicentennial visit of a European Chief of State, the visit of President Kekkonen of Finland, occurred. While Ford would have working meetings at the White House with Foreign Minister Genscher of the FRG, Foreign Minister Forlani of Italy, Foreign Minister de Guiringaud of France, and the USSR's Foreign Minister Gromyko in the autumn of 1976, he now turned almost every ounce of his energy and every minute of each day to his re-election campaign. When the votes had been cast and he had been denied a second term, he found time at the end of his Administration to write me the letter he quoted in his Introduction to this work. Service to one's country is high honor. Acknowledgment such as this is the summit sherpa's highest reward.

End Notes

1. Skytte, Karl, President of the Danish Parliament and Chairman of the Danish Bicentennial Committee, *Denmark Gets the News of '76*, Danish Bicentennial Committee, Copenhagen, 1975, page 7.

2. Notice to Press, *Office of the White House Press Secretary*, September 10, 1975.

3. Exchange of Toasts between the President and Liam M. Cosgrave, Prime Minister of Ireland, *Office of the White House Press Secretary*, March 17, 1976.

4. *200 Years of Franco-American Friendship*, William W. Davenport, Director, Northwood Institute Europe, Secretariat d'Etat au Tourisme, France, 1975.

5. Press Conference by His Excellency Jacques Kosciusko-Morizet, French Ambassador to the United States, Washington, January 12, 1976, Ambassade de France Service de Press et d'Information, 972 Fifth Avenue, New York.

6. Exchange of Toasts Between the President and Giscard d'Estaing, the White House, *Office of the White House Press Secretary*, May 17, 1976.

7. Address of His Majesty King Juan Carlos I to Joint Session of Congress, *Congressional Record—House H 5121*, June 2, 1976.

8. Ibid.

9. Text of Remarks by the President, Honor America Program, the Kennedy Center, July 3, 1976.

10. Magna Carta, from Reference Division, Central Office of Information, London, October 1975.

11. Exchange of Remarks Between the President and Helmut Schmidt, Chancellor of the Federal Republic of Germany, the White House, *Office of the White House Press Secretary*, July 15, 1976.

CHAPTER SEVEN
Mondo Mondale — 1977

I will not cease from mental fight,
Nor shall my sword sleep in my hand
Till we have built Jerusalem
In England's green and pleasant land.

Milton
William Blake, 1804

On March 1, 1977, the AP wire ran the following story: "President Carter, meeting in the White House Tuesday with Soviet dissident Valdimir K. Bukovsky, said that he would not be 'timid' in his pronouncements on human rights but wanted them 'to be productive and not counterproductive.'

"In the face of strong Soviet protests over human rights pronouncements, Carter told Bukovsky he wanted 'to assure that our own nation and countries other than the Soviet Union are constantly aware that we want to pursue the freedom of individuals and their right to express themselves.

"Carter's ten minute visit with Bukovsky in the Roosevelt Room, across a hallway from the Oval Office, was in marked contrast with former President Gerald R. Ford's refusal to meet Soviet dissident Alexander Solzhenitsyn during the height of the detente policy.

"But the White House has been sensitive to the way the Bukovsky meeting is viewed and refused to allow photographers and reporters into the meeting for even a brief period.

"Pictures were taken, however, during a 30-minute meeting between Bukovsky and Vice President Mondale. Carter walked into the meeting during its last ten minutes."[1]

The story went on to mention that I, as Vice President Mondale's Assistant for National Security Affairs, had also taken part in the meeting. Carter's entrance—it was my first fact-to-face meeting with America's new President—had been dramatic. The door to

129

the Roosevelt Room had opened, and he had appeared alone without any retinue whatsoever, crossed the room to where the Vice President and Bukovsky were seated, extended his hand, projected his famous smile, and said, "Hi, I'm Jimmy Carter."

It had been apparent to me in late 1976 that knowledge of Bicentennial affairs, however expert, did not promise a lasting professional future. By then, I had served with the Eisenhower, Kennedy, Johnson, Nixon, and Ford Administrations. I arranged a meeting with the Head of the President-elect's NSC transition team, David Aaron, who would soon be named as Deputy Assistant to the President for National Security Affairs. I had known him as a colleague on President Nixon's NSC staff. I told him that I hoped to continue in government service, and I expressed a particular interest in the position of Assistant to the Vice President for National Security Affairs. I had a good sense of the responsibilities of that position, having provided considerable NSC staff support to Vice President Nelson Rockefeller. I was informed that the new Vice President would be closely linked to the President on all foreign policy and NSC issues, and the the initial thinking of the transition team was that there would be no need for a full-time professional on the Vice President's staff, that the various NSC staff members would provide support as required.

I outlined my thoughts supporting a full-time staff member in a note to Aaron in early 1977. The Vice President, I suggested would be a busy man carrying out a multitude of domestic, foreign and political responsibilities. In the foreign policy/national security field, I suggested, he will need top quality, fast-response assistance from his own staff to ensure that his requirements were being fully met; I set forth the following examples:

The formal business of the National Security Council: The Vice President is a full member of the National Security Council and brings an independent judgment to NSC meetings. It cannot be assumed that the papers prepared by the NSC staff for the President and the Assistant to the President for National Security Affairs will automatically meet every staffing requirement of the Vice President. It can be assumed that preparation of such papers may sometimes run late; there will be tight deadlines. It can be assumed that the Vice President may wish to have further information on certain aspects of the papers. Who will do this staffing?

Requests for meeting by Ambassadors and foreign visitors in Washington: Because of his office and the importance it is being accorded in the Carter Administration, the Vice President can expect a steady flow of requests from Ambassadors and foreign visitors in Washington. Briefing papers will be required—often on a tight deadline. While the State Department can be given the primary tasking for such papers, it cannot be automatically assumed that the paper forwarded will fully cover the issues the Vice President may wish to address. Who will keep an eye on the preparation of such papers? Who will revise and expand them when required?

In this category, one also has to take into account the continuing flow of the social invitations the Vice President and Mrs. Mondale will receive from Ambassadors and foreign visitors in Washington. If the Vice President wants background information on short notice, if the Vice President needs a toast on short notice, who will do the staffing? If during office meetings and social events with foreign officials issues come up or requests are made of the Vice President, who will he turn to for follow-up staffing?

Of importance in this category, when the President invites Heads of Government or Chiefs of State to Washington for formal visits, the Vice President can expect to be heavily involved both in substantive talks and in social events. Background papers and toasts tailored to his individual style will be required. Who will oversee this staffing?

Correspondence: Who will be charged with staff responsibilities for the correspondence from American citizens, foreigners and foreign leaders that the Vice President can expect to receive in considerable volume on matters of national security and foreign policy? Who will be involved in the staffing process in which such correspondence is sent to State or elsewhere for reply, or is forwarded to the Vice President for his personal attention?

Press Guidance: Who will be assigned to work with the Vice President and his press secretary to ensure that press guidance on major foreign policy issues, on international crises and fast-breaking events is available when required and takes into account the guidance being provided by the President and the guidance being used, for example, by the Secretaries of State and Defense?

Daily Intelligence: The Vice President will have available to him on a daily basis the same intelligence information that is provided to the President. Who at the staff level will provide quick follow-up when the Vice President has questions about a specific issues, when he wants fuller information. Who will draft the information memorandums day in and day out?

Commissions: Vice President Rockefeller was a Member of the Murphy Commission and headed the CIA Commission. Considerable personal staffing was involved. Who will be the focus for such staffing if Vice President Mondale is given similar responsibilities?

Official Missions Abroad: From the outset of the Carter Administration, the Vice President can be expected to undertake major foreign missions. State and the NSC staff and other departments will be involved in the staffing of such missions. Will the Vice President wish to have new players, depending on the region to be visited, for each mission—people who may not know his preferred work style; or will he additionally wish to have a member of his own staff who is able to take a hand in preparations—in the drafting of public remarks, substantive papers, the shaping of foreign schedules—and who will be along on each mission to provide continuity and more efficient support by the party accompanying the Vice President?

I concluded by recommending that the Vice President must at least have one full-time staff member in the foreign policy/NSC field in addition to his military aide or aides. In my discussions with the Transition Team, I also offered my observations on the incoming President's communications with foreign leaders. I suggested, based on my work involving the communications of several past Presidents, that the substance and style of a President's communications with foreign leaders become a distinguishing characteristic of his Administration. Some Presidents have allowed the pace of events to dictate the frequency of such communications, and they have looked to their advisers for recommended draft correspondence whenever it is required. Other Presidents have added a significant dimension, taking greater personal initiative in their contacts with selected foreign leaders, such as (1) staying in touch on a continuing basis, (2) taking a personal hand in the drafting of letters and messages, discussing noteworthy domestic as well as for foreign events, (3) developing a relationship which the history of the period would indicate has led to greater understanding, personal friendship, and an ability to deal with major issues and crises with greater flexibility and understanding whenever they may occur.

A new President, I suggested, had the opportunity from the outset of his Administration to take initiative in the timing, style and substance of his contacts with selected leaders abroad rather than allowing less-productive approaches, be they communications dictated solely by response to events or by the momentum of bureaucratic activity, to become established procedure. Foreign leaders look to a new President for the fullest possible statements of his views. They will want to ensure that they have the best possible understanding of his policy and program directions. They will want to develop a relationship of frankness, trust, and confidence; often placing a great premium on discretion because of the sensitivity of the issues in involved.

A new President's primary purpose in initiating contact with selected foreign leaders is to open lines of direct communication, to indicate that he will value such contact throughout his Administration, and to review issues of importance to him and issues which he believes are of interest to both parties, even though no specific decision may be required. He also had the opportunity to take the lead in proposing new undertakings and in reaffirming certain government-to-government commitments already in existence. Such action by the President sets a positive and forward-looking tone and pace to his leadership.

Channels of Communication: It is useful to bear in mind the many channels available to the President for communication with foreign leaders. They include (1) personal contact with foreign leaders—formal and informal bilateral meetings in the United States and abroad, multilateral meetings in the United States and abroad, and telephone conversations, (2) written communications with foreign leaders—direct communications via the White House Communications Agency (WHCA), signed correspondence, telegraphic messages via the State Department, and messages and correspondence via foreign Ambassadors in Washington, (3) communications via emissaries—the Vice President, Secretary of State and other Cabinet officers, U.S. and foreign ambassadors, White House assistants and personal emissaries, and Congressional emissaries, (4) indirect communications—messages to Congress, speeches, press conferences, and interviews.

The matter of personal style: If the President takes the initiative of direct early contact with selected foreign leaders, in addition to the normal flow of State Department recommended responses to all foreign leaders following the receipt of messages of congratulations in his Inauguration, he will probably choose to do so via message and letter. In considering such communications, the President may wish to establish procedures that will ensure from the outset his personality, his style, and his hand are clearly reflected in every document. If variations are readily discernible, even on such matters as salutations and closings, and unless the style is consistently the President's, the staff product is seen for what it is at the receiving end. The entire communications process loses some of its effectiveness, and the uneven quality is recorded in the President's permanent papers.

At the same time that this exchange was taking place between myself and the head of the NSC Transition Team, the President-elect was in the process of selecting the members of his Administration and, with them, beginning to shape the principal policies of his foreign and national security programs. With the Inauguration still weeks away, Carter took the decision to send Vice President-elect Mondale on a mission to NATO Headquarters, the capitals of our principal NATO Allies and Japan personally to convey and to discuss the new President's thinking and proposed directions on key issues. With the concurrence of General Scowcroft, I became a member of the team of incumbent NSC and staff officials and incoming foreign policy, economic and defense experts assembled to prepare the senior Senator from Minnesota for this first assignment in global summitry.

In mid January, Governor Carter placed personal telephone calls from his transitional Washington headquarters at Blair House to Prime Minister Callaghan, President Giscard d'Estaing, Chancellor Schmidt, Prime Minister Andreotti, and Prime Minister Fukuda to establish contact on the eve of his Presidency and to receive their ready concurrence in his proposed mission for Vice President Mondale. With the green light from all concerned, Fritz Mondale set an intense pace in preparing for the trip, with a steady flow of background papers, briefers, and experts heading to his Senate Office and, on the weekends, to his Lowell Street residence: international finance, trade and economic issues; North-South issues; the key concerns before NATO Alliance; non-proliferation; our relations with Japan and the nations of the Pacific; Southern Africa; Greece, Turkey, Cyprus; the Middle East; and, of course, strategic arms issues, the Soviet Union and the Warsaw Pact.

January 1977 was a frigid month in Washington, and the snows and challenge of the rutted, icy streets remain in my memory as part of the background of four weeks' intense work. As one of our teams was preparing to depart the Senate Office late one afternoon, with the initial round of briefings drawing to a close, Mondale told me that I had been recommended to him because of the NSC-staff experience in summitry. He said he was depending on me to oversee the overall arrangements for the trip. "If you do well," he said with a smile, "you'll go far." I knew from the start that the nation's newly elected second highest official had a good sense of humor. He had reserved for my own contemplation the 'if you don't do well' option.

At the same time that I was putting the finishing touches on drafts of recommended farewell letters from President Ford to each of his European colleagues, I was helping to guide the drafting and assembly of the papers for Vice President Mondale's mission under the following major headings: PRE-DEPARTURE: Scope memo for Mondale, Mondale to Carter memo—this would be a very detailed paper sent to the President-Elect in Georgia seeking his concurrence on the recommended positions to be taken on each major issue with the leaders in each nation, and pre-departure press guidance; BRUSSELS, January 23–24: Arrival and Departure Remarks, Book for Meeting with Tindemans, Book for NATO Secretary General Luns, Speech to North Atlantic Council, Book for Jenkins/EC Commission, and Book for van der Stoel of the Netherlands; BONN, January 24–25: Arrival and Departure Remarks, Book for Schmidt, Dinner Toast; BERLIN, January 26: Arrival and Departure Remarks, Book for Meetings with Mayor Schuetz and Senate President Lorenz; Berlin Speech and Proposed inscription for Berlin Golden Book; ROME, January 26–27: Arrival and Departure Remarks, Dinner Toast, Book for President Leone and Prime Minister Andreotti, and Book for Meeting with His Holiness Paul VI; LONDON, January 27: Arrival and Departure Remarks, Dinner Toast, Book for Prime Minister Callaghan; PARIS, January 28: Arrival and Departure Remarks, Toast, Books for President Giscard d'Estaing and OECD Secretary General van Lennep; ICELAND Stopover; TOKYO, January 30–31, Arrival and Departure Remarks, Dinner Toast, Book for Prime Minister Fukuda; POST-RETURN, Presentation to President Carter.

Time magazine's January 31, European edition did its cover story on the Vice President's trip, with the subtitle, 'Getting to Know You.' *Newsweek*'s January 31, edition carried a photograph of me discussing plans for the trip with the Vice President, together with a map entitled *Mondo Mondale* showing the global route, more than 24,000 air miles, seven nations plus Berlin in little more than seven days.

On Inauguration Day, as the transfer of the Presidency and Vice Presidency proceeded on Capitol Hill, I was at work in the Old Executive Office Building drafting a detailed set of talking points on the foreign mission for the Vice President's use at the first Cabinet Meeting of the Carter Administration the following morning. I stepped out on to the balcony of the office to watch the helicopter bearing the former President and Mrs. Ford on a farewell look at Washington. Hours later, with my drafting nearly completed, I watched President Carter and his family, at the conclusion of their inaugural stroll down Pennsylvania Avenue, walk along a wooden boardwalk that had been constructed over the ice and snow on the White House's north lawn for the new First Family's use at the time of the Inaugural parade. At 8:00 a.m., Sunday morning, January 23, 1977, I was at Andrews Air Force Base ready for our 9:00 a.m. departure for Brussels aboard Air Force Two. To say the least, the Vice President's mission less than three days after his swearing in was newsworthy. A chartered jet press plane took off one hour prior to the Vice President's departure, and press coverage would be heavy at every stop on his itinerary.

With the time-consuming obligations of the inaugural now fading with each mile of the trans-Atlantic flight, the Vice President spent several hours reading and discussing each leg of the trip with members of his embarked staff. The following morning, seated at the oval table of the North Atlantic Council in Brussels, he began his address to America's NATO allies:

Mr. Secretary General, Members of the Council:

In behalf of President Carter, I have come to NATO Headquarters as a matter of first priority. I have come to convey to you and the Member Governments of the North Atlantic Alliance:

- The President's most sincere greetings;
- His commitment—and the full commitment of the United States—to the North Atlantic Alliance as a vital part of our deep and enduring relations with Canada and Western Europe; and
- his dedication to improving cooperation and consultations with our oldest friends, so as to safeguard our peoples and to promote our common efforts and concerns.

The President's conviction concerning NATO's central role is deep-rooted and firm. As he stated in his message to the NATO Ministers last month: "Our NATO Alliance lies at the heart of the partnership between North America and Western Europe. NATO is the essential instrument for enhancing our collective security. The American commitment to maintaining the NATO Alliance shall be sustained and strengthened under my Administration."[2]

The Vice President emphasized the success the Alliance had realized in deterring war. He stated Carter's readiness to increase American investment in NATO, with a comparable increase by each of the allies. He stated the President's commitment to the strategic arms limitations negotiations—the SALT talks, and to both the

MBFR negotiations and the process of monitoring implementation of the 1975 Helsinki Agreement. He closed his address to the council with a quotation and a forecast: "Years ago," he said, "Jean Monnet, the father of Europe, spoke eloquently of the problems facing us; 'Europe and America must acknowledge that neither of us is defending a particular country, that we are all defending our common civilization.' We have acknowledged that basic truth, and it will bind us ever closer together in the years to come."[3]

The first day in Brussels was packed: the working breakfast with Belgium's Prime Minister Tindemans, the NATO address, the talks with Secretary General Luns and General Haig, Supreme Allied Commander Europe, afternoon sessions with the European Commission's Permanent Representatives at EC Headquarters in Brussels, a wide-ranging press conference testing Mondale's ability to handle detailed follow-up questions on the specifics of his morning's address—probing the position he would take on the problem of nuclear proliferation with Chancellor Schmidt and President Giscard d'Estaing, testing his knowledge on the state of play in Cyprus and the Middle East, checking on the possibility of any government-to-government consultations on the possibility of Spain's membership in NATO, the prospects for SALT and for a new Allied summit. Before departing for the airport, he had a dialogue in his hotel suite with the Netherlands's Foreign Minister van der Stoel.

Night had fallen when Hans Detrich Genscher, Foreign Minister of the Federal Republic of Germany, greeted the Vice President upon arrival of Air Force Two at Cologne/Bonn Airport. Genscher was warm in the satisfaction he expressed with this visit by the President's most important emissary so soon after the Inauguration, and in the FRG's special gratitude that Berlin would be on the Vice President's schedule. Upon our arrival at the night's hotel, my new staff colleagues and I made our way to the staff room and worked well into the night reviewing and adding polishing touches to the drafts prepared—seemingly months before—in Washington in advance of our departure for Mondale's discussions with the German Chancellor, his Berlin speech, and his entire set of papers for Rome and the Vatican on January 26–27. A hard look at such papers close to the time of each event is absolutely essential to good staffing. Substantive issues must be updated; toasts and addresses must be purged of the generalities and 'canned language' that are an understandable if unacceptable shortfall of early drafts. Once on the summit trail, the staffer must be in touch with American colleagues—the traveling party, the advance team, the Embassy staff—and with contacts in each host country to obtain the background information and the updates required for sharper detail and greater relevance and color in the papers actually to be drawn on during each visit.

The Vice President reserved the morning of January 25, for a final review of the issues he would be raising with Schmidt on behalf of the President. The afternoon's atmosphere was cordial, but the talks were long and serious, moving beyond fundamental areas of U.S.-FRG agreement to differences not easily resolved. Carter had entered office determined to realize more stringent international control over nuclear proliferation, and he saw the FRG's pending $4.8 billion sale of nuclear fuel and reprocessing equipment to Brazil as an important test case. Additionally, on the international economic front, the President wanted Schmidt to stimulate the German economy at a greater rate, in keeping with U.S. and Japanese plans, to contribute to a coordinated improvement in employment, trade, and economic growth among the major democracies.

The fact that America's new President had entrusted such prickly summit-level issues to this Vice President was important from the outset in establishing Mondale's role and credibility as international statesman. While Schmidt, of course, had not been expected to agree immediately to the new U.S. Administration's proposals, the United States attached importance to having the views of its Government presented authoritatively, and on the record. Mondale had studied hard and had handled the issues well, both at the Federal Chancellery and in his press conference with Helmut Schmidt. "Despite such apparent divergence, both Mr. Mondale and Mr. Schmidt went to great lengths to establish a cordial basis for future dealings between their governments."[4]

Mid-morning on the 26th, the Vice President was in West Berlin at Rathaus Schoeneberg to convey President Carter's eagerly awaited message: "Our President, Mr. Carter, visited Berlin four years ago and has the fondest memories of this great city. He knows first hand your determination to be free. In the words of his Inaugural Address: 'Because we are free we can never be indifferent to the fate of freedom elsewhere.' I am here, barely hours after our new government has assumed office, in his behalf, to assure you that the United States' policy is based on our full support for your city, a policy that guarantees with our Allies your freedom and security."[5]

It was a strong address detailing America's commitment and the deeply rooted ties between the people of West Berlin and the United

States. It was important that such words again be spoken by an American statesman. Nothwithstanding my years of travel with U.S. Delegations across the Soviet Union and nations of the Warsaw Pact, until the visit in January 1977 to the Berlin Wall I had seen nothing that so starkly defined the differences between East and West. The chill of death present in the no-man's land shaped by guards' towers, concrete walls, barbed wire, and other grotesque obstacles so methodically erected to deny the freedom of people to move from East to West could not help but give fresh meaning to the importance of democracy and to the commitment of America to the people of Berlin.

At 1:40 p.m., on the 26th, Air Force II rolled to a stop at its appointed check marks for the arrival ceremony at Ciampino Airport, Rome, at 4:05 p.m.. Following a quick swing by our hotel 'base-camp', we entered Palazzo Chigi with the Vice President for his meetings with Prime Minister Andreotti; three and one-half hours later I was eye to eye with one of the largest fish ever poached by a renowned chef at President Leone's dinner in honor of the Vice President at the Quirinale Palace. At 10:30 a.m., the following day, His Holiness Paul VI received the Vice President at the Vatican and, at the end of the audience, greeted the members of our delegation, presenting each of us with a bronze medal that had been struck to commemorate his visit to the United Nations. Paul VI was frail and spoke very softly: "I am a numismatic expert," he told the Vice President with a self-deprecating laugh. The Vice President turned to the member of our Party who had assumed iron-clad responsibility for the custody of the specially bound copies of President Carter's Inaugural Address prepared for presentation at each key moment in the global mission. His Holiness' copy had been left at the hotel—a minor slip-up, but not the kind to be repeated.

The black iron picket fence with its ornamental arch supporting a lamp over the black doorway of the brown brick face of Number 10 Downing Street, offers a most unpretentious face to the official residence and elegant townhouse of the British Prime Minister. Upon our arrival in London from Rome, Vice President Mondale held an afternoon round of talks with Prime Minister James Callaghan, which he would continue over dinner. Callaghan's reception could not have been more cordial. There were no major, potentially contentious issues of the type that had been raised with the German Chancellor. The Labor Government in Great Britain looked forward to doing business with the Carter Administration.

There were 31 of us around the mahogany table in Number 10's dining room that evening. Spirits were high, good yarns were spun and laughter flowed over the dinner of consomme demidow, filet of sole Elizabeth, breast of duck with apricots, and profiteroles with chocolate sauce. Mondale recalled some of the songs he had learned when visiting Great Britain as a young man, and almost immediately the room filled with song as the Prime Minister led the evening's company in a round of lusty after-dinner singing. Whistles were further whetted by the service of a Hennessy Grand Fine Champagne 1912 cognac from Churchill's cellars.

As we prepared to leave the table I commented to one of my dinner partners, Mr. Roger Stott—a political adviser to the Prime Minister: "About the only good song we haven't sung this evening is Blake's 'Jerusalem'. He took the comment aboard and asked; "You know it?" I nodded and his voice rang out; "Prime Minister, Mr. Clift knows 'Jerusalem'."

Sunny Jim Callaghan pushed away from his chair. He smiled broadly and said, "do you?" In that resonant chamber of Number 10 Downing Street the song burst forth:

Bring me my bow of burning gold!
Bring me my arrows of desire!
Bring me my spear! O clouds unfold!
Bring me my chariot of fire!
I will not cease from mental fight,
Nor shall my sword sleep in my hand
Till we have built Jerusalem
In England's green and pleasant land.[6]

The British Prime Minister and I gave full voice to both verses, undoubtedly the finest duet accompanied or unaccompanied I will ever be privileged to sing!

During the course of the London visit, Prime Minister Callaghan and the Vice President held a press conference, with a normal healthy London turnout swollen by the press corps traveling with the Vice President. Callaghan was pleased to report that he had accepted an invitation from President Carter, extended by the Vice President, to visit the United States in March and that he would be doing so both in his capacity as head of the British Government and as President of the European Community.

Still in the first week of his new role of national U.S. leadership, the Vice President fielded a number of important questions during the conference, including one on southern Africa that he would have reason to recall a few weeks later.

> QUESTION: Mr. Vice President, on the question of southern Africa, I understand that Mr. Andrew Young has been invited to South West Africa. Is he likely to take that up? And I understand on American television he said, and I quote: "The Cubans bring a certain stability and order in Angola." Is that the view of the new Administration?

> VICE PRESIDENT MONDALE: May I say that I am not familiar with what the schedule of the new Ambassador to the United Nations, Mr. Young, might be, nor had I heard that particular comment. But may I say this about Mr. Young. We are very, very proud of our new Ambassador to the United Nations, Andrew Young, who happens to be very familiar with the politics and the leadership of southern Africa. And in the United Nations we expect him to be a very effective leader and counselor in our common effort to bring about a responsible settlement within the context of a majority rule.[7]

We departed London for Paris, for the Friday afternoon meeting with the OECD Secretary General and talks the following morning with Giscard d'Estaing. As the Vice President was preparing to board his motorcade for the short drive to the Elysee Palace and his appointment with Giscard d'Estaing, I asked my colleague, the keeper of the presentation copies of the President's bound Inaugural Addresses, if all was in order for the Elysee. He confidently produced a leather folder from his briefcase and offered me a look...he had the copy addressed to Prime Minister Fukuda! The necessary change was made and from that moment on my responsibilities included a field promotion to custodian of such documents.

On Saturday afternoon, heading into our second week on the road, we took off for Tokyo on an overnight transpolar flight from Europe, with refueling stops set at Keflavik, Iceland, and Elmendorf Air Force Base, Alaska. Near-gale-force winds were tearing across the runway when we deplaned at Keflavik; the honor guard of Icelandic motorcycle police looked like a line of airborne ski-jumpers with their bodies at attention uniformly planing forward against the blast. Prime Minister Hallgrimsson was at the entrance of the terminal building to greet the Vice President, and he escorted us to a lounge for 15 minutes of conversation during which both leaders emphasized their deep interest in working to assure that U.S.-Icelandic relations would prosper.

On the night flight, 30,000 feet over the North Pole our entire party draped, slouched, and slumped throughout Air Force Two catching a few desperately needed hours of sleep. I drew on the mountain goat in me, managing to stretch out on a storage bench, not more than 14 inches wide running along the aircraft's passageway outside the Vice President's cabin. Upon departure from Paris, we had exchanged some of our European experts for new Asian hands, and by the time of our arrival in Tokyo at 9:45 p.m., Sunday night, the Vice President had devoted several in-flight hours to preparing for his talks with Prime Minister Fukuda, talks which would involve a strong signal of concern from the new Administration over the U.S.-Japanese trade imbalance. In the event, the Japanese were splendid hosts, more pleased perhaps than any of the other nations we had visited that the President and Vice President had seen fit literally to go the extra mile to include Japan in this diplomatic mission of such symbolic as well as substantive importance.

On Tuesday, February 1, we headed back to Washington at 1:00 p.m., for the final legs of our marathon air odyssey back across the international dateline, refueling again in Alaska, and flying on back through the time zones to be met by the President at 1:35 p.m., the same afternoon at Andrews Air Force Base. We had devoted many hours of the return flight to drafting different sections of the Vice President's report to the President and, following the Vice President's review and revisions, assembling them into a combined draft to be typed in final at the White House Monday night to be available for the scheduled meeting between Mondale and Carter at 7:30 a.m., Tuesday morning.

The mission had without doubt been successful. In Tokyo, a correspondent had noted to the Vice President that this had been the first time he had undertaken a foreign policy mission of such magnitude, and had asked if the trip had left the Vice President with any dominant observation. Mr. Mondale, in reply, emphasized the value of having immediately established a close cooperative relationship with some of America's best friends and allies, including the value of having immediately raised concerns and problems rather than allowing them to 'continue to tick away'. More specifically, the Vice President said that the mission had enabled the Carter Administration to begin discussion on some of the key issues that would be formally addressed at the economic summit of the major Western nations later in 1977.

As we headed east across the United States, I was not unaware that I might be on the street looking for a new job within the next 24 hours. I was bone tired after the intensive work of January. I felt the trip had gone extremely well, although it had had its harrowing moments at the staff level. On Friday morning, January 28, in London, for example, the Vice President had added to his schedule a telephone call from his hotel suite to Prime Minister Soares of Portugal in Lisbon to exchange greetings, to express regrets that it had not been possible to include Portugal on this mission and to state that he looked forward to visiting Portugal in the very near future. The traveling press was to be invited to the London hotel suite to report on the Vice President's end of the conversation. To ensure the connection, we had already put through the call and the phone receiver was already off the hook at our London hotel and in Lisbon, where the Prime Minister was with our Ambassador waiting for the appointed moment. With the press coming down the hall about to be ushered into the Vice President's suite, I picked up the receiver and there was no one at the other end of the line. Shouts through the receiver produced nothing, although I could hear voices very faintly in the background. What I could not know was that the Prime Minister and our Ambassador were enjoying a chat standing on a balcony.

The door to the Vice President's suite opened, and in came the traveling press. They couldn't be escorted out again. I whispered our dilemma to one of my colleagues, said that the Vice President would have to chat with the press, stall until we had the problem sorted out. I then slipped out of the room, ran down to our Secret Service Command Post, put a call through to Embassy Lisbon and had the Embassy get immediately in touch with the Ambassador. A long minute passed. Then, the Prime Minister was on the line and a most successful, well-reported conversation ensued.

As Air Force II was banking for its final approach into Andrews Air Force Base, Vice President Mondale mentioned that he had been observing me throughout the trip, that he was aware of my contributions, pleased with the part I had played, and thought that I would make a good member of his new staff. With this initial global mission now history, he invited me to become his Assistant for National Security Affairs.

At 6:30 the following morning, our global team—at least the majority—was with the Vice President in his new White House West Wing Office, a seasoned oak fire crackling in the fireplace, again reviewing his trip report; at 7:30, with the sun just rising he left for the new 100-foot walk to the Oval Office, his meeting with the President. The tempo of that first day back in Washington would continue for many, many months—staying power is essential to the sherpa's psychological and physiological kit—for the President and Vice President had from the outset shaped history's first genuinely important U.S. Vice Presidency.

There had been at least half a dozen major contenders for the Democratic Vice Presidential nomination. Governor Carter had interviewed each in Plains, Georgia, exploring their personalities and testing their views against his on the key issues they could expect to face if elected. "The night before I was to announce my preference," Carter later wrote, "I settled on Senator Mondale. When Fritz came down to Plains he had really done his homework about me and the campaign. More important he had excellent ideas about how to make the Vice Presidency a full-time and productive job....He did not wish to be sidetracked into heading up one or two trade councils or special study commissions. Instead, we agreed that he would truly be the second in command, involved in every aspect of governing. As a result, he received the same national security briefings I got, was automatically invited to participate in all of my official meetings, and helped plan strategy for domestic programs, diplomacy and defense."[8]

Every aspect of this decision by the President was precedent-setting. Not only would the Vice President participate in the occasional meetings of the National Security Council and the Cabinet, he would also be welcome to participate in the President's meetings with every foreign official and leader, and in every meeting that might fall in my new field of responsibility to the Vice President for foreign policy, intelligence, and defense affairs.

The President instituted a Friday morning working breakfast to discuss the national security agenda with the Vice President, the Secretary of State, the Secretary of Defense, the Assistant to the President for National Security Affairs and other senior members of the White House staff. A working lunch between the President and Vice President was scheduled for each Monday. Of prime importance, Carter directed that Mondale be fully involved, together with Harold Brown the incoming Secretary of Defense, in all briefings and support involving the President's responsibilities for the possible use of nuclear weapons in the defense of the United States and its Allies—the President's ultimate responsibility for nuclear command and control.[9]

After six years with the National Security Council staff, one of my most immediate challenges was training myself to get off the elevator at the second floor rather than the third of the Old Executive Office Building. The Vice President, his Executive Assistant Jim Johnson, and his Secretary Penny Miller, were in the West Wing. My colleagues on the Vice President's Senior Staff, Richard Moe, the Chief of Staff; Deputy Chief of Staff and Counsel Michael Berman; the Assistant for Domestic Affairs, Gail Harrison; and Press Secretary Al Eisele—who had pitched for the Cleveland Indians' farm club—had their offices in close proximity to mine on the second floor. We worked well together from the days of our first Saturday staff meetings and would remain intact as a senior staff team for the next four years.

From the post-World-War-II of the NSC system, it had become expected professional practice for each new, incoming U.S. Administration to launch an all-encompassing review of existing policies and to set new policy directions. In the first months of the Carter Administration as invariably had been the case, this process produced a giant bow wave of draft policy papers for heated work and debate at the action officers' level, for review at the Assistant Secretary and Under Secretary's level and for decision at the formal sessions of the NSC chaired by the President. Papers for these meetings had already started to come forward in number to the White House for review upon our return from Japan. Staffing the Vice President for these sessions of the NSC and its committees—and quickly learning the essential requirement as a senior member of his staff of ensuring that the necessary times on his calendar were confirmed with those of my colleagues responsible for juggling the endless competing demands for his schedule—demanded a good part of each week in February and March 1977. In turn, the formal work of the NSC system was a subset of my larger, ongoing, mulitiered staffing responsibilities.

Upon the Vice President's arrival in the West Wing each morning Monday through Friday, often on Saturdays, and otherwise at his residence on weekends, I would see that he had the morning's update on international developments: State Department telegrams, Department of Defense messages, the latest current CIA intelligence, and important wire stories. Here again, the Vice President's staffing was dovetailed with the President's to keep the Vice President fully informed. "My first scheduled meeting in the Oval Office each day," President Carter would write, "was with Zbigniew Brzezinski when he brought me the Presidential Daily Briefing (known as the P.D.B.) from the intelligence community...a highly secret document distributed to only five people: the President, the Vice President, the Secretaries of State and Defense, and the National Security Advisor."[10] The P.D.B. would be hand-delivered to the Vice President immediately following the President's reading, and I would stand by for any directions or requests for follow-up information. Additionally, working with staff of the White House Situation Room, I would provide the Vice President subsequent international updates at noon and 6:00 p.m., each working day, augmented, of course, in times of crisis.

The third tier of day-to-day staffing involved the enormous business of the Vice President's dealings with policy-level foreigners in Washington: substantive talks, arrival ceremonies, toasts, press remarks, departure ceremonies—meetings outside the business of the formal NSC system—and all of the Vice President's meetings with U.S. officials, Members of the Congress, and private citizens on foreign policy, intelligence and defense affairs. This involved background papers and talking points for his use, for example, at each Friday's Cabinet Room foreign policy breakfast with the President; for the Monday lunches with the President; for his use in each of the President's meetings with foreign leaders—in his own, separate meetings with such leaders, and in his meetings with American officials.

The fourth tier of staffing included the continuing responsibility for the Vice President's correspondence in the defense and foreign policy fields—correspondence including a heavy volume of replies to interested and concerned Americans on the broadest spectrum of issues. Press guidance had to be provided to the Press Secretary on the issues discussed with foreign leaders; questions and answers had to be drafted as contingency press guidance, in keeping with the key issues of the day. Recommended draft language had to be provided to the speechwriters for the Vice President's heavy schedule of public addresses.

The Vice President, of course, required 24-hour-a-day support for the national command responsibilities assigned to him by the President; these fell to my office and to the operational support of the Military Aides to the Vice President who were part of the operational responsibilities of the Assistant to the Vice President for National Security Affairs.

Additionally, the sixth tier of staffing was perhaps the most challenging—the shaping and conduct of the Vice President's summit missions on behalf of the President. The next mission was already on the horizon.

President Carter's first Secretary of State Cyrus Vance went to the heart of the challenging overseas assignment that Carter gave to Mondale in the spring of 1977—two days of talks with Prime Minister John Vorster of the Republic of South Africa:

> Vice President Mondale met with Prime Minister Vorster in Vienna on May 19 and 20 to discuss our policy toward southern Africa. Mondale told Vorster that our future relations would depend on Pretoria's actions and attitude toward political and racial change in southern Africa, including the beginning of a progressive transformation of South African society away from apartheid. Mondale emphasized that we intended to vigorously assist British efforts to negotiate majority rule in Rhodesia, and would participate actively in the efforts of the United Nations to secure independence for the South-African controlled territory of Namibia. He underscored the fact that our policy was rooted in our view of human rights and was not solely based on anti-communism....He added that in the absence of significant progress in these three areas, there would be an inevitable deterioration in U.S. relations with South Africa.[11]

The process that we instituted to prepare the Vice President for these complex, extremely important talks would set a pattern that we would continue to follow in preparing for each subsequent summit mission. The talks with Vorster were central to the goals of the new Administration. The President and the senior members of his national security team were agreed not only on the importance of progress on peace in the Middle East, in the strategic arms talks with the USSR, in relations with Latin America and with the People's Republic of China; "[they] were determined to demonstrate also the primacy of the moral dimension of foreign policy."[12] As soon as the decision was taken to schedule the talks with the South Africans, we engaged the best minds in the government to assist with the preparations. Given the Vice President's unprecedented role in foreign affairs from the outset of the Administration, I worked hard to ensure that on all key issues he received the same papers and same NSC staff/State/Defense support available to the President. And, on missions such as the Vorster talks, where he would be taking the lead for the President, we worked with the key members of the Administration to ensure support equal to that which would have been given to the President.

The support process for the talks on southern Africa was pyramidal in design, starting in early March with a flow of background reading. The Vice President liked to begin such work with non-governmental readings—major histories of the nation and region, historical novels, and political science essays and other works by the world's internationally recognized talents and authorities. Next the Vice President called for detailed background papers on the key issues in each of the regions and nations to be visited. Following this second stage of preparatory reading, he would assemble the government's experts to discuss the objectives of the overseas mission and the nuances of the reading just completed. We then would move to the preparation of specific issues papers, including the recommended position to be taken by the Vice President. Invariably, this set of papers would receive a critical review; he would seldom be satisfied with the positions initially recommended—they would be too 'soft', not designed to take maximum advantage of the opportunity afforded by his head-to-head talks with whichever the foreign leader. Then, there would be another lengthy round of talks with the experts supporting the mission. As we neared departure and the tip of the pyramidal process, I would refine and redraft the cover 'checklist' paper, seldom more than two pages in length, summarizing the key points the Vice President would wish to bear in mind on each of the key issues. Finally, I would summarize these points further on one, possibly two, three-by-five inch cards, as a final memory aid for him to carry in his pocket to the meeting. It was a process that worked most impressively; Vice President Mondale seldom needed to refer to the papers available to him as a back-up during the course of a meeting.

On May 13, 1977, the Vice President's Press Secretary released the itinerary for the Vorster mission. Having decided with the South Africans on Vienna, Austria, as the most suitable site for the talks, we had developed the mission into a five-nations visit, with arrival in Lisbon, Portugal for meetings with President Eanes and Prime Minister Soares on May 15–16; meetings with King Juan Carlos and Prime Minister Suarez in Madrid, Spain on May 17; on to Vienna, Austria on May 18 for a working lunch with Chancellor Kreisky and a courtesy call on President Kirschlaeger; with the first round of talks with Vorster scheduled for the morning of May 19, an afternoon session, a dinner in honor of the U.S. and South African delegations; a third round of talks on Friday May 20, to be followed by the Vice President's press conference, departure for Yugoslavia; talks with President Tito on the 21st; departure for London and consultations with Prime Minister Callaghan at Chequers on the 22nd; with return to Washington on the 23rd.

We reviewed this itinerary and goals for the mission in a background briefing for the U.S. press, in which I participated with David Aaron; William Bowdler, the U.S. Ambassador to South Africa; and Tony Lake, the State Department's new Director of Policy Planning. The Hofburg Palace in Vienna was the site of our talks. The advance team had chosen a conference room above an inner courtyard. It was a warm spring morning when our two delegations introduced ourselves prior to the opening round. A rhythmic clopping of hooves could be heard through the open windows. White Lippizaner stallions were engaged with their riders in their daily training—a brush stroke of European culture against which we would then grapple for more than eight hours with the political vestiges of Europe's African empire. Vorster and Mondale, while civil and diplomatically correct, were candid to a point of sharpness in the language they chose to present their opposing views on the internal situation in South Africa. On Namibia and Rhodesia, there was not agreement, but diplomatic formulations were accepted by either side for further exploration. There could be no doubt that each nation, while not encouraged, knew clearly where the other stood by the end of the third round. I would be with the Vice President many months later at the British Embassy in Washington at a Luncheon honoring Great Britain's new Prime Minister Margret Thatcher when Foreign Secretary Carrington would excuse himself to take a call bringing the news of a decisively successful breakthrough in the Rhodesian negotiations—and with the President and Vice President still months later when Prime Minister Mugabe of newly independent Zimbabwe paid his first official to the United States to offer his thanks for America's support.

We would not see such progress on either Namibia or South Africa. At the end of his lengthy news conference on May 20th, which had opened with the reading of a precisely drafted statement on the tenor and results of the talks, the Vice President was asked and responded affirmatively to the question: Is the U.S. really pressing for a 'one man, one vote' in South Africa? This was a dramatic departure from the official U.S. position that there should be progress toward majority rule in South Africa. But, there was no confusion on Mondale's part; I am sure he knew he reflected the sentiments of most Americans in providing the world's press with the answer he gave.

Upon completion of this second major assignment, the balance of the Vice President's 1977 foreign policy involvement focused on meetings with foreign leaders in Washington. Similarly, President Carter, with the exception of his travel to the U.K. for the mid-May economic summit, with a side trip to Geneva for talks with Syria's President Assad, would remain in the United States until the end of December 1977, when he would depart on Air Force One for a summit journey through Poland—where faulty interpretation of his arrival remarks would detract from the world's coverage of his visit—still another reminder of the endless pitfalls that lurk in the path of a sherpa's summit staffing—Iran, for meetings with the Shah; India, Saudi Arabia; Egypt; France and Belgium.

On December 8, 1977, with planning already underway for new foreign assignments early in the new year, I took off from Andrews Air Force Base with the Vice President aboard one of the Joint Chiefs of Staff's modified 747 National Emergency Airborne Command Posts—the NEACP, or 'Doomsday Plane'—for an orientation flight en route to further briefings by the Strategic Air Command at Offutt Air Force Base, Nebraska. The event was announced by the President's Press Secretary. There was value to be had from reminding both friend and foe that the United States continued to attach the most vital importance not only to deterrence but to the readiness of U.S. strategic forces.

End Notes

1. A.P. WIRE, 2233G, 1 March 1977.
2. Address by Vice President Walter F. Mondale before the North Atlantic Council, NATO Headquarters, Brussels, January 24, 1977.
3. Ibid.
4. Broder, David S., and Getler, Michael, *International Herald Tribune*, Paris, January 26, 1977, page 1.
5. Address of Vice President Walter F. Mondale, Golden Book Ceremony, Rathaus Schoeneberg, Berlin, January 26, 1977.
6. Blake, William, *Milton*, 1804.
7. Press Conference of Vice President Walter F. Mondale, London, January 27, 1977.
8. Carter, Jimmy, *Keeping Faith, Memoirs of a President*, Bantam Books, Inc., New York, 1982, page 37.
9. Ibid., page 40.
10. Ibid., pages 51, 55.
11. Vance, Cyrus, *Hard Choices*, Simon and Schuster, New York, 1983, page 265.
12. Brzezinski, Zbigniew, *Power and Principle*, Farrar, Straus, Giroux, New York, 1983, page 81.

CHAPTER EIGHT
Camp David — 1978

I never pass an Arab ploughman or reaper
without greeting him "Saha badhu" (Health
to your body) and hearing his reply, "Badnu
salmo" (Peace to your body).

Living With the Bible
Moshe Dayan, 1978

Wilting, steamy heat invaded Air Force Two, then opened the pores as I moved through the receiving line with Vice President and Mrs. Mondale at Jakarta International Airport Halim Perdanakusuma, to be greeted by Foreign Minister Malik and the resident Diplomatic Corps. Sunset, May 5, 1978, Jakarta, the island of Java, Indonesia—we had just arrived from Bangkok, Thailand, midway through a two-week swing through Hawaii, Guam, and five nations of the Pacific. The front pages of the Jakarta press were carrying the unbelievable photograph of a giant python, its belly slit, exposing the legs and torso of an adult male villager the snake had caught on a jungle path, crushed and ingested.

This mission to the Pacific had come with the Carter Administration at full foreign-policy stride. In the face of tremendous domestic controversy, the President had pushed ahead in September 1977 to terminate prior treaties pertaining to the Panama Canal and to conclude a new treaty with the Government of Panama safeguarding America's strategic interests. This would provide for the permanent neutrality and operation of the Canal, and ensure Panama's rights as a territorial sovereign.[1] Early in 1978, the President and Vice President had shaped a complementary schedule of summit travels for the first half of the year that would take the President to Venezuela, Brazil, Nigeria, and Liberia in late-March and early-April, and to Panama City in mid-June to confirm the exchange of documents ratifying the Panama Canal Treaties.

In January 1978, I was with the Vice President for two, intensively prepared working visits to Canada and Mexico—visits which had coincided with the loss of one his most important guiding lights and friends, Hubert H. Humphrey. Summit principals are human beings, not robots. The staffer, with responsibility rising in accordance with position, must help to shape the professional calendar to ensure that his principal's concerns day-to-day are understood and anticipated, so as to contribute to the broader national objectives both staffer and principal share. I had had the pleasure of knowing Hubert Humphrey. As a graduate student, I had written him in 1967 in his capacity as Chairman of the National Council on Marine Resources and Engineering Development during his Vice Presidency to apply— successfully as it turned out for an Executive Office staff position in international marine science affairs. In December 1968, Vice President Humphrey had written to thank me for my contributions to the Council. In December 1977, I had been aboard the Air Force Two flight, with Vice President Mondale, that took Humphrey back to his home in Minnesota for the final time. His spirit, the spark in his eyes, were still there despite the ravages of illness to his body as he spoke with us on that flight—a splendid man. I was impressed by the tributes he received from the Vice President's hosts in Ottawa and Mexico City.

1978 would be, for me, a year of important diplomatic endeavor, the opening of new vistas, the culminating experience of the Middle East summit at Camp David—and more, including the strategically important visit by the Vice President to the Pacific. On February 17, 1978, the Office of the White House Press Secretary advised: "The President today announced that the Vice President Walter F. Mondale will visit New Zealand, Australia, Indonesia, Thailand, and the Philippines. Here is the text of his statement: Since my schedule will not permit me to travel to the Pacific area during 1978, I have asked Vice President Mondale to serve as my personal representative on a trip to this region in mid-April....His mission underscores the importance my Administration attaches to this region of the world where we retain vital security interests and where we have very large and rapidly growing commercial ties...."[2] America's withdrawal from Vietnam had caused other friends and allies in the Pacific to sense a greater abandonment. And, the limited record of American visits to the region, mostly at the sub-Cabinet level, in 1977 had added to the uncertainty.

The Vice President, in fact, would undertake the mission in early May so as to avoid any suggestion of U.S. interference in the Philippine elections scheduled for that April. It was a fast-paced trip—May 3-4, the Philippines; May 4-5, Thailand; May 5-7, Indonesia; May 7-9, Australia; May 9-10, New Zealand—spanning many thousands of miles, with dramatic time zone changes and accompanying jet lag, and with a heavily loaded security, economic and human rights agenda. By this time, I had adopted the practice of preparing two, complete duplicate sets of all the classified and unclassified papers prepared for each event in the mission. I had learned that even in the close, airborne confines of Air Force Two, key papers had a way of disappearing at crucial times. I gave the greatest care to the preparation and assembly of the folders in each of the large rectangular carrying cases; their well-being was paramount. Each folder contained the desired end-result for each stage of the journey.

Mondale's fundamental message, publicly and privately throughout the mission was that the United States is unalterably a Pacific power; we are a nation of the Pacific; the freedom of the seas and the prosperity of our trade in the Pacific are essential to our interests; and our Asian alliances are central to the stability of the Pacific and to the global balance. To underline the vital nature of these interests, the Vice President reached an understanding with the Philippines' President Marcos breaking an impasse over the renewal of U.S. base rights at Clark and Subic Bay. Careful preparation had been required. Renewal of comparable base agreements with Turkey, Greece, and Spain earlier in the 1970s on generous terms not unnoticed by the Philippines required the crafting of a skillful diplomatic compromise in Manila, and this was accomplished. In Bangkok, the Vice President assured Prime Minister Kriangsak that the United States would continue to be a reliable supplier of defense equipment, as the Prime Minister would confirm in his press conference following their talks:

REPORTER: The issue of military assistance is included, isn't it?

KRIANGSAK: It is a talk satisfying to both sides, including military affairs, such as the purchase of weapons and ammunition.

REPORTER: Including airplanes?

KRIANGSAK: They will supply one squadron of F5E's

REPORTER: Eighteen planes?

KRIANGSAK: Yes, eighteen, but probably more for spares.

REPORTER: How about other weapons? Are they going to sell them to us?

KRIANGSAK: Yes, they are. The detail is not yet known. They will try to sell more of other weapons.[3]

In Jakarta, the Vice President advised President Suharto that the United States would deliver more A-4 aircraft. And, in Canberra and Wellington, with his Australian and New Zealand hosts, he reaffirmed the U.S. commitment to the ANZUS alliance, calling attention to joint naval exercises soon to be held off the west coast of Australia.

In Manila and Jakarta, a fresh dimension of economic assistance accompanied the security understandings. Mondale and President Marcos signed agreements on rural road development aimed at expediting farm crops to market, on the development of farm cooperatives similar to those in the U.S., on water purification for the people of the Barangay, and on a nonconventional energy project aimed at providing energy sources other than fossil fuels and nuclear power—energy from solar, wind and biomass sources—for rural Philippine areas. Energy cooperation was also on the agenda in Jakarta, and the Vice President and President Suharto signed an $30 million rural electrification loan. On this Pacific mission I took the sherpa's initiative of assisting in the formal signing ceremonies, the staffing task under the eyes, lens, and recording equipment of international media, of ensuring that the right page was opened with the right spot identified for the signing of the duplicate copies of the multiple agreements. In such events, instant, correct action is the only standard to be accepted by the media and to avoid 'color commentaries on slip-ups today during and important overseas mission;' with the fast pace of the summit events it is unrealistic to expect more sophisticated coverage. Presidents command coverage by their very office. Vice Presidents, Cabinet Officers, and officials at sub-Cabinet rank compete increasingly with other stories, and the reporters covering these officials work hard to develop the story angle—too often the 'color' angle—that will be equal to the competition.

Human rights was the third, principal dimension of the Pacific mission. Following his May 3 talks with Mondale, Marcos moved to take the initiative: "In a 45-minute free-wheeling conference at Malacanang yesterday afternoon, the President told local and foreign newsman, including some White House reporters, that if there were cases of human-rights violations here, these were the exception rather than the rule....The subject of human rights was reportedly one of the matters contained in the letter of President Carter, which Vice President Walter F. Mondale delivered to the President. The President said that he and Mondale had 'lively discussions' on this and other matters."[4]

The Vice President took a different tack in his press conference: "I emphasized that the United States had no plans for how the people of the Philippines should conduct their internal affairs, and I think I was able to convey the fact that the concern of the American people for human rights is a measure of the affection and respect we have for the Philippine people. To this end I will be meeting with several religious and other political leaders this afternoon."[5] That meeting, in the Vice President's hotel suite, began on a strained note with the Vice President's guests asking how he could condone human rights abuses by his very presence in Manila. He asked in return if the very fact of his presence and the fact that he was raising the issue did not offer an entirely different signal—and the tone of the meeting, confirmed by the report of these leaders to the awaiting media, warmed immeasurably.

Again, in Indonesia, the Vice President addressed the issue, stressing the importance attached to the rights of the individual by Americans, noting the encouragement that Americans took from the holding of the elections and from the recent release of some 10,000 detainees in East Timor. The human rights commitment extended beyond rhetoric. In Bangkok, the Vice President had informed Kriangsak of America's readiness to expand its quota of Southeast Asian refugees by 25,000 a year, and of the immediate offer of two million dollars to assist the Thais in the development of their longer-term plans for handling the flood of refugees still fleeing Vietnam and Cambodia.

The hedges, sculpted into ornamental elephants at the Royal Palace in Bangkok, the freighters of the world being lighted in historic Manila Bay, the urban bustle of Jakarta against the jungles of Java, the journey back through the years in the tunnels of Corregidor, were all part of the vivid impressions. On May 4, we had helicoptered with Marcos and Foreign Minister Romulo from the President's grounds in Manila to Corregidor to pay tribute to those who had died 36 years before. Romulo, now in his late 70s, had fought with General Wainwright at Corregidor, and served as the Vice President's guide through the main wing and laterals of Malinta Tunnel.

"It was damp in the tunnel and the ventilation was often bad," Wainwright had written. "By April 25, the tunnel hospital had been expanded until it was handling a thousand wounded men. It made you weep to see them in there, trapped, while the place shook from the bombing and shelling outside. More than once the tunnel's shaky lighting system, through protected by Brigadier General Beebe's improvisations with small generators, failed and cast all of us into the most Stygian blackness imaginable—a fearful hardship on the hospital, where blood-stained doctors and nurses worked day and night."[6] We emerged from the tunnel and proceeded to the site of the commemorative ceremony. In his speech, the Vice President honored the courage and the memory of the defenders of Corregidor praising their perseverance in the face of the horrendous shelling and bombardment by an overwhelmingly more powerful Japanese force as one of the brightest, enduring symbols of the indominability of the human spirit. On May 4, 1978, a page in history turned; for the first time since the battle, a representative of the Government of Japan had been invited to participate, and was with us to honor the memory of those who had given their lives.

The visits to our ANZUS allies in Australia and New Zealand marked a change of gears in the swing through the Pacific, with more informal, more colleagial consultations. While there were, as always, bilateral trade issues and other minor bilateral irritants to be pursued, the talks permitted both sides to take stock of broader international issues of shared interest and concern—in Asia and the Pacific, in the Middle East, in the security and political relations between the nations of the West and the Warsaw Pact.

The day-long flight across the vast red-brown of Australia's interior brought us to Canberra, the nation's planned national capital, on Sunday, May 7 at 7:45 p.m., Monday was given to talks with Prime Minister Frazer and members of his Cabinet, a luncheon hosted by the U.S. Ambassador followed by consultations with the Leader of the Opposition, a wreath-laying at the Australian War Memorial and a dinner hosted by the Prime Minister and Mrs. Frazer. On Tuesday morning, following the 1,200-mile flight across the Tazman Sea, Air Force Two began its descent into the Royal New Zealand Air Base at Ohakea. Mondale, who had grown up in the bountiful farmlands of southern Minnesota, looked out on the lush green countryside dotted with sheep, impressed by what he saw, commenting; "The entire place looks like a grass factory."

Prime Minister Robert Muldoon, a delightful, bluff political figure, was at the Air Base to greet us. By the time of our visit he had already spun and published the second of his autobiographies—the first, *The Rise and Fall of a Young Turk*, and the second, even more to the point, *Muldoon*—a thoughtful appraisal of the success of his public years with fair warning in the preface; "I have tried to be impartial in writing this book, but I will in no way be offended if any critic claims that I have not succeeded."[7]

While in Wellington, we received the grim news from halfway around the world of Prime Minister Aldo Moro's murder by terrorists in Rome. And, as the program with Prime Minister Muldoon and the members of his government proceeded, we were in repeated contact with the White House to determine if the President would wish the Vice President to proceed immediately to Italy to lead the U.S. Delegation to the Moro funeral. The decision was taken that the Vice President should complete the Pacific mission as planned. At 6:00 p.m., May 10, Air Force Two was wheels-up for the long night flight back across the international dateline, north to Hawaii with a refueling stop in Pago Pago, to meet the Vice President's schedule for an address to the East-West Center at 10:00 a.m., May 10. The speech, which reviewed the goals and the accomplishments of the five-nation visit just completed, was addressed not only to all in the packed auditorium at the University of Hawaii, but also, through resulting press coverage, to the nations of the Pacific reaffirming the priority importance the United States attached to its role of leadership among the nations of the Pacific community.

Within days of our return to Washington, I was on the phone to Simcha Dinitz, Israel's Ambassador to the United States. From June 30–July 3, 1978, the Vice President would lead the U.S. Delegation to honor Israel's 30th Anniversary of Independence. America's recognition of the anniversary called for a national gift equal to the importance of the event, and I was probing the minds of as many experts as possible to develop some good recommendations for White House consideration. Dinitz underlined the importance that the people of Israel attached to their history. He steered me in the direction of Daniel Boorstin, the Librarian of Congress. This, in turn, led to the recommendation of the gift of a copy of the first Hebrew-language edition of the Bible to be published in America, in the first decade of the 1800s. A copy of this extremely rare edition was located in Philadelphia, and the proposal was approved by the President and Vice President, as well as the loan for a year to Israel from the National Archives of President Truman's instruction to Secretary of State Marshall directing formal U.S. recognition of the State of Israel.

From the outset, there was little question of this being solely a ceremonial trip for the Vice President; too much was at stake in the Middle East. President Carter had worked hard, but with little to show by the Spring of 1978, to further the peace process. Sadat's historic visit to Jerusalem in November 1977 had shown that direct talks between Egypt and Israel were possible, but the U.S. was still searching for the right context, channels and venue to make such talks a reality. And, given several controversial positions that President Carter had taken publicly on issues key to such talks, Prime Minister Menachem Begin was not as comfortable with the prospects of the U.S. as middleman as was Sadat.

On June 21, 1978, Secretary of State Vance had sent messages to Tel Aviv and Cairo proposing that the Israeli and Egyptian Foreign Ministers meet with him in London in mid-July. As the time of the 30th Anniversary visit neared, the President asked the Vice President to carry letters to both Begin and Sadat placing the Vance invitation on a personal leader-to-leader basis.[8] Alexandria, Egypt was added to the flight plan, as each additional dimension of the mission developed. In addition to the official staff party, the Vice President would be accompanied by a special delegation of private American citizens—we would be traveling aboard two Air Force jets with a refueling stop in the Azores en route to Tel Aviv—further underscoring the importance American attached to the independence anniversary. The itinerary would take the delegation from Tel Aviv to Jerusalem; with additional travel by helicopter to Ben Gurion's beloved Sde Boker Kibbutz overlooking a great cut in the Negev, much like the Grand Canyon; a visit to Beersheva for the unveiling of a plaque at Ben Gurion University's Humphrey Institute; back to Jerusalem for the State Dinner in the Knesset Building on the evening of July 2; and a very somber visit to Yad Vashem Memorial, to honor those lost in the Holocaust, the following morning.

On a mission such as this, where a goodly number of private citizens were included in our traveling party, additional staff members were also included to look after the details of their program. This proved to be both efficient and successful. Important guests of the U.S. Government received the minute-to-minute attention they deserved. At the same time, those of us professionally responsible to the Vice President for his support in the business of the mission were able to carry out our duties without such predictable distractions. And, there was much business to be conducted.

At the public level, is his July 2 Knesset address, Mondale delivered a major statement of U.S. Middle East policy, aimed at dispelling any confusing signals that might have been earlier received from Washington. In so doing, and in keeping with his pattern in all major speeches to foreign audiences, he quoted the President:

> For thirty years we have stood at the side of the proud and independent nation of Israel. I can say without reservation, as the President of the United States, that we will continue to do so, not just for another thirty years, but forever.

He firmly reaffirmed America's commitment to U.N. Resolution 242 as the framework for peace in the Middle East:

> Resolution 242 is an equation. On the one hand, it recognizes the right of every state in the area to live in peace within secure and recognized borders free from threats or acts of force. We believe such peace must include binding commitments to normal relations. In return, Israel would withdraw from territories occupied in the 1967 war. We believe that the exact boundaries must be determined through negotiations by the parties themselves.[9]

Of equal importance, the Vice President devoted long hours to discussion with Prime Minister Begin. He began these discussions from the very moment our motorcade departed Tel Aviv for Jerusalem, winding its way through the hills past the hulks of armored vehicles and transports dotting the route, preserved in red lead paint from the time of the war of independence, past Bedouin camps— discussing America's commitment to working with Israel. Wolf Blitzer of the *Jerusalem Post* would later report Begin as saying that this car ride with the Vice President had turned everything around, that he had seen no chance of progress before. The official talks proceeded with Begin and his Cabinet in the Prime Minister's office and in tete-a-tetes at the Prime Minister's residence. President Carter's letter of invitation to the London talks was delivered, and the Vice President continued to exercise his personal diplomacy in a final private meeting just before our departure for Egypt. In Mondale's own words: "I made a strong plea that he trust Carter....I tried to interpret Carter to him....I believe I made an impact on him, because I think he was beginning to doubt us in our commitment to Israel."[10]

It was a short hop in Air Force Two from Ben Gurion Airport to the military base in Egypt, and President Sadat was at his expansive best when we arrived by Egyptian helicopter at his Mediterranean seaside villa outside of Alexandria. Our delegation of private citizens had proceeded directly back to the United States. Sadat showed the

Vice President and members of our official party to a lawn setting of arm chairs and end tables for talks and refreshments, talks punctuated by the boisterous shrieks of Honey and Sonny, two handsome chimpanzees in a large, domed, outdoors barred cage on the villa grounds. Sadat the statesman then escorted Vice President Mondale to a bank of microphones prepared for his statement to the awaiting members of the press: Yes, he had received a communication from his friend President Jimmy Carter; yes, he would agree to the proposed London talks. Secretary Vance would meet with Foreign Ministers Moshe Dayan and Muhammed Kamel in mid-July, and in August would convey President Carter's invitations to Begin and Sadat to meet with him at Camp David that September. Our 30th anniversary mission had made a significant contribution to the launching of this summit process.

In mid-1978, President Carter had undertaken additional summit travels: to Panama in mid-June to sign the Protocol confirming the exchange of documents ratifying the Panama Canal treaties, with meetings on the fringe with the Presidents of Venezuela, Colombia, and Mexico, and the Prime Minister of Jamaica; and, in mid-July, to the Federal Republic of Germany for the 1978 Economic Summit of the industrialized democracies in Bonn.

In August 1978, puffs of white smoke from the Vatican announced that a new Pope had been chosen by the College of Cardinals to succeed the late Paul VI. Newly elected, appearing at the Papal balcony to greet the masses in St. Peter's Square waiting to see him, Pope John Paul raised his hands in the familiar Papal gesture of greeting, then illuminated his face—and the spirits of all who witnessed—with the broadest of engaging smiles, a smile that would forever hold him in the world's memory.

The President named the Vice President to head the U.S. Delegation to the ceremonies marking the installation of Pope John Paul, and selected Americans from across the United States to accompany the Vice President as members of the Presidential Delegation: Senator Pell of Rhode Island, Senator McIntyre of New Hampshire, Senator Hathaway of Maine, Congressman Conte of Massachusetts, Congressman Zablocki of Wisconsin, Congressman Rodino of New Jersey, Congressman de la Garza of Texas, Governor Byrne of New Jersey, Notre Dame University President Father Theodore Hesburgh, Mayor George Moscone of San Francisco, the list went on—a fascinating Air Force Two manifest, embarking on a joyous occasion. It would be a very quick mission, with departure from

Andrews Air Force Base to Rome and the Vatican via Shannon, Ireland at 4:00 p.m., Saturday, September 2, 1978, and return to Andrews again via Shannon at 8:00 p.m., Monday, September 4. As ever, I guided the drafting, assembly, and final review of the background papers for each event, including the Papal Audience, as well as talks on the fringe with Prime Minister Andreotti and a working breakfast with Chancellor Helmut Schmidt. As ever, there was the question of the best gift from the nation. My mind kept returning to the smiling John Paul—the very special moment in history that had been captured. I asked the State Department's Chief of Protocol, Ambassador Kit Dobelle, if we could ascertain whether newspapers in each of the nation's 50 states had carried that photograph on their front pages. She did, and more; on Air Force Two we carried with us a custom-built mahogany portfolio containing those front pages from each of the 50 states, a spontaneous tribute from all of America.

Upon the Vice President and Mrs. Mondale's arrival in St. Peter's Square at 6:00 p.m., on September 3, our delegation was shown seats among heads of State and Chiefs of Government close to the platform erected for the Inaugural Mass. A copy of the Vatican's 93-page richly illustrated text and music of the Mass, *Messa Celbrata dal Papa Giovanni Pauli I per l'Inizio del Suo Ministero di Supremo Pastore*, was at each place and the Square soon filled with the multitude of joyful voices:

Veni, creator Spiritus, mentes tuorum visita,
imple superna gratia, quae tu creasti pectora...

The towering statuary of St. Peter's Square was dressed in the gold of sunset. Only the passage of a large balloon, beyond the Square, protesting the presence of Argentina's President Videla momentarily intruded on the spectacle of John Paul I's installation. Few could know that I had been in touch with a member of Videla's staff to confirm the details of a meeting with the Vice President on September 4.

Chancellor Schmidt joined the Vice President at his hotel suite for breakfast the next morning. It was clear to me from the ease of conversation that the two Administrations had come to know each other better, free of the protocol of formal diplomacy; following which we departed for the Palazzo Chigi and talks with Andreotti. Such opportunities for informal contact on the fringe of international occasions are an important dynamic to summit life. The positive chemistry of such meetings, unburdened by the heavy logistics in every respect of more formal state-to-state discussions, contributes uniquely both to continuing dialogue with ensuing productive results on matters of shred interest, and to advances resulting from face-to-face exchanges on differences not susceptible of resolution by bureaucracies. On this mission, the former would be the case with both Schmidt and Andreotti, the latter with Videla.

The military takeover of Argentina and the resulting hard reports of human rights abuses, 'disappearances' and confirmed heavy loss of life in the government's 'anti-terrorist' campaign had compelled President Carter, reinforced by punitive action of the U.S. Congress, to chill U.S.-Argentine relations. Military sales were canceled, and the entire future of the government-to-government contacts became conditioned to the requirement of internationally credible evidence of an improvement in respect for human rights by the Argentine Junta.

The Vice President had one of his most capable, most experienced advancemen, Mike Murray, in Rome to pave the way for the September 1978 mission. Upon our arrival, Murray buttonholed me: Videla's aide had been in touch and wanted me to call as soon as possible to confirm the time, place and any other particulars of the meeting. Second, Murray's ex-Marine voice dropped to a disparaging growl, our Ambassador thought that the meeting was a bad idea and, specifically did not want to have his official residence as the meeting site. I told Mike that the President, the Vice President, the Secretary of State, and the Assistant to the President for National Security Affairs thought that the meeting was a good idea, that the Ambassador was out voted on this and on the venue; there was no other logical site given the need for discretion and the Vice President's tight schedule. In less than an hour, Mike was back in touch; all was in order.

Upon the Vice President's return from the Palazzo Chigi, he joined with Mrs. Mondale and the members of our distinguished Presidential delegation and departed for the Papal Audience in the Sistine Chapel. John Paul I reached out in his greeting to the delegation. Congressman Conte mentioned that his family had come from Vincenza, the Pope's very roots in Italy. "John Paul grabbed both his hands and said, 'I can't tell you how proud I am that a family from my province went to America and elected their son to the Congress.'"[11]

A reception had been planned from the outset to conclude our delegation's visit, and as the delegates enjoyed midday refreshments in the Ambassador's gardens, the Vice President and I proceeded to a second-floor drawing room where we were joined by President

Videla. Mondale's message was polite but to the point—much along the lines of his message to Vorster of South Africa a year before. Argentina's internal affairs were for Argentina to decide, but America could not be indifferent to the outcome. The Vice President told Videla we wanted to return to the traditionally good relations between the U.S. and Argentina; we wanted to give favorable consideration to requests in this context from Buenos Aires; however, we needed evidence of Argentina's good faith on the issue of human rights. To launch this process, the Vice President urged Videla to agree to a long-standing request by the Inter-American Human Rights Commission for a visit to Argentina. Videla, soft-spoken and polite throughout, listened carefully. Within a very brief time following his return to Buenos Aires, the commission's request for a visit was granted. Characteristically, following the discussion in the residence in Rome, the Vice President told the members of the press prior to his departure for the airport of his discussions, of their purpose and of his hope for progress. Thirty-four days later, the mission to Rome and the Vatican was jolted by the news of John Paul I's heart attack and death. "The Pope had a message to give our world," said Cardinal Francois Marty of Paris. "He gave us the smile of God. In the grayness of these days, this smile will remain like a beam of light."[12]

Marine Two, the Vice President's helicopter, made a quick journey of the 65 miles from Washington to Camp David. I arrived with the Vice President on September 7; I would remain through September 17, the conclusion, the stunning success of the summit. Within 24 hours of our return from the Vatican, I had been at Andrews Air Force Base to assist the Vice President in his reception ceremonies first for Sadat, then for Begin. President Carter had invested his prestige and the prestige of the United States; he would break the stalemate in the Middle East or he would be broken politically by his failure to do so. The very fact that I was at Camp David was testimony to the partnership between the President and Vice President and to the integrated working relationship between the President's and the Vice President's staffs, a relationship virtually unparalled in U.S. history. Carter had correctly predicted that the summit would take time, and he knew that if it were to succeed drum-tight integrity would have to be maintained throughout the summit process "because hundreds of other bureaucrats and would-be advisers from all three countries were struggling to find an excuse to join the historic deliberations. [He was] remarkably successful in keeping them out and in minimizing visits to and from our private place."[13] The President had asked the Vice President to divide his time between Washington and the summit, to help ensure that the routine business of government flowed smoothly in the President's absence, and to be a participant and of counsel in the negotiations with Begin and Sadat. This meant that the Vice President would have to be kept fully abreast of hour-by-hour developments at the summit; the President agreed that to make this possible I should be admitted as a member of the summit staff.

The Camp David Summit was a unique diplomatic experience. Normal summit schedules, calendars, and timetables were set aside. The hours of the day and night and the days of the week were far less relevant to the summit's participants than the non-stop dynamics of consultations, of the drafting of new proposals, the analysis of Egyptian and Israeli proposals, the informal, continuing mission-oriented dialogue between participants at all levels of the delegations, all keyed to support the President's negotiations with Begin and Sadat. With very few exceptions, the U.S., Egyptian, and Israeli delegations remained within the confines of the Presidential retreat from start to finish; the Israeli Prime Minister would dub Camp David a 'concentration camp de luxe'. Contact with the media was limited to the briefings that the President's Press Secretary Jody Powell provided in the press center established miles away at Thurmont, Maryland. This 'lid' on the news of the summit was virtually absolute. Americans—the world—did not know what was transpiring in the talks beyond the information provided by the one agreed-upon press spokesman, and the absence of thousands of conflicting, inevitably controversial news stories freed each of the three summit leaders from having to posture publicly or to take irreversibly unbending stands—for reasons of domestic politics—during the negotiations. The press was kept in the waiting room during the summit's labor.

President Carter guided the Camp David process with a deep intensity and sense of purpose, 24 hours a day from start to finish, a remarkable feat both of diplomacy and endurance. I was seated perhaps four feet from him at the large round conference table in Holly Lodge at a night strategy session early in the summit. He sketched the wide differences, clearly evident between Begin and Sadat, that he had encountered in the opening rounds of their talks. He stressed his total trust in the integrity and skill of his American team, and his dedication to sharing his innermost thoughts and the most sensitive information with this team in pursuit of the summit's goal. His pale gray-blue eyes probed our faces as he spoke. He would pause, very briefly, holding his words until he had driven his mind to shape each of the precise thoughts he wished to impart. I wondered to myself at the time if anyone's health could be equal to such strain.

The President's principal lieutenant throughout the summit, Secretary of State Cyrus Vance, played a role second only to the President's in achieving the Camp David accords. Vance worked day after day, with no more sleep than that of a destroyer skipper's in combat, at three different levels of the summit process: with the President, Begin, and Sadat; with the Israeli, Egyptian, and U.S. Delegations at the ministerial and expert's levels—political intent had to be meshed with international law and the code of formal diplomacy—and late into the nights, early into each new morning with the U.S. team reviewing tactics, revising draft texts and shaping new formulations in light of each preceding day's discussions. An electric golf cart, not an Air Force jet, was to be the chosen vehicle for Vance's successful Middle East shuttle diplomacy. He was a veritable demon of the cart, at the controls, whizzing along the asphalt footpaths among the cabins, among the delegations. Camp David lent itself to such travel.

Franklin Delano Roosevelt had been the first President to motor to this picturesque site in the Catoctin Mountains of northern Maryland to find brief respite from the era-of-depression and wartime pressures of the Presidency, and from the humid summer heat of Washington. Navy stewards from the President's yacht had traveled with him to the summer cottages, which Roosevelt had named Shangri-La, to staff his visits. The retreat, renamed Camp David by President Eisenhower, had become a favorite of each successive President. By the time of the Carter Presidency, Camp David had evolved physically into one of the world's most exclusive, secluded year-around 'resorts', which the Navy by tradition and expertise continued to manage for the White House.

Within its fenced, carefully guarded perimeter, the Camp at one end had a fully equipped helicopter landing pad and hangar facility set in an open field that would be the site of the Marine Corps' silent drill performed in the evening of September 7, in honor of the summit leaders. A narrow, vehicular service road led from the landing pad to the heart of Camp David. The President's lodge, Aspen, commanded a view of many miles out over the ridges to the south, with a terraced patio, swimming pool and putt-and-pitch golf range at the foot of the lodge in a clearing of the Catoctin forest.

Beneath the towering hardwood trees along the roads and footpaths curving from Aspen, upwards of a dozen separate guest lodges with subtle exterior and interior variations in their rustic, comfortable designs—each with carved wood address plaques—Maple, Elm, Red Oak, Walnut, Hemlock, Hickory, Hawthorn, and the rest—were 'home' for the members of the three delegations. Laurel Lodge, a relatively recent addition to the Camp, provided the main dining room and lounge for the participants. Tennis courts, a bowling alley, horse shoe pitch, swimming pool with bath house, the Camp Commander's quarters, a dispensary, and barracks for additional personnel were all placed discreetly in the heavily treed mountain side landscape. There could be no finer place to relax—or to work—free from distraction.

Carter's trilateral talks with Begin and Sadat were adjourned early in the summit after two sessions; the wide gaps between the Egyptian and Israeli positions could not be bridged so early on by personal diplomacy; the three would not meet again together until the final day. The U.S. offered the first of a score of compromise texts to the Israeli Delegation on Sunday, September 10. The Vice President met early into Monday morning with Begin and Carter then, as would be the case for the next week and one-half, departed later in the day for Washington to pick up the other business of government.

Upon each of these departures, I remained glued firmly to the evolving talks. This was not difficult, as I knew and worked easily with the experts on our delegation: Ambassador at Large Roy Atherton, Assistant Secretary of State Hal Saunders, Bill Quandt of the NSC Staff, and our Ambassadors to Israel and Egypt, Sam Lewis and Hermann Eilts. Attending our delegation's meetings, working late into the nights during the preparation of new drafts, sitting in on a round of talks between Secretary Vance and the Egyptians, receiving a summary of other such talks from various participants, and dining with different members of the three delegations at Laurel, I was able to maintain a fairly detailed status report on developments that I would present to the Vice President each time he returned via helicopter to re-enter the talks.

The hard work of the summit was leavened by the experience of working side by side with the Egyptians and the Israelis for so many days. These were not just political figures. Men such as Sadat, Begin, Dayan, and Weizman had fought for their countries' independence and for their countries' existences. Their beliefs on the issues of the Middle East ran to the deepest veins of human existence. They had many good stories to tell. Ezar Weizman, who had commanded Israel's Air Force, before becoming Minister of Defense, told us that he had been a truck driver for the Royal Air Force in Egypt during World War II. Weizman, with his military secretary Colonel Ilan Tehila, took the pressures of Camp David in stride. On Sunday, September 17, President Carter suddenly appeared at Holly Lodge and asked me where he could find Weizman. I pointed to Sycamore, and he was at the door in a second or two, with Weizman urging him not to come in. "We laughed because the cabin was in such a mess."[14] The President had achieved his breakthrough to success but he was leaving nothing to chance, seeking and receiving the Minister of Defense's word that he would do everything possible upon his return to Israel to have the decisions of the summit approved by the Israeli Knesset.

Menachem Begin, invariably accompanied by his wife, strolled the Camp's grounds and often dined with us at Laurel, always maintaining a very courtly, 'old world' manner. It was hard to believe that he had been one fiercest of the guerrillas in Israel's war for independence. Moshe Dayan was truly a grand, charismatic figure who delighted in discussing his real interest in life—the archaeology of Israel and the Middle East, and who recounted various adventures and misadventures in literary efforts intended to augment his government salary. Dayan, to me, exuded the spirit of Israel. His words were not the words of an individual but of a people. President Sadat, throughout the summit, remained in relative seclusion; I would only catch a glimpse of him from time to time during his morning strolls. And, among them, day after day, President Carter kept the process going. Israel's withdrawal from occupied territories—the Siani foremost in this category in terms of issues vital to Sadat—was clearly the most difficult issue confronting the negotiators. The status of Jerusalem was a close second. On Thursday, the 10th day of the summit, the Israelis agreed that they could withdraw their airbases from the Siani provided the United States built new military bases in the Negev, but Begin insisted that the Jewish settlements would have to remain. When Sadat received this news, only Carter's personal intervention kept the Egyptian President from demanding a helicopter for his immediate departure.

On Friday, I accompanied the Vice President on a mission as unique as the summit itself. The President had penned a personal letter to Sadat and Begin setting a deadline of Sunday for the conclusion of the summit; this was done not out of optimism but as a last-ditch effort to produce concessions from Israel and Egypt. Mondale delivered these letters to each leader discussing their contents and receiving comments, first to Sadat at Dogwood, then to Begin at Birch. Late Saturday, Begin agreed that the question of the settlements could be put to a vote by the Knesset, and if the Knesset approved, Israel would depart. The President somehow found time to dictate the following note to the American team: "There is one major issue on which agreement has not been reached. Egypt states that agreement to remove Israeli settlements from Egyptian territory is a prerequisite to a peace treaty. Israel states that the issue of the Israeli settlements should be resolved during the peace negotiations. Within two weeks the Knesset will decide on the issue of the settlements." To which he added in his own hand; "This is the only statement to be made by any of the U.S. Delegation regarding the Sinai settlement issue—whether on or off the record. *J.C.*"

Sadat agreed to this formulation on Sunday morning. The status of Jerusalem could not be resolved, but all at Camp David knew that what had already been achieved was too important to let slip away. The parties agreed that the issue would remain unresolved with both Egypt and Israel including side letters stating their positions as part of the summit's formal documents.

In a Wagnerian finale, thunderstorms tore through the Catoctin skies Sunday evening as the delegations prepared to depart, at last, for Washington and the White House. The dash south by helicopter was as rough as the very worst I had endured during my Antarctic years; however, we were soon on the ground and euphoria was on every face in the East Room of the White House late that evening when President Carter, President Sadat and Prime Minister Begin entered to sign the Camp David Agreements.

The Framework for Peace in the Middle East pointed the road to a comprehensive peace settlement. It established principles to guide the process, for example:

> The agreed basis for a peaceful settlement of the conflict between Israel and its neighbors in United Nations Security Council Resolution 242 in all its parts...

> Peace requires respect for the sovereignty, territorial integrity and political independence of every state in the area and their right to live in peace within secure and recognized boundaries free from threats or acts of force. Progress toward that goal can accelerate movement toward a new era of reconciliation in the Middle East marked by cooperation in promoting economic development, in maintaining stability, and in assuring security...

The Framework offered each stage of the process to peace in the West Bank and Gaza, as agreed to by Begin, Sadat, and Carter:

Egypt, Israel, Jordan and the representatives of the Palestinian people should participate in negotiations on the resolution of the Palestinian problem in all its aspects. To achieve that objective, negotiations relating to the West Bank and Gaza should proceed in three stages....[15]

Carter, Begin, and Sadat also signed the Framework for the Conclusion of a Peace Treaty Between Egypt and Israel that evening, providing for the withdrawal of Israeli Armed Forces from the Sinai, for return of sovereignty over the Sinai to Egypt and for the negotiation and signing of a Peace Treaty Between Israel and Egypt within three months. This towering achievement hinged, even with the September 17 signing, on Knesset approval of the Camp David accords, including the dismantling and removal of all Israeli settlements from the Sinai. On September 28, after many hours of impassioned debate, the Knesset would vote its approval.

President Carter had achieved the near-impossible, bringing great honor to the United States at home and abroad, and dramatically demonstrating anew the unique diplomatic opportunities afforded by negotiation at the summit. I returned from that summit with a prized expedition jacket—the navy-blue windbreaker with the Seal of the President, topped by the words Camp David framed in anchors. The President would send me another trophy, a photograph of Begin, Sadat, and Carter in front of Aspen, smiling broadly, inscribed by each leader. The total experience of that summit will never fade. However, one conversation with Prime Minister Begin remains etched in my memory. On the final evening, just before our departure, I was in laurel Lodge enjoying a cup of coffee with Ed Sunders, President Carter's principal staff liaison officer with the Jewish-American community. Prime Minister Begin and an aide entered the dining room and we invited them to join us. Begin shook our hands warmly; he was still absorbing the splendid meaning of his actions that day. "For years," he said, "all the time I was in the Opposition, they said, 'Don't elect him; he will bring war.' Last year I was contemplating retirement, and now, I am bringing peace!"

End Notes

1. Text of Treaties Relating to the Panama Canal, Selected Documents No. 6., Bureau of Public Affairs, September 1977.

2. The White House, *Office of the White House Press Secretary*, (Providence, Rhode Island), February 17, 1978.

3. Interview given by Prime Minister Kriangsak Chomanan at Government House, Bangkok, Thailand, May 4, 1978, United States Information Service.

4. *Bulletin Today*, Vol. 67, No. 4, Manila, Philippines, May 4, 1978, page 1.

5. Vice President Mondale's Press Comments following meeting with President Marcos, *Office of the Vice President's Press Secretary*, Manila, May 3, 1978.

6. Wainwright, General Jonathan M., *General Wainwright's Story*, Greenwood Press, Publishers, Westport, Connecticut, 1945, page 96.

7. Muldoon, Robert D., *Muldoon*, A.H. & A.W. Reed, Wellington, 1977, page *x*.

8. Vance, Cyrus, *Hard Choices*, Simon and Schuster, New York, 1983, page 214.

9. Speech delivered by Vice President Walter F. Mondale, Knesset Building, Jerusalem, July 2, 1978.

10. Lewis, Finlay, *Mondale, Portrait of an American Politician*, Harper & Row Publishers, New York, 1980, page 259.

11. *Newsweek*, October 9, 1978, page 73.

12. Ibid.

13. Carter, Jimmy, *Keeping Faith, Memoirs of a President*, Bantam Books, New York, 1982, page 324.

14. Ibid, page 398.

15. *The Camp David Summit*, Department of State, Washington, D.C., September 1978.

CHAPTER NINE
Crisscrossing the Continents

We were all delighted, we all realized we
were leaving confusion and nonsense behind
and performing our one noble function of
the time, *move*.

On the Road
Jack Kerouac, 1957

Only the sounds of the light lapping of waves and my feet hitting the moist, hard sand intruded on my thoughts during the run along the empty Copacabana Beach in the early morning of March 14, 1979. I was again on a Presidential mission—this time to Venezuela and Brazil—headed by Mrs. Joan Mondale and Secretary of Labor Ray Marshall. I traced the schedule of the day ahead: upon return to the Copacabana Palace Hotel, a call to the White House Situation Room for an update on the President's mission to the Middle East as well as any other news events that might be raised in Mrs. Mondale's news conference later in the day.

The sun was already burning through the morning haze on the return lap, and the Corcovado statue of Christ the Redeemer had emerged atop Rio de Janerio's magnificent skyline. Following the call to the U.S., I would meet with Mrs. Mondale and her chief of staff, Bess Abell, to review the news, the schedule, the plans for the delegation of U.S. citizens accompanying her—and a brief review of likely issues that she would encounter with Rio's press corps. We would also discuss the line she would wish to take, the route of the morning's motorcade, the meeting with Brazilian artists and their expected request for a statement of Mrs. Mondale's support for their right to true artistic liberty; the exhibit at the Museum of Modern Art; the call at the offices of the U.S. Consul General; the Press Conference; departure for the airport and the flight to Brazilia: and the reception for the U.S. Delegation in Brazilia; and the reception for the U.S. Delegation in

Brazilia that evening to be hosted by the U.S. Ambassador at his residence.

By early 1979, the diplomacy implementing the Camp David Accords had been intense and sustained. Only hours after the September 17 East Room signing ceremony, Secretary Vance had departed for the Middle East to enlist the support of the moderate Arab States. Israelis and Egyptians set to work in respective capitals, and then together at the negotiating table, to come to grips with the vital language that would terminate the state of war and establish peace between their nations.

The United States kept a close eye on this process, and with the first signs of deadlock, Carter persuaded Begin and Sadat to move the negotiating teams to Washington where the United States could perform most effectively as middleman. The talks continued at an intense pace. Late in the fall, I had a call from the Ambassador of Egypt asking if his delegation might have permission to stroll the grounds of the Naval Observatory from time to time to relieve the close, near-continuous confinement of hotel and negotiating rooms. The call need not have been made; the Vice President was delighted to offer the hospitality not only of the Observatory grounds but also of his residence.

While the Camp David process moved carefully forward, the rest of the world's pressing issues—the SALT negotiations, formal relations with the People's Republic of China, developments of international concern and importance in Europe, Africa, Asia, and the Western Hemisphere—demanded White House attention, including attention at the summit. One of the challenges of summit diplomacy is that it is a process that is self-generating. Talks at the the summit are a measure of international recognition and prestige. With each new U.S. Administration, as months turn into years, many nations not yet included in the process steadily increase pressure through public and private channels for a summit with the U.S. leadership. While informal talks with a good number of foreign leaders either in New York or Washington on the fringe of each autumn's United Nations General Assembly session help to ease the pressure, they do not solve the problem.

Further complicating the schedule of an American President, those nations that have enjoyed a summit early in the days of an Administration often press for further rounds of talks citing not only the merits on their substance but also the perils to the bilateral relationship if another round does not occur. The White House will be warned that the foreign leader's domestic political standing will suffer if he or she is not seen as sustaining personal diplomatic contact with the President. The positive results between the two nations flowing from the first meeting may seep away if a populace believes that it is being ignored or taken for granted because of the absence of further face-to-face talks between leaders. Press commentaries in this era of near-instantaneous, global, electronic, radio, television, and newspaper communications, fuel the demand for further summit contact.

These considerations were duly weighed with President Carter's Administration now in its third year. The months that followed were heavy with official overseas travel by the Vice President: Brazilia, Caracas, Reykjavik, Oslo, Bergen, Stockholm, Copenhagen, Helsinki, The Hague, Geneva, Tokyo, Beijing, Xian, Guangzhou, Hong Kong, Panama City, Belgrade, Dakar, Niamey, Lagos, Kano, and Cape Verde would be among the jet ports of call. Wherever the Vice President traveled, he carried the full authority of the President of the United States. President Carter would say: "The leaders of other nations...recognize that Fritz indeed speaks for me. I doubt that this has ever been the case in the history of our nation with another Vice President."[1]

Having already made summit visits to Venezuela and Brazil, the President, desiring to maintain high visibility in each of these bilateral relationships, named the Vice President to lead the U.S. Delegations to the mid-March-1979 inaugurations of President-elect Luis Herrera Campins in Caracas, and President-elect Joao Baptista de Oliveira Figueiredo in Brazilia. However, diplomatic disaster loomed high in the Middle East, with Egyptian-Israeli peace negotiations deadlocked. All that had been achieved at Camp David the preceding September was about to be destroyed. With little hesitation, Carter again gambled the entire prestige of the U.S. Presidency with the announcement that he would go to Jerusalem and Cairo personally to take charge of the peace process. By custom and for sound reasons of national security, the United States carefully avoids having both the President and the Vice President simultaneously overseas. On March 6, the White House announced that the Vice President would remain in Washington while the President was in the Middle East, and that Joan Mondale and Secretary Marshall would lead the inaugural delegations.

The inaugural swings through Venezuela and Brazil were festive occasions. Our advance teams had smoothly worked the triangular coordination of all changes in the schedules with Washington, the

U.S. Embassy teams, and the host governments—who fully appreciated the reason for change in delegations. A charming lady, very active in the United States in her role as spokesperson for the arts, Mrs. Mondale had traveled with the Vice President on several of the earlier foreign missions, and she took these new responsibilities in stride, as did the Secretary of Labor. Their principal task was to convey America's respect, friendship, greetings, and best wishes to both new leaders; this they did most ably. On the day of Herrera's inauguration, the Vice President called for a status report, and I was pleased to advise him that his wife and son William had dominated front-page coverage that morning. The Vice President was obviously pleased: "Tell them I'm proud of them," and he added with a laugh, "keep that delegation out of trouble."

The delegates, for the most part a cross-section of some of the nation's finest hispanic-American leaders, enjoyed themselves thoroughly and added a very positive special dimension to America's representation. It was a happy company aboard our Air Force jet, and to this day I have the mounted piranha with jaws spread baring its needle-sharp triangular teeth—first prize, coveted by all, for having come closest to guessing the precise minute and second we would pass over the Equator on our flight from Caracas to Rio.

In her calls on the new Presidents, Mrs. Mondale presented each with a letter from President Carter, which had been entrusted to me to be retrieved from out traveling files, and told each that she was receiving word of favorable Middle East developments, and that the Vice President looked forward to following through with an official visit upon the President's return to Washington. On our flight home, I finished drafting the delegation's report to the President. As soon as it had been retyped Mrs. Mondale and Secretary Marshall signed the report for delivery to the Oval Office the following morning. The President had, indeed, wrought another miracle. I would watch Begin and Sadat sign the Egyptian-Israeli Peace Treaty beneath the bright spring sunshine of March 26, in a ceremony on the White House lawn. On March 16, the foreign ministries of Venezuela and Brazil announced that the Vice President would be making a visit. On March 22, I again stepped from a motorcade at Planalto Palace in the new capital city of Brazilia—laid out in the middle of the Brazilian jungle in the shape of a giant flying bird—accompanying Vice President Mondale to his talks with President Figueiredo.

The benefit of having this high-level U.S. visit so soon after the Inaugurations became obvious immediately. While the flush of inaugural excitement still remained in both capitals, the Vice President and his hosts, and new Presidents, were free to devote fulltime to serious discussion—with the Vice President now not relegated to the time-consuming role of spectator at the elaborate ceremonies of little more than a week before. His March 22 schedule told the tale: 9:30 a.m., meeting with Vice President Chavez; 10:15 a.m., meeting with the President of the Chamber of Deputies Flavio Marcilio; 10:30 a.m., meeting with leader of the opposition; 11:00 a.m.–12:00 p.m., at the hotel suite; 12:30 p.m., meeting with Foreign Minister Guerreiro; 1:00 p.m., lunch hosted by the Foreign Minister; 3:00 p.m., meeting with President Figueiredo; 5:00 p.m., press conference; 8:00 p.m., dinner in honor of Vice President Chavez hosted by the Vice President.

Air Force Two departed for Caracas early the next morning. Following meetings and luncheon with leaders of the Venezuelan Congress, Mondale entered into a full afternoon and evening of talks with President Herrera and the Ministers of his Government. These were opportunities for straightforward conversations; there was much to celebrate, even more still to accomplish given the fact that the 'new moral dimension' of the Administration's foreign policy had included Brazil among its early targets. Upon the Vice President's return to Washington, the *Los Angeles Times* published an editorial, "Mondale Mends Some Fences," analyzing the results of the mission. The *Times* recalled that the earlier strains in the U.S.-Brazilian relations prompted by criticisms of Brazilian human rights violations, that U.S. efforts to block the $4.8 billion nuclear fuel and reprocessing sale from the FRG now appeared to be easing, and that with Mondale's visit; "President Figueiredo's acceptance of an invitation to meet with President Carter in Washington suggests that U.S. relations with this important country may indeed be on the mend." The editorial examined the importance of Venezuela as a member of the Organization of Petroleum Exporting Countries, against the background of the Mondale's forward-looking talks with Herrera, and suggested, "Venezuela's desire for U.S. participation in the costly development of the Orinoco 'tar belt' with its huge reserves of heavy oil, should be treated sympathetically to the degree consistent with he development of this country's own nonconventional energy sources....Vice President Mondale's trip to Brazil and Venezuela was inevitably overshadowed by more dramatic events elsewhere in the world, but it was an important demonstration of the Administration's interest in good relations with both countries."[2]

There were other fences to be tended, not mended. On Good Friday, April 13, I was enjoying the snap of the Vice President's flag flying at the yard and the cold mist driving across the bow of our fast, Norwegian coastal charter boat pushing north through the gray coastal seas of Iljeltefjord, Fedjefjord. We nosed out briefly into the open waters of the North Atlantic before our starboard turn into majestic Songnefjord on the four and one-half hour run to Fjaerlandfjord and the Vice President's ancestral home in the fjord's headwaters village of Mudal. A sleek, gray-green 100 ton Snogg-Class fast-attack missile gunboat of the Royal Norwegian Navy rode shotgun on this passage. Iceland, Denmark, Finland, and Sweden—had with immense pride been attempting to lure America's Scandinavian-American Vice President into paying a visit from the moment of his election in 1976. In 1977 and 1978, dates had been explored, then evaporated. As guest of honor at a working luncheon of the Nordic Ambassadors at the residence of Iceland's Ambassador Hans Andersen in February 1979, I had assured them that the visit would come to pass in April.

The White House announced that the President had asked the Vice President to make the visit in his behalf. The Netherlands, a close friend and ally too often bypassed because of its adjacency to the international hub of Brussels, was included from the outset. Air Force Two brought the Vice President and Mrs. Mondale to Iceland on April 11; to Norway on the 13th; to Denmark on the 18th; Sweden on the 19th; Finland on the 20th and the Netherlands on the 21st. This was the stuff of good, American diplomacy. It was a week of tribute to the Vice President, a continuum of cordial meetings, receptions and glittering banquets in the palaces, official residences and halls of government of Kings, Queens, Presidents, and Prime Ministers. Added to this and reflected in Mondale's warm reception, the Nordic countries and the Netherlands were demonstrating the degree of national satisfaction each took from the U.S. Administration's foreign policy, with its emphasis on fundamental respect for human rights; on the 'North-South dialogue', that is to say the initiative of the United States and other industrialized nations in seeking improved patterns of cooperation with the poorer developing nations of the world; the new era of relations, with its favorable implications for U.S. relations with all of Central America; and the continued dedication to the success of the Strategic Arms Limitation Talks with USSR.

The Vice President repaid these compliments, choosing Oslo City Hall on the evening of April 17 to deliver the major address of his

Scandinavian mission, with King Olav, members of the Norwegian Royal Family, and the Prime Minister and Members of his Cabinet in attendance, with particular emphasis on the security of the Western democracies:

> Throughout the history of the Alliance, Norway has stood firm against all challenges, from the very first efforts to keep you from signing the North Atlantic Treaty, until today, and we in the United States, together with our other allies, will continue to support that courageous Norwegian resolve to maintain your security, independence and liberty—wherever the challenge, whatever the need.
>
> We also value deeply the contributions Norway and your Nordic colleagues have made to regional stability. Indeed, the Nordic States deserve special praise, far more than is usually accorded to you, for your major contribution to East-West stability.[3]

The visit went far deeper. From the Vice President's first day of talks with Prime Minister Johannesson in Reykjavik through his final session with Prime Minister van Agt in the Hague, the defense objectives and requirements of the West and the resulting steps being taken to enhance NATO security were a central topic of discussion. Although U.S. and Soviet negotiators were finally gaining the momentum required for agreement in SALT II, the Alliance—and Western Europe specifically—faced the stark growing presence of an entirely new generation of highly capable Soviet mobile, 5,000-kilometer range SS-20 missiles, each with three independently targetable nuclear warheads, a fundamentally destabilizing act on the part of the Soviet Union—free from the constraints of the intercontinental strategic arms talks—that would require a response in the form of upgraded NATO deterrent forces. This mounting challenge from the East was also the subject of discussion in Stockholm.

In the NATO capitals, the Vice President took stock with each ally of the efforts being made to realize the Alliance's goal of three percent real growth annually in each nation's defense budget. He reviewed the progress on NATO's "two-way street" providing for better sharing among the allies of increasingly expensive weapons systems production and purchasing. The F-16 Fighting Falcon supersonic jet fighter program offered a classic example of what could be achieved by the allies. In 1975, Norway, Denmark, Belgium, and the Netherlands chose the F-16 package as the most capable new fighter for each of their air forces. Such decisions do not come easily. Development and integration of such highly advanced, extremely expensive weapons systems take virtually a decade of political, military and economic commitment on the part of each nation. As part of the F-16 package, it had been agreed that ultimately more than 20 European companies would have a part in the production of F-16 components and that both Belgium and the the Netherlands would build and operate F-16 final assembly lines.

In Iceland, the Vice President met with Rear Admiral Martini, the American Commander of the NATO Icelandic Defense Force in the North Atlantic. He boarded one of the U.S. Air Force's new Boeing E-3 Sentry Airborne Warning and Command System (AWACS) jets, which had just arrived at Keflavik from Tinker Air Force Base, Oklahoma. The commander of the four-engine jet—with its large discus-shaped down-looking radar mounted on a perpendicular knife-edged pedestal atop the fuselage—provided a crisp review of the mission and capabilities of this complex airborne radar, command and control, and battlefield communications station designed to guide high-performance aircraft such as the F-16 to their targets.

Following these briefings, Mondale met with the officers, men and their families of the defense force in one of the Keflavik hangars, choosing very special words to state the nation's appreciation for their dedicated service, away from homes, as the United States began the celebration of the Easter holiday. And, eight days later at Soesterberg Airbase in the Netherlands he boarded the single-seat F-15 Eagle supersonic air-superiority fighter of the U.S. Air Force's 32nd Tactical Fighter Squadron, talked with the pilots on their mission in a nearby ready room then watched as they raced for their aircraft at the sound of the battle claxon. The F-15 Eagles, 'cocked' in their revetted hangars, ready for action, were on the main runway in less than two minutes and airborne in less than 1,000 feet climbing almost vertically with flames bursting from the afterburners of their twin engines. The bond of U.S.-Dutch friendship and alliance was captured in the Squadron's crest—the head of a ferocious wolf topped by the crown and wreath of laurels and oranges of the Royal House of Orange. The visit to Soesterberg concluded with another very warm, informal session with the Squadron's families with more warm words of praise for their sacrifices and the contribution all were making to America's security. The following morning, immediately prior to his return to Washington, the Vice President echoed these words in a large breakfast session with the American community in the Hague.

Despite the success of the mission, I was still muttering to myself on the return flight across the Atlantic about an event that had occurred in the village of Mundal a week before. Following the presentation of awards at the Easter ski competition, the Vice President and Mrs. Mondale had adjourned to the packed local meeting hall to hear a speech in his honor and to join in a reception by the people of Fjaerlandfjord. At the conclusion of these festivities, the Vice President took the microphone to express his thanks and, to commemorate his visit, to present to the local meeting hall the Vice President's flag that had flown on the boat bringing him to Mundal. Prior to the visit I had attached importance and given personal attention to ensuring that a flag would be available, even overseeing the addition of two grommets to receive the clips of the coastal ferry's yard halyard. I had overlooked the fact that the flag was a multi-colored silkscreen, not multiple panels of different color cloth. When we retrieved the flag for its Mundal presentation, I was appalled to find that the brilliant seal had dissolved into an indistinguishable blur during the misty, windy voyage—there is no limit to the sherpa's continuing responsibility for attention to detail!

President Carter had begun his summit travels in 1979 joining Giscard d'Estaing, Helmut Schmidt, and Callaghan at Guadeloupe for four-power consultations in early January. In mid-February he met again with Lopez Portillo and addressed the Mexican Congress. Following his urgent mission to the Middle East a month later and the signing of the Israeli-Egyptian peace treaty, his administration turned top priority to the SALT II negotiations, and in mid-June 1979, Carter flew to Vienna, Austria to join Brezhnev at a U.S.-Soviet summit marked by the signing of the SALT II Treaty. Upon the President's return, I began many days of travel with the Vice President as he crisscrossed the United States aboard Air Force Two rallying domestic public opinion in support of SALT II, which still required ratification by the U.S. Senate. Half a world away, a grim human tragedy was swiftly growing to global crisis proportions with thousands upon thousands of men, women, and children attempting to escape from the threats of murder, of prison, and the totalitarian hardships of the Communist rule in Vietnam. Where possible, they fled or were driven across land borders. They put out to sea in the most perilous of cockleshells, drowning, starving, dying of thirst, being raped and murdered by pirates on the high seas. They arrived sick, without possessions in numbers that created deep political problems and a near-crushing imposition on the Governments of Thailand, Hong Kong, Malaysia, and Singapore. The United States acted decisively:

I am proud that our nation responded as it did. During the Tokyo Economic Summit in June 1979, President Carter authorized us to double our intake of Indochina refugees to 17,000 a month—an annual total of 168,000. A month later, Vice President Mondale led our delegation—and the world— in a historic conference in Geneva that, I believe, forced changes in Vietnamese policy, saving countless lives and forcing open the doors of other countries to larger resettlement efforts. Mondale's moving speech in Geneva brought tears to the eyes of many in the audience; the policy he outlined that day will long stand as one of the most significant acts of the Carter Administration.[4]

Detailed planning for this mission to Geneva had begun via telephone from the West Coast while I was with the Vice President on the SALT II speaking tour. During a return stopover in Philadelphia, Air Force Two took aboard the new members of the party who would accompany us to Geneva. Before departure, I went through the cases of documents that had been developed by State, the NSC, White House and Vice Presidential staffs, carefully checking each set of papers for the conference and for the accompanying bilateral talks the Vice President would hold in Geneva pressing for an international response sufficient to meet the refugee crisis. Shortly after take-off, the Vice President called me forward to brief the distinguished private Americans who had been invited to accompany the U.S. Delegation, on the situation in Indochina and our goals in Geneva.

On July 21, 1979, the Vice President was recognized by the chair and began his address to the delegates to the U.N. Conference on Indochinese Refugees assembled in the great assembly hall of the Palais des Nations in Geneva. And, he began with a stark reminder:

> Forty-one years ago this very week, another international conference on Lake Geneva concluded its deliberations. Thirty-two 'nations of asylum' convened at Evian to save the doomed Jews of Nazi Germany....At stake at Evian were both human lives—and the decency of self-respect of the civilized world....The civilized world hid in the cloak of legalisms....
>
> As the delegates left Evain, Hitler again goaded 'the other world' for "oozing sympathy for the poor, tormented people, but remaining hard and obdurate when it comes to helping them." Days later, the 'final solution to the Jewish problem' was conceived, and soon the night closed in.
>
> Let us not re-enact their error. Let us not be the heirs to their shame. [5]

Mondale laid fundamental blame for the 'boat people' crisis on Vietnam, and he called for an immediate moratorium on expulsions from Vietnam. He urged the countries of first asylum in the region to rise to their responsibility and to provide safe haven. And, he urged all other countries to rise to their responsibilities by assuring the nations of Southeast Asia of a global long-term resettlement commitment, as the United States already had done. He stressed the need for larger national contributions to the U.N. High Commissioner for Refugees, and the need for new transit centers in the Pacific to assist the refugees en route to more permanent homes. "Today," he said, "I am especially pleased to announce that we are requesting more that $20 million from the Congress to finance our share of such new UNHRC facilities."[6]

Mondale said that President Carter would be requesting an additional $20 million from the Congress as an initial contribution to a U.S.-proposed International Refugee Resettlement Fund. Finally, he said that the President, as Commander-in-Chief of the armed forces, was ordering U.S. warships and patrol aircraft to intensify their search for refugee boats on the high seas. It was a powerful address that brought a thunder of prolonged applause, highly unusual in the staid decorum of U.N. conferences. "History will not forgive us it we fail." he concluded. "History will not forget us it we succeed." No voice spoke out more stridently in support of the Vice President's condemnation of the Vietnamese that did that of Ambassador Zhang Wenjin, head of the Delegation of the People's Republic of China.

Zhang, a very refined 64-year-old diplomat, who had been present during Zhou Enlai's conversations with General George Marshall during World War II, served as the PRC's ambassador to Pakistan and Canada, and was now Vice Minister of Foreign Affairs, was among the several heads of delegation who paid bilateral calls on the Vice President in his hotel suite during the course of the refugee conference. This was important for the support he would give the U.S. position in the Palais des Nations; it was also an excellent diplomatic opportunity in terms of the objectives the United States was setting for the Vice President's official visit to the People's Republic of China in August 1979. This would be the first summit-level mission to the PRC since the commencement of formal U.S.-PRC relations and Vice Premier Deng Xiaoping's visit to the United States in January 1979, and we wanted the visit to highlight the progress in relations. In Washington we had been working hard to this end; however, our proposals seemed to be met by bureaucratic lethargy on the part of the Chinese.

When Mondale and Zhang had completed their consultations, David Aaron, Assistant Secretary of State Richard Holbrooke and I took the Vice Minister of Foreign Affairs aside. At the invitation of my American colleagues, and drawing on memory, I sketched out in considerable detail each of the proposals the U.S. had advanced the Chinese side for the Vice President's visit, and the benefit to both sides if these proposals were to be accepted. With an aide taking notes, Zhang listened most attentively, seeking an occasional clarification or confirmation of the points being made. It was time well spent. Within a very few days the diplomatic logjam began to break in Beijing.

On long overseas journeys through many time zones, there is an effect on the human body's biological rhythm that should be understood and calibrated from the outset if a summit is to experience minimum adverse impact from the phenomenon of 'jet lag'. Simply stated when you are at a conference table in, for example, Hong Kong, at 2:00 p.m., Hong Kong time, and you have just arrived from the East Coast of the United States, your mind and body silently but forcefully advise you that it is really 2:00 a.m., and that you should be asleep. Formulas for successfully contending with jet lag rival those for hangovers. The only formula that has ever made sense to me in my official travels is to accept instantly the local time as your own preferred time and to got to bed, whether your body says you are tired or not, when it is night and the correct bedtime locally, ignore even an hour of wakefulness and then sleep hard until the alarm orders you up and into the traces again.

Air Force Two departed Andrews Air Force Base for the People's Republic of China at 8:45 a.m., on Friday, August 24, 1979. The first leg of the journey was seven hours and 15 minutes with a time change of minus five hours; destination Elmendorf Air Force Base, Alaska. Following one hour's ground time for refueling, we departed Elmendorf at noon for Yokota Air Force Base, a journey some 100 miles longer than the first leg— 3,683 miles—a flying time of seven hours and ten minutes, a time change of minus six hours and a gain of a day, with touch-down at Yokota at 1:10 p.m., Saturday, August 25, 1979. There were typhoons to the south, and we extended our start at Yokota by little more than an hour, departing Yokota at 3:00 p.m., for the final 2,071 mile leg to the PRC spanning four hours and 25 minutes flying time and an additional minus one hour of time change. There were full honors complete with military honor guard for the Vice President at Beijing International Airport, and the motorcade then took us through the sunlight countryside to the villas, walks, ponds, streams and gardens of the walled Diaoyutai Guest House. Following a shower and a change of clothes, we were again on the road en route to the Li Guan restaurant on Kumming Lake at the Summer Palace for an informal dinner in honor of the Vice President given by Foreign Minister Huang Hua. Sleeping was not a problem that night. By the time of the next formal event, the welcoming banquet at the Great Hall of the People at 7:30 p.m., Sunday evening, the body clock had made an excellent adjustment. It would only be in the midafternoons during the trip through China—the dead of night in Washington—that my eyelids would grow heavy for a moment or two.

We had worked hard to ensure that the Vice President's mission would be fully productive. In the first half of 1979, a trade agreement had been signed and joint U.S.-PRC commissions on economic and scientific and technological relations had been informed. Many hours of interagency meetings and consultations would now further this process. The President would authorize Mondale to inform the PRC that the United States would be requesting Most Favored Nation treatment of the Congress for the PRC before the end of the year, as well as the guarantees and insurance of the U.S. Overseas Private Investment Corporation for U.S. firms wishing to do business on China. Further, the United States was now prepared to establish Export-Import Bank credits, keyed to the growth in commercial development, as much as $2 billion over five years. The Vice President would also announce that the United States wish to push ahead with the negotiation of textile, maritime, and civil air agreements—and I would personally see one of the PRC's big 747 Boeing clippers at San Francisco International Airport in January 1981. In addition to these announcements, there were ribbons to be cut and formal agreements to be signed.

The Vice President's first round of substantive talks with China's political leader, Vice Premier Deng, ran three hours, from 9:00 a.m., to noon in an airport-terminal sized conference room of the Great Hall of the People. Deng, physically a tough little chestnut of a man, demonstrated anew the toughness and sharpness of mind that had led to his role as 'first among equals' in China's thousands of millions. Chain-smoking *Panda* cigarettes, keeping a benevolent eye on the steady refilling of the large china cups of green tea at each place on each side of the long, green-felt covered table, Deng would invite the

Vice President's views, quietly gauge—depending on the issue—whether he would respond at that instant or set the issue aside for a response later in the visit, then launch into fast-clipped deliveries of his own on the crucial points to be addressed in U.S.-PRC relations or the world more generally.

After a formal luncheon hosted by Vice Premier Fang Yi at the Diaoyutai Guest Compound, the Vice President departed for Beijing University, and I felt very much like a trustee, seated behind him on the stage of a university auditorium as he made history becoming the first American leader ever to address not only the University but also the people of China via radio and television. In his eloquent address, he reviewed the past, present, and future of the relationship; the fundamental difference between the political systems; the fundamental congruence of views on issues of global strategic importance; the milestones that would be passed during his visit; and the progress still to be realized. He went further, placing America's perception of China's security in the context of the emerging bilateral relationship:

> For Sino-American relations, that means that we respect the distinctive qualities which the great Chinese people contribute to our relationship. And despite the sometimes profound differences between our two systems, we are committed to joining with you to advance our many parallel strategic and bilateral interests.
>
> Thus any nation which seeks to weaken or isolate you in world affairs assumes a stance counter to American interests. This is why the United States normalized relations with your country, and that is why we must work to broaden and strengthen our new friendship....
>
> Let there be no doubt about the choice my country has made. The United States believes that any effort by one country to dominate another is doomed to failure.... Normalization signals our understanding that American security in the years ahead will be attained not by maintaining the status quo; not by colluding for purposes of domination; but by fostering a world of independent nations with whom we can build positive relations.[7]

Secretary of State Vance would describe the Vice President's mission as "one of the most important and successful trips ever made by an American Official to China."[8]

Artists for the Chinese Opera and Ballet Company and the 4th Troupe of the Beijing Opera Company presented an evening of music and dance for our delegation; Tuesday morning, a motorcade again carried us along Beijing's broad avenues, our official cars almost an extinct species in the swarming two-way traffic of bicycles. The enormous outdoor portraits of Marx and Lenin peered down on us as we neared the Great Hall of the People once again for the Vice President's second three-hour round of consultations with Deng.

The Great Hall is a massive, fascinating urban labyrinth of conference halls, conference rooms, banquet halls, reception rooms, offices, and professional suites. And, it was in one such drawing room within this revolutionary-era complex that we settled into heavily upholstered Victorian-era armchairs dressed in antimacassars for the Vice President's tete-a-tete with Premier Hua Guofeng. "Policy and tactics are the life of the Party;" Mao had written, "leading comrades at all levels must give them full attention and must never on any account be negligent."[9] Clearly, Hua had many political opponents in the jockeying for the post-Mao reins of power that continued in China in 1979. He had been Mao's personal choice as successor, and, in addition to his role as Premier, occupied two positions critical to political dominance—Chairman of the Chinese Communist Party Central Committee and Chairman of the Military Commission. His manner on the afternoon of August 27, was very much that of Chief of State, removed from the day-to-day detailed work of the government, yet, judging by the posing of his questions, he had been fully briefed on every minute of the Vice President's six hours with Vice Premier Deng.

At the conclusion of this conversation, we adjourned to a larger conference room that had been readied for a formal signing ceremony—U.S. and PRC flags on the ample felt-covered table, and risers behind the table on which our Chinese hosts, the American Ambassador Leonard Woodcock, and members of his Embassy staff, and members of our traveling delegation took their places. Given the political competition between Deng and Hua, our diplomatic colleagues whispered their amazement that the Chinese Premier had joined the Vice Premier for this occasion. They could not recall an earlier instance during this period of internal Chinese political struggle when Deng and Hua had permitted themselves to be photographed together, a reaffirmation of this significance attached by the Chinese to this visit.

A member of the PRC's Ministry of Foreign Affairs and I hovered over the Vice President and Vice Premier, turning the pages of the duplicate copies of the heavy parchment legal-sized diplomatic documents to the correct line for signature by each, then exchanging the documents and repeating the signing process. With this ceremony, Mondale and Deng expanded the formal framework for cultural exchanges and reached formal agreement on a program for the development of hydroelectric energy in the People's Republic of China—in effect, resuming the pre-World War II efforts of the Army Corps of Engineers to assist the Chinese in harnessing the potentials both for tremendous energy and destruction of such great rivers as the Yangtze—with the provision that the PRC would now compensate the U.S. for the new program of assistance.

If there is a knack to establishing the right biological rhythm for successful, distant summitry, there is an even finer art to the business of setting summit schedules to a pace that produces the best news coverage. By 1979, banquet toasts in the Great Hall of the People and visits to the Great Wall were no longer the news events they had been in U.S.-PRC relations half a decade before. Immediately following the August 28 signing ceremony, the Vice President proceeded to a news conference in the Minzu Hotel, the residence of the moment for our traveling party of correspondents, who had been joined by a sizable gathering of the Chinese and international press corps resident in Beijing.

The combination of the summit talks with Deng and Hua, together with the 'meat' of the agreements just signed, was newsworthy. This, coupled with the fact that August is traditionally a slow news month, led to excellent coverage of the visit now shifting from the conference tables of the Great Hall of the People in Beijing to the distant cities of Zian and Guangzhou.

Once again, now closer than ever to the Himalayas, my sherpa's existence took me to three wonders of the world—the Forbidden City, the Great Wall, and the Qin Tomb and its Army Vault. Half a millennium of Chinese history is captured in the preserved, former imperial palaces of the Forbidden City in Beijing. Our guides would tell us that construction began in the Ming Dynasty with one million laborers and one hundred thousand artisans impressed in their building. Three palatial structures with golden tiled roofs and red exterior columns—the Hall of Preserving Harmony, the Hall of Middle Harmony, and the Hall of Supreme Harmony—formed the nucleus of the Palaces' ceremonial quarters. White structural and ornamental stones, dragged overland from distant quarries with great loss of life, shaped the palaces' terraces and broad stairways, including one massive slab of more than 200 tons, its face transformed into clouds and dragons, adorned the center of the stairs of the Hall of preserving Harmony. These majestic stairways proved good training for the Great Wall.

The Great Wall is one of the most celebrated, photographed manmade structures. Despite the many, many times in my life that I had had occasion to look at photos of this unique defensive barrier snaking along 4,000 miles of China's mountains, I had never imagined I would find it so steep in its journey up and down these mountains. Walking along its top—a 20-foot-wide stone paved highway broad enough for ten foot-soldiers marching abreast within its protective crowning sidewalls—was decidedly difficult. There are, in fact, lengths of the Wall steeper still where steps have been cut into the surface of the top. There was little more than time for this discovery. Our motorcade soon whisked us back to Diaoyutai Guest House, and shortly after 3:00 p.m., we were airborne on a jet flight of the Chinese Government bound for Xian, capital of Shensi Province, one of the oldest cities in the world.

The following damp, gray morning the cavalcade taking us through the farmland of north-central China along a road dotted with pedestrians and worn farm wagons, with heavy truck tires, being hauled by livestock, slowed and turned onto a dirt sideroad approaching a structure similar in appearance to a university field house. Our host, the Chairman of the Revolutionary Committee of Lintong County, guided the Vice President and Mrs. Mondale and their daughter Eleanor into this building with the rest of our party in tow—onto the site of an archaeological dig creating incredulity and excitement the world over. We were privileged to gaze upon the Army Vault of the Qin Tomb. Our hosts told us that Qin Shi Huang had ascended to the Qin Throne in 246 B.C., and that the tomb he commissioned upon becoming Emperor took 11 years to build. Its ceilings depicted the heaven's constellations in compositions of pearls. Its palaces were constructed on a floor designed as a physical map of China, with the rivers created from mercury. The mound of the tomb was 300 feet high and a mile and one half in circumference, and the Emperor Qin had ensured that he would not enter the hereafter unescorted. The Army Vault, discovered in May 1974, contained an entire Army of life-sized terra cotta warriors and their horses, with the digging, as of the summer of 1979, indicating that his force numbered at least 6,000.

Before reboarding our Chinese flight on the next leg of this Chinese odyssey, the Vice President returned to the city of Xian to tour the General Factory of Petroleum Exploration Instruments. The inclusion of Xian on the itinerary had involved an additional dimension of planning, staffing, and logistical support both for our party and our Chinese hosts. To cite just one example, we had to ensure the same reliability of communications in Xian as in Beijing. In summitry, however, such side visits have an important purpose in the business of nations and involve far more than a relaxed interval of sightseeing in the midst of high-pressured formal diplomatic discussions.

In January 1978, during his working visit to Mexico, the Vice President had included a visit to the Mayan ruins at Uxmal and Chichen Itza on the Yucatan Peninsula at the suggestion of President Lopez Portillo. The Vice President's tour of these historic sites would not only be a fascinating experience for him personally but also through its coverage by the media would manifest America's interest in the entire nation of Mexico and would remind travelers and tourists around the world of Mexico's archaeological treasures. This, too, was the case with our visit to Xian. At a time when the relations between the PRC and the United States were on the verge of considerable expansion, such side visits made a substantial contribution to the goals both nations shared. And, it was in this spirit, with even more specific objectives that we continued on to the commercial/industrial city of Guangzhou—formerly Canton—on the Pearl River, 75 miles northwest of Hong Kong, a city of importance to America not only for the potential of trade but also because the Guangzhou region is the place of origin for the ancestors of most Chinese-Americans. Here, in this setting of heavy commercial river traffic and buildings whose architectures were a reminder of the European and American presence at the beginning of the century, we realized one of the important objectives that I had discussed with Ambassador Zhang in Geneva— a ribbon-cutting by the Vice President marking the opening of the first U.S. Consulate in the new era of U.S.-PRC relations. Following this ceremony, the Vice President addressed a luncheon of American businessmen, many of the pioneers in the developing commercial relationship, outlining the steps the U.S. Government was taking to encourage such bilateral trade.

On Saturday, September 1, we boarded a special train, complete with a fringed white canopy on the open observation platform of the Vice President's parlor car, for the quick run to Hong Kong. We had been joined by another American party making its own diplomatic success—Abe Pollin and his Washington Bullets basketball team—at the end of exhibition tour of several Chinese cities.

Little more than a month had passed since the Vice President's address to the U.N. Conference in Geneva. The United States was pressing forward with the refugee rescue effort on every possible front. Hong Kong had become one of the largest transit centers, with thousands of Vietnamese safely ashore but restricted to packed barracks awaiting acceptance by other nations for permanent resettlement. From the traveling documents cases came the background papers prepared for a series of meetings aimed at keeping full pressure on all concerned. At 2:00 p.m., the Vice President met with the American Ambassadors to the Philippines, Malaysia, Singapore, Thailand, and Indonesia; then, an hour later, a meeting with the regional representatives of the International Organizations and Voluntary Agencies grappling with the refugee crisis. A message was drafted to be sent to the U.N. High Commissioner on Refugees.

The following morning the Vice President traveled by harbor launch to the Shamshuipo and Jubilee Transit Centers. Thousands of faces, thousands of cheers, thousands of outstretched hands were everywhere. At noon, I continued on with him for an assessment of Hong Kong's future role over lunch with Sir Murray MacLehose, Governor of Hong Kong. At 1:30 p.m., U.S. Navy helicopters took us from the landing pad at the Royal Navy's Hong Kong Headquarters, HMS *Tamar*, for the 15 minute flight the aircraft carrier USS *Midway*, anchored in the Hong Kong roadstead. The Vice President was escorted to Flag Quarters where he was given a status report on the 7th Fleet's at sea record of refugee rescues. He returned to the flight deck to address the carrier's company. It was Labor Day weekend in the United States. He praised them for their service to the nation; he praised them for the success of their humanitarian refugee mission recognizing the demands it superimposed on the *Midway's* already crowded responsibilities as an attack carrier of the 7th Fleet. The helicopters lifted off again. At 5:00 p.m., the Vice President held a wide-ranging press conference at the Hong Kong Hilton, reviewing the success of the mission to China and the great challenge still to be met if the refugees were to be saved and assisted to find decent lives in new homelands. We were up early on September 3, and soon winging northward to Tokyo for the Vice President's consultations over lunch at Akasaka Palace with Prime Minister Ohira, en route back to Andrews Air Force Base and Washington. This final meeting of the swing through Asia again recognized the requirement for close consultations with Allies on issues of common interest and concern as an essential ingredient of successful summitry.

On September 19, 1979, the Vice President and Prime Minister Muldoon met again for the unveiling of the commemorative marble plaque bearing the date and their names, marking the opening of the

New Zealand Chancery in Washington—a signal, enduring footnote to the diplomatic advances realized as a result of Mondale's official travels through Asia and the Pacific. On October 1, 1979, Air Force II took us to Central America, to Panama for the ceremonies marking the formal entry into force of the 1977 Panama Canal Treaties. We toured the length of the Canal by ship and helicopter, observed the passage of ocean traffic through the Miraflores Locks, a towering engineering achievement so flawless in its basic logic drawing on nothing more than the everlasting force of gravity to fill the locks from reservoirs at higher altitudes in the Panamanian countryside then to drain each lock down into the sea.

In his address to President Royo, the Heads of State from several nations among the delegations, and the Panamanian people, the Vice President again underscored the political significance of the treaties, quoting President Carter's judgment that the treaties "mark the commitment of the United States to the belief that fairness, and not force, should lie at the heart of our dealings with the nations of the world."[10] He closed underlining the lasting importance of the Canal to all peoples, drawing on the words of David McCullough, perhaps the Canal's finest historian, who was with us as a member of the U.S. Delegation:

> The creation of a water passage across Panama was one of the supreme human achievements of all time, the culmination of a heroic dream of four hundred years and of more than twenty years of phenomenal effort and sacrifice. The fifty miles between the oceans were among the hardest ever won by human effort and ingenuity, and no statistics on tonnage or tolls can begin to convey the grandeur of what was accomplished. Primarily the canal is an expression of that old and noble desire to bridge the divide, to bring people together. It is a work of civilization.[11]

With the coming of the first week of November, force replaced fairness halfway around the world. America was stunned by the invasion of the U.S. Embassy in Tehran. On November 9, the White House issued an official Statement: "The seizure of more than 60 Americans in our embassy in Tehran has provoked strong feelings here at home. There is outrage. There is frustration. And there is deep anger....The President shares these feelings. He is pursuing every possible avenue in a situation that is extremely volatile and difficult....He calls on all Americans, public officials and private citizens alike, to exercise restraint, and to keep the safety of their countrymen uppermost in their minds and hearts."[12] The nation's frustration would grow, and it was mirrored on television and in the press in every town, city and state. The December 1, 1979, edition of *The Oregonian* was illustrative. Its front page carried photographs of young Iranian boys beating themselves with heavy chains in a Moslem religious rite fueled by anti-Americanism, and in the right-hand columns American women in Washington standing beneath the American flag and a placard "Nuke the Ayatollah." The headlines of three front-page stories pointed to the different dimensions of the the crisis: "U.S. Demands All 50 Hostages Be Seen," "Iran to Boycott Meeting of U.N. Security Council," "Shah Asks Carter's Aid in Leaving Country."[13] The hostage crisis would dominate U.S. foreign policy concerns over the next 12 months. However, it was not alone in the challenges facing the White House.

Armed Forces of the Soviet Union invaded Afghanistan in late December 1979. As part of the U.S. response, the President requested the U.S. Senate to set aside its consideration of the SALT II Agreement. With the turn of the year, the national debate mounted on additional steps that might be taken—the boycott of agricultural sales to the USSR, the boycott of the 1980 Moscow summer Olympics. The nation seized America's spectacular hockey victory over the USSR in the winter Olympics with feverish pride. In the midst of this turmoil, the President and Vice President began their quest for re-election. There was a pause in overseas summitry.

Following the SALT II signing with Brezhnev, the President had flown to Tokyo in late June 1979 for the annual Economic Summit of the industrialized democracies. On June 30, and July 1, he had traveled on to Seoul, Korea for consultations with President Park. He would not again depart the United States until mid-June 1980 for the Economic Summit in Rome, an audience with Pope John Paul II, and official visits to Yugoslavia, Spain, and Portugal. In the final overseas summit mission of his Administration, the President would board Air Force One to fly again to Tokyo for the Memorial Services for the late Prime Minister Ohira.

As the complex international problems of late 1979–early 1980 continued to unfold, my responsibilities to ensure that the Vice President was fully abreast of the very latest information on all critical issues were more important than ever. Such staffing ranged from monitoring the international wires and electronic media, to the quality of current intelligence reporting in the President's Daily Brief. In late March, the Vice President passed along a note he had just received from the Director of Central Intelligence:

The Director of Central Intelligence
Washington, D.C. 20505

25 March 1980

The Vice President
The White House
Washington, D.C. 20500

Dear Mr. Vice President;

In response to a note from the President, we have completely revamped the PDB to provide a more complete review of the developments around the world and to do so in as brief a form as possible. A new PDB will be circulated this week.

In this connection, I want you to be aware that Denis Clift provided very useful insight and a number of useful suggestions on ways to improve the PDB. A number of Denis' suggestions have been incorporated into the revised PDB.

Please convey to Denis my appreciation for the time and effort he very kindly volunteered to assist us.

Yours sincerely,

/s/ Stan
STANSFIELD TURNER

On May 4, 1980, President Tito—Marshal Tito, Josip Broz Tito, leader of the partisans' struggle against the Nazis in World War II, leader of Yugoslavia throughout the entire post-war ear—died at the age of 87. U.S.-Yugoslav relations had been a real part of my professional work from 1971 on: Tito's visits to Washington; President Ford's and Vice President Mondale's visits to Yugoslavia; the staffing of bilateral issues year after year requiring the attention of the NSC and the White House. Tito had 'bucked' the Soviets following the war, resisted the Warsaw Pact nations sirens' song, and together with Nehru and Nasser founded the 'non-aligned movement' as an international political force independent of either the United States or the Soviet Union. Yugoslavia's place on NATO's southern flank was critical to U.S. and Allied strategic interests. At every occasion, America stressed its commitment to Yugoslavia's independence, territorial integrity and unity—no mean goal given not only the pressure from the Pact but even more importantly the centrifugal forces among the peoples of the Yugoslav republics.

President Carter named Vice President Mondale to lead a U.S. Delegation that would include Secretary of the Treasury William

Miller, the President's mother Miss Lillian and America's distinguished statesman Averill Harriman. Our advance team departed immediately—its role more central than in almost any other summit-level event—given the precise dictates of the host nation's funeral arrangements. The team's messages via Embassy Belgrade advised us of the central elements of the ceremony prior to our departure. The peoples of Yugoslavia were grieving the passing of a leader who had towered among them for generations. Papers were prepared for the Vice President's talks with Yugoslavia's new leaders. Following our arrival, before the Vice President's wreath-laying at Tito's bier, I penned suggestions for the words he might choose in inscribing his entry on behalf of the American people in the formal book of condolences. The role of the staffer is not one of presumption but of assistance. The words suggested for such a moment may not be chosen; that is not the point. It is the staffer's responsibility correctly to frame the event; it is the leader's responsibility to represent the nation, fully advised on all key aspects of the issue.

The world's leaders came to Belgrade from Europe, from Africa, Asia, and the Western Hemisphere to pay their last respects to Marshal Tito—Prince Philip, Prime Minister Thatcher, former Prime Minister Callaghan, Prime Minister Suarez, Chancellor Schmidt, President Kaunda of Zambia, First Secretary Gierek, General Secretary Brezhnev, King Husseain, King Olav, U.N. Secretary General Waldheim, President Caramanlis, and the list went on and on.

Early on the day of the interment, the Delegations were assembled for the procession that would take Tito's flag-draped coffin from the great hall where he had lain in state, through the black-draped streets of Belgrade lined on either side by the peoples of a mourning nation, to the hillside mausoleum erected as his final resting site. There were several hundred of us—Kings, Queens, Presidents, accompanying delegation members, military aides, body guards and staff—being carefully sheparded by Yugoslav protocol officers into various reception rooms to await further marshaling for the start of the procession, all according to careful plan, all designed to permit the somber ceremony to proceed as scheduled.

As we entered the large sitting room assigned to the Vice President and the U.S. Delegation, to the consternation of our Yugoslav escort, we immediately turned as a body and departed for another chamber. One of my colleague's eyes had been even quicker than my own; our decision was instantaneous. Yasser Arafat and the PLO Delegation had been ensconced in the first chamber. U.S. policy denied official contact with the PLO; to have permitted such an encounter would have been a serious U.S. diplomatic error. The fact that such an encounter would have become world news almost instantly, meant that straightforward coverage of the funeral would have been intruded upon, magnifying any such error into an international blunder of considerable dimensions. The error was neatly avoided, with few the wiser. At the Vice President's request, I returned to the first chamber, introduced myself to Prime Minister Thatcher, and extended the Vice President's apologies for his sudden exit. With a glance across the room, she laughed: "I only wish my staff had told me."

While the Iranian hostage crisis and the demands of domestic affairs would keep the President and Vice President in the United States for much of the remainder of 1980—with staffing required for the continuing flow of high-level visitors to Washington, there would be one more overseas mission with the Vice President—to Africa: Senegal, Niger, Nigeria, and Cape Verde in July 1980.

The rusted hull of an ocean freighter driven onto the beach from the Gulf of Guinea broke the otherwise tranquil seascape view from our hotel in Lagos, Nigeria. The Vice President's talks had gone well in Senegal and Niger. Nigeria was the focal point of this mission to Western Africa. The world's fourth largest democracy, the second largest oil exporter to the United States, a powerful political voice in the international issues of importance to the African nations, Nigeria was important to the United States in 1980. Mondale's program aimed at progress on both bilateral and broader issues. The capital of Lagos, a port city born of British and Portuguese empire trade, a city built on a cluster of coastal islands, had boomed with Nigeria's oil wealth, and with the boom had come incredible urban congestion manifested most vividly by the traffic jams on the city's web of bridges and elevated highways. This offered a new page of learning to the student of motorcades. Truckloads of Nigerian soldiers accompanied us throughout the visit, plowing ahead to part the traffic, and swooping in on cars whose drivers were not quick enough in their reactions to pound on the roofs of such cars with their rifle butts. I could only wonder what possible contribution this might make to the strengthening of relations.

The United States continued to press South Africa both on the requirement for majority rule and for independence for Namibia. "The clock is ticking in South Africa," the Vice President told Nigeria at a banquet in his honor. "We know there is no simple answer.... We see the need to resolve a problem, and we believe that only blacks and whites, talking and reasoning together, can find its solution." And, he again stressed the policies stressed by President Carter during his visit to Nigeria in 1978—respect for human rights, mutually beneficial economic progress and freedom from war and foreign domination.[14]

On July 21, we had flown to Kano, Nigeria's third largest city—a thriving modern city set in Nigeria's cattle grazing plains, and ancient Hausa city that had served for centuries as a principal terminus of trans-Saharan trade. The opportunities for new fields of cooperation and for Nigerian investment in American technology to help balance U.S. purchases of Nigerian oil were reviewed with the Governor of Kano State as they had been with President Shagari in Lagos. Both sides were enthusiastic. As we exited the conference hall at Kano, my enthusiasm vanished. The American flag, side by side with the Nigerian on two tall poles, was flying upsidedown. The Vice President had not yet emerged with the Governor of Kano. The word was passed to our lead advance man to have them linger for a few more moments inside.

One of our military aides sped over to the Nigerian officer in charge with the request that he immediately correct the flag. I watched the officer sight up along the flag pole, laugh, then indicate that there was no need to make the change; he wished to get on with the pomp of the departure ceremony. I then offered a few words which do not now bear repeating. They were relayed to the officer. The flag was run down, turned rightsideup, and run up again. The Vice President and the Governor appeared, and it was a splendid departure ceremony. The insult—really, the error, had been inadvertent. Whether or not the press had been there, there would have been no room for compromise. With the press there, any resulting wire story photographs would have undone all that was being accomplished.

The results of the mission to Nigeria were considerable. The Joint Communique ran three, single-spaced legal-sized pages. The visit had elevated Nigeria above the status of oil supplier to a valued friend among nations with whom the United States wished to work more closely across the board, on science and technology, agriculture, education, energy, trade, and investment. The person-to-person dialogue of summitry had politely pushed past the barriers erected by the complex Nigerian bureaucracy, with candid appraisals of problems inhibiting greater trade and effective arrangements for U.S. Nigerian business contacts. The dialogue had reaffirmed the strength of America's commitment on international political issues of vital importance to Nigeria. The results of the visit went far beyond these already realized through day-to-day diplomatic channels. For me, it symbolized the positive, forward-looking character of almost four years of official overseas travel with Mondale.

On December 12, 1980, he wrote as follows:

THE OFFICE OF THE VICE PRESIDENT
Washington, D.C.

December 12, 1980

Mr. A. Denis Clift
Assistant to the Vice President
for National Security Affairs
The White House
Washington, D.C.

Dear Denis;

As my Assistant for National Security Affairs during the years I have been privileged to serve as Vice President of the United States you have, indeed, distinguished yourself.

Your role in every aspect of my defense, intelligence, and foreign policy responsibilities has been invaluable; outstanding.

We have circled the globe together in behalf of the President. We have worked hard together in Washington in the development of policy, in time of international crisis and in time of historic achievements. Where history records the results as good and lasting, you should take great and deserved pride. You helped in your positive, professional way to shape that history.

With thanks, with friendship and with best wishes for your future success.

Sincerely,

/s/ Fritz
Walter F. Mondale

The arrival of 1981 would also mark the drawing to a close a full decade of summit staffing. Unique to me throughout those years had been the very special character of the relationship between the United States and Canada as reflected in the summits guiding the dealings between our two countries.

End Notes

1. Lewis, Finlay, *Mondale: Portrait of An American Politician*, Harper and Row Publishers, New York, 1980, page 260.

2. Editorial, *Los Angeles Times*, Monday, March 26, 1979.

3. Address of Vice President Walter F. Mondale, Oslo City Hall, Oslo, Norway, *Office of the Vice President*, April 17, 1979.

4. Vance, Cyrus, *Hard Choices*, Simon and Schuster, New York, 1983 page 126.

5. Address of Vice President Walter F. Mondale, United Nations Conference on Indochinese Refugees, Palais des Nations, Geneva, *Office of the Vice President's Press Secretary*, July 21, 1979.

6. Ibid.

7. Address of Vice President Walter F. Mondale, Beijing University Beijing, PRC, August 27, 1979.

8. Vance, Cyrus, *Hard Choices*, page 115.

9. *Quotations from Chairman Mao Tsetung*, Foreign Languages Press, Peking, 1972, page 7.

10. Address of Vice President Walter F. Mondale, Panama Canal Ceremony, October 1, 1979.

11. McCullough, David, *The Path Between the Seas*, Simon and Schuster, New York, 1977, pages 613–14.

12. White House Statement, *Office of the White House Press Secretary*, November 9, 1979.

13. *The Oregonian*, Vol. 129, No. 37, 268, Portland Oregon, December 1, 1979.

14. Gupte, Pranay B., *The New York Times*, Lagos, Nigeria, July 22, 1980.

CHAPTER 10
Honorable Obligations

That long frontier from the Atlantic to the Pacific Oceans, guarded only by neighborly respect and honorable obligations, is an example to every country and a pattern for the future of the world.

> Winston S. Churchill
> Canada Club, London, 1939

In November 1979, at the height of the confusion and violence accompanying the seizure of the U.S. Embassy in Iran, six of the Americans slipped the net and made their way undetected to the Canadian Embassy where they took refuge for two months while the chaos of the revolution continued to swirl through the streets of Tehran. For President Carter, the release of all the American hostages would, in his words, become almost an obsession. As tense days slipped from 1979 into 1980, the President personally monitored the critical steps required for the extraction of the "Canadian six."

> This was a real cloak and dagger story, with American secret agents being sent into Iran to rehearse with the Canadians and Americans the plans for their safe departure. The agents and those being rescued would have to be furnished with disguises and false documents that appeared authentic, and they needed enough instruction and training to convince the Iranian officials that they were normal travelers and business visitors from other countries, including Canada. There were several delays and many adventures as our plans were put into effect.[1]

The escape plan worked. On January 31, their rescue was announced, and America sang the praises of Canada—deservedly so.

America's partnership with Canada, and the strains, pleasures, and shifting demands of that relationship as manifested in U.S.-Canadian dealings at the highest levels had, for me, a special place in my professional interests—for no larger reason that the fact that we were and are good neighbors. In my earliest memories, Canada had meant red-jacketed Mounties on chestnut steeds with haunches brushed into maple leaf pattern for the parade drill in Madison Square Garden, a Garden whose floor could be miraculously transformed into the frozen playing surface of Canada's 'super-human' professional ice hockey players. Canada was also the home of distant relatives I would never know, but who always were spoken of by my family with approval.

During a teenager's summer 'walloping pots' in the roasting kitchen of a resort hotel on the upper reaches of Lake Champlain, Canada was a ten-minute drive from Vermont across the border into Quebec, rich farmland and good beer, rides on spotless electric trains to the sophisticated bilingual city of Montreal, with customs and immigrations formalities at the border less imposing than those required to pass from Arizona to California through interstate agricultural inspection stations.

As reported in the press, Canada was Campebello where FDR fished and sailed; Argentia where FDR and Churchill plotted the strategy of democracies; Canada was America's partner in the harnessing of the Great Lakes and the opening of the St. Lawrence Seaway; Canada was Ottawa where Jack Kennedy had sacrificed his back to the bilateral protocol of a ceremonial tree-planting ceremony.

The focus of these hazy, rosy, positive impressions would sharpen and be calibrated. In the mid-1960's, while on assignment from my magazine to ride the nuclear ship *Savannah* from Port Everglades, Florida, to Mobile, Alabama. I would watch the Rolls Royces of vacationing Canadians be swung aboard as so much baggage. I would learn from these millionaires of the extent of Canada's wintertime sunbelt presence in America and of the extent of Canada's investments in the United States. In late November 1970, the sight of a military column grinding across Ontario farmland at sunset in the wake of the political murder of a Canadian minister would underline the reality of Canada's internal problems.

As I entered my sherpa years, Canada was still in its political adolescence, engaged in shaping a new relationship with its parent, the British crown; engaged in discovering its individuality, and in establishing more clearly its place as a sovereign nation among nations; and engaged at the level of national government in asserting its requirement for respectful recognition of this individuality from its neighbor to the south. At the level of daily commerce, daily interaction between peoples, the U.S.-Canadian relationship is a giant engine that does not depend on the stiff limited steps made possible by protocols and treaties to carry forward the shared interests of the millions of North Americans on both sides of the border. At the national cultural level, the relationship is different. Canada's late Prime Minister Lester Pearson summed it up succinctly: "We worry when you look hard at us, but we are also touchy about being over-looked."[2] At the summit, Canada's relationship with the United States throughout the 70s was dominated by one individual—Pierre Elliott Trudeau.

As Prime Minister, Trudeau was a potent force who inspired the passions of both love and hatred among his people. Earlier in his life, he had described himself as "a man who always rowed against the current, whose thought had only one consistent principle—that of opposing prevailing ideas—to counter-balance."[3] At home Trudeau would provide the creative, far-sighted leadership shaping a just future for French-Canadians within the Canadian nation, a dramatic political struggle culminating in the spring of 1980, the results captured in *The New York Times*, May 21 lead story headline: "QUEBECERS DEFEAT SOVEREIGNTY MOVE BY A LARGE MARGIN—Balloting Peaceful—Trudeau Played a Key Role in Campaign to Protect the Federal System." This would be his most important legacy to Canada. In his dealings with the United States as Prime Minister—with Presidents Johnson, Nixon, Ford, Carter, and Reagan—Trudeau combined the pursuit of distinct Canadian policies, variously merging and separating from those of the United States, with the underlying friendship and pleasure he took from America and Americans.

During his first visit to Washington as Prime Minister in 1969, Trudeau was faced with trends troubling to Canada in the bilateral economic relationship. As America's largest trading partner, Canada was extremely sensitive to any shifts in American economic, industrial, and financial policy. "Living next to you," Trudeau told his National Press Club audience, "is in some ways like sleeping with an elephant: No matter how friendly and even-tempered the beast, one is affected by every twitch and grunt."[4]

With America's trade deficits of the early 1970s, the twitches and grunts became more pronounced. My first exposure to the occasional sparks of U.S.-Canadian summitry came on December 6, 1971. Trudeau had again come to Washington, bringing with him Finance Minister Edgar Benson and Deputy Finance Minister Simon Reisman. Canada had chosen not to follow America's recommended lead on certain international monetary actions; the United States had chosen to levy a ten percent surcharge on all imports—a heavy blow for its largest trading partner. While Prime Minister Trudeau and President Nixon conferred with great civility in the Oval Office, I was across the hall in the Roosevelt Room of the West Wing of the White House witnessing a head-on clash between the Canadian Finance team and Secretary of the Treasury John Connally. Benson and Reisman found their arguments rewarded only by stronger counter-arguments. "Show them that next graph, Paul," Connally would say again and again. He had prepared carefully for the session, was in no mood for a compromise, and one of the world's most illustrious graph flippers, Under Secretary Paul Volcker, produced a succession of charts. Tempers flared; the President and the Prime Minister rode serenely above the fray. In the words of the President's Press Secretary Ron Ziegler, "when the Prime Minister and the President met together, they talked more in the context of the general economic trends and general positions that the Governments hold, and allowed the working level then to get into specific discussions."[5] And, this is as it should have been. The dynamics, the contacts at all levels in all walks of life every day of every year, the strength and enduring friendship of a relationship created by two peoples not by two governments, did not call for a harsh split between Nixon and Trudeau as might have been the case if two other nations had drawn opposing lines on such important issues. The U.S.-Canadian relationship had an instinctive knack for absorbing such moments of friction and pushing ahead with the shared interests of the two North American neighbors.

Canadian affairs were an important part of my NSC staff responsibilities, and U.S.-Canadian relations did see important progress on the occasion of U.S.-Canadian summits. I had been appalled to learn in the late 1960s that Lake Erie was so polluted that a plastic curtain had been immersed off one of the beaches near Cleveland to permit enough chlorine to be introduced into the water so that it would be safe for swimmers. The Great Lakes Water Quality Agreement signed by Nixon and Trudeau during the President's visit to Canada in the spring of 1972 involved a tough economic price on the part of both nations. It would lead to the far greater good of lakes a decade later that would again be capable not only of delighting swimmers, but also providing an uncontaminated fishery for sport and commercial fishermen. Helping to guide the interagency review of the draft agreement, working with the speech writers on the President's address to the Canadian Parliament, even drafting a few presumptuous witticisms for Dr. Kissinger's use during the Ottawa summit's social occasions were all part of the 1972 staffing. Such assignments came in addition to, not in place of, continuing contact with members of the official Canadian-U.S. establishment, whether a periodic talk with members of the Canadian Embassy in Washington, similar contacts with my own colleagues in Ottawa and 'the experts on Canada' scattered throughout the agencies and departments of the U.S. Executive Branch, informal addresses to visiting Canadians such as a class of the National Defense College—face-to-face contacts at the staff level absolutely invaluable to gaining greater insights and the great possible appreciation of differing—or shared—U.S. and Canadian perceptions of world events and bilateral affairs requiring the attention of the White House.

I was quick to learn that in official contacts between our nations, when actual meetings were not possible, the telephone was the preferred medium of official communications. Messages, telegrams, correspondence, the written word—paper flow—dominate to the point of overwhelming the routine conduct of international relations—with the exception of U.S.—Canadian relations. When it is as quick and near-automatic to dial directly any office in Ottawa as it is the person next door, the practice becomes near-automatic, a blessing and a curse. Important work would surge ahead—work central to the interests of both nations; yet there was often not the printed record, the reference of the message or the diplomatic cable one could expect in the case of U.S. dealings with any other foreign country.

The use of telephones extended to all levels of the relationship, and I was far from excluded. I recall, for example, in the early spring of 1973 my first important 'ring' from Ottawa, a call from Timothy Porteous, Prime Minister Trudeau's executive assistant, advising that the Prime Minister wished to place a call to the President that morning to discuss a decision he would be presenting to the Canadian Parliament that afternoon; and the calls I would make half a decade later to Ivan Head, the Prime Minister's foreign policy assistant, and to our Ambassador and Deputy Chief of Mission in Ottawa to shape the detailed arrangements for the Vice President's official visit to Canada in late January 1978.

Prime Minister Trudeau captured the flavor of these dealings during his first visit with President Ford on December 4, 1974. Looking to the benefits to be expected from continuing close contacts, he said, "Mr. President, we hope...that you will find it convenient, as your predecessor did, to talk on a very informal basis even by phone or by quick visits which do away with all formalities, permitting us to come to the point right quickly and to solve whatever small problems we my have."[6]

The papers we had staffed for the President's talks with the Prime Minister earlier in the day had included both 'small problems' and the broader international subjects of shared interest on which the President wished to consult as part of his opening round of consultations with key allies—the results of the Vladivostok summit and their implications for East-West relations, the priority NATO agenda, the problems of Cyprus and the Middle East, and the West's struggling efforts to extract itself from the global energy crisis, both through the work of the International Energy Agency and through national efforts aimed at reducing dependence on imported oil. Here, the broader international agenda merged with a very real bilateral problem of the moment. Canada wanted to cut back on its oil imports and to make greater use of domestic oil that traditionally had been sold to U.S. refineries along the northern tier of American states. This could not be solved in the course of an afternoon in the Oval Office, but the two leaders could and did agree to have both governments give closer attention to the issue—to place it and address it in the low-keyed framework of neighborly respect and honorable obligations in which such 'small problems' were best suited. And, at the State Dinner, I would listen to Trudeau's explanation for this practice. "You, as President, have been exposed to the electorates much more frequently than I have. I dare say that I have walked in the valley of the shadow, and feel a little more closer than you have. But I think we would both agree that our peoples, Canadian and the American peoples, will cease to support us overnight if they thought that we were embarking on courses which were not friendly, which were not based on cooperation and understanding; on the desire to solve any differences that arise in that spirit of friendship rather than the spirit of hostility."[7]

Ford would next meet with Trudeau on the fringe of the May 1975 NATO Summit, and that October, I would find a new dimension of U.S.-Canadian consultations, joining Secretary Kissinger on his official visit to Ottawa. Telephones were not the only innovation in the relationship. Canada's officialdom had genuine respect for the Secretary of State and his influence on world events. Secretary of State for External Affairs Allan MacEachen let it be known that his Ministry was taking the occasion of the Kissinger visit to put into play the freshly tailored protocol, ceremonies and social events that would become standard Canadian practice thereafter for visits by foreign Heads of Government.

Accordingly, when the Secretary and Mrs. Kissinger's Air Force jet arrived at Canadian Forces Base Ottawa, the red carpet literally had rolled out to its fullest in Hangar 11; the military guard of honor came to attention; the band played; and welcoming remarks were delivered in a very fine arrival ceremony.

That evening, Secretary MacEachen welcomed the Kissingers and the rest of our delegation to the ninth floor of the Lester B. Pearson Building, new headquarters for the Ministry of External Affairs. I asked about the building, which seemed to be almost on the outskirts of the capital, and was told by my hosts that the move from the Ministry's old offices on Parliament Hill had produced many of the same withdrawal symptoms as those experienced by America's diplomats in their westward migration from the Old Executive Office Building adjoining the White House to their new post-World War II home in Foggy Bottom.

Nonetheless, MacEachen's dinner for the Kissingers— Canadian duck a l'orange—was a refined, congenial affair with generous toasts offered both by MacEachen and Kissinger. In the interest of capturing these *bon mots* for posterity and for the next morning's media headlines, microphones at the head table were wired to carry the exchange to reporters standing by at the press center. The following morning, as we worked our way with Kissinger through two business sessions, the first with Allan MacEachen and his External Affairs deputies and then an expanded session with the principal ministers of the Canadian Cabinet, almost all concerned were appalled to learn that the mikes had been 'live' throughout the entire dinner and that at least one enterprising correspondent had captured and was now reporting the highlights of Secretary Kissinger's incidental dinner conversation, much of which clearly had not been intended for public consumption. En route to Canadian Forces Base Ottawa for the return flight to Washington that afternoon I constructed the image of a gathering of Canadian sherpas undoubtedly assembled somewhere in Ottawa at that very moment, conducting a *post mortem* on the visit, discovering or rediscovering a critical lesson of summitry—any microphone intended for the press must be assumed to be a live mike unless checked and specifically proven dead—this with the broader understanding implicit in both the United States and Canada that the press will report what it considers newsworthy, not necessarily what the distinguished speaker of the moment would choose to have reported.

Seven months later, the Canadian Government created a publishing masterpiece in its pictorial reporting of the U.S.-Canadian relationship *Between Friends/Entre Amis*, Canada's official Bicentennial gift to the American people. Bound in the red of the Canadian maple leaf with its title in gold, 10" x 14" in size, in a navy blue cloth-covered slip case bearing the American and Canadian flags, the book was a credit to the printer's art and a statement on the U.S.-Canadian relationship to be treasured for generations to come. Turning its pages, the reader embarked on a journey of thousands of miles from the Beaufort Sea along the border country of Alaska and the Yukon territories; then eastward to the Rockies across the lands joining British Columbia and Alberta with Washington, Idaho, and Montana; eastward across the borderlands between Saskatchewan and Manitoba to the north with North Dakota and Minnesota; snaking through the Great Lakes country of Ontario, Wisconsin, Michigan, Ohio, Pennsylvania, and New York; into the border country of Quebec, New Brunswick, Vermont, New Hampshire, and Maine to Quoddy Head and Campebello Island in the Bay of Fundy opening on the Atlantic Ocean.

More than 260 full-color photographs captured the grandeur, richness, and staggering beauty of these borderlands, the many faces of the American and Canadian peoples; the endless threads of shared experiences creating the interwoven pattern of their lives; the variety and the color of both distinct and shared traditions; and the size and strength of the great engine of U.S.-Canadian trade, transport, and industry.

On June 16, 1976, Prime Minister Trudeau joined President Ford in the Rose Garden of the White House. To honor the daring eras of exploration that had opened both America and Canada, Trudeau presented the President with an explorer's desk, a light-weight, collapsible wooden 'office' of the kind used by explorers to record their discoveries during their harrowing journeys by canoe across the Canadian wilds. And, the Prime Minister officially delivered the first copy of *Between Friends/Entre Amis*.

> This book is about people—about the Canadians and Americans who live in harmony close to that long thin line known as the International Boundary....This book is also a celebration—a joyful recognition of that striking triumph of the human spirit reflected in the atmosphere of peace and friendship which pervades the many relationships between two proud and free nations....No one should think it strange that Canadians should involve themselves

in the observance on an American anniversary. Over hundreds of years we have worked and played together, laughed and mourned together, fought side by side against common enemies. Out two peoples have helped each other repair the havoc of natural disasters, inspired and applauded each other, opened our hearts and our homes to each other as two valued and welcome friends."[8]

The Prime Minister would open the doors of his official residence at 24 Sussex Drive to me on the evening of January 17, 1978, on the occasion of a dinner in honor of Vice President Mondale. The Vice President, as a former border state senator, was very knowledgeable of key U.S.-Canadian issues when he took office. In an early meeting with Canada's Ambassador to the United States Peter Towe, he told the Ambassador that he wanted to do all possible to further the relationship to the benefit of both countries. He encouraged Peter to contact him or me anytime there was a matter requiring the Vice President's attention. The Ambassador would exercise this privilege on numerous occasions, including the consultations aimed at solving 'small problems' in the context of the Vice President's official visit in 1978.

An understanding of U.S.-Canadian relations requires at the outset an understanding of the limited authority of Canada's Federal Government over certain of the actions of each of the Canadian Provinces—more limited on some matters than that of the U.S. Government over each of the States. At the time of our visit, for example, the United States had an interest in a greater flow of natural gas from the gas fields of Alberta to the American midwest. The Albertans, in turn, wanted greater access to American markets for their beef. This was not an issue that could be quickly resolved in Ottawa by a meeting of U.S. and Canadian leaders. Alberta, not Ottawa, controlled the policy over its resources, and Alberta was vigorously exercising its voice in Canadian affairs. "The fact that Edmonton, Alberta's capital, and Calgary, Canada's energy capital, witnessed building and employment booms, with construction cranes reeling over mounting battalions of modern skyscrapers, only served as a heightened symbol of the new West's increasingly assertive—and increasingly resented—demands for a realignment of national political and economic power. 'It's the West's time in Confederation,' said Peter Lougheed, Alberta's premier, 'and it's about time.'"[9]

Talks in Ottawa would help to set the tone for more detailed discussion with the Premiers of the Provinces, but the quest for improved understanding on the arrangements for the sale of gas and beef meant that we would include Edmonton and a working session with Lougheed on the Vice President's itinerary. Such was the nature of the discussions over cocktails at 24 Sussex. The Prime Minister's young sons appeared for a moment to say good night to their father. Trudeau then escorted our party—the Vice President, Senator Hathaway of Maine, Senator Stafford of Vermont, Senator Anderson of Minnesota, Ambassador Tom Enders, Assistant Secretary of State George Vest, David Aaron and myself—together with members of his Cabinet and other Canadian leaders to dinner. The Prime Minister casually set the pace of this select company's conversation turning first to one minister with the suggestion that he touch on the subjects of primary concern to him at the moment, then to another with the same request. This process opened a high-spirited colorful exchange among all concerned. However, honors for the evening went to Ambassador Marcel Cadieux, Canadian Chairman of the Maritime Boundary Talks with the United States, and former Ambassador to the United States. In recounting the details of the talks and the impasses between Canada and the United States, Cadieux, in his French Canadian accent painted a canvas of the absurd, the improbable and the hilarious. By the time he had finished, every one at the table was doubled over in laughter. He had captured the essence of the frustrations and the barriers encountered in trying to deal with any number of the bilateral 'small problems' at the federal level. He received a rousing round of applause for his effort and, needless to say, Canada and the United States would successfully negotiate a maritime boundary agreement.

We were scheduled to depart for Edmonton early the following morning. One of the conveniences—and challenges—of such official travel to foreign lands is the baggage call process. Luggage going aboard Air Force One and Air Force Two receives a careful security check at every stop. To facilitate this process and to free delegation members from the task of hauling luggage at the same time that they are moving from one event to the next during tightly scheduled visits, the administrative members of each delegation slip notices under hotel room doors advising each participant of the hour the bags must be in the hall outside of each room. The hour is so early and return to the room the night before is usually so late, there is often the temptation just to lie out in the hall with your bags to be scooped up and deposited on the plane in the morning.

Concentration, protocol, and survival all fold into the process of setting aside everything you will require in the morning—from shaving gear to rain gear—wherever you may be in the world, before you consign your luggage to the hall and fall into bed. Colleagues have been known to appear in suit, tie, and pajama shirt—and even rarer regalia—as a result of the process. It was snowing when the Prime Minister's dinner ended. The baggage call notice, of course, had been slipped under my door upon my return to the Chateau Laurier. I adjusted my packing slightly with this turn of the weather, and the faithful flight bag which had been my road companion for 20 years again took its post outside my door.

Meeting the baggage call is important; catching the plane is essential. Tales abound of staff members just 30 seconds too late who have had grim, career-chilling experiences of watching the tail of their intended jet disappear into the skies. The snowfall had been a heavy one, and while the center of the storm had passed, the flakes continued to fall in the early morning of January 18, adding to the three foot shoulder of plowed snow en route to the airport. While the wings of Air Force Two received a final sweep and de-icing, we were shown into a reception room looking out on the airfield and offered a welcome cup of coffee. Within a few minutes, the Air Force jet started its engines and began to taxi slowly through the swirls of snow to its boarding chocks. Then, in a moment of delightful drama, we witnessed a colleague who—we would learn—had slept through his wake-up call and missed the motorcade, charge through the terminal out onto the taxiway furiously waving his arms at the cockpit, the wind fanning his hair as he desperately insisted that the big jet stop and take him aboard before continuing on its departure. Ground crew, concerned for his safety, intercepted him and led him inside where, purple-faced, he received an unmerciful reception. Such is the sherpa's life.

The traits that go into the distinctive character that Canadians both pride themselves on and continue to search for are very real and many in number. From my professional vantage point, Canadians beyond any doubt, among the world's free and democratic peoples, are good partners sharing the same deep enduring values of the American people. The United States would work in earnest to ensure that Canada was permitted to join that closely drawn circle of major Western democracies meeting annually at the economic summit, and Canada would be a good partner at those summits. Trudeau would rank them ahead of NATO summits in terms of their importance to the West. Carter would note—almost as a given—the common interests that he and Prime Minister Joe Clark, Canada's Prime Minister for less than a year, enjoyed at the 1979 Economic Summit.

Joe Clark had reconfirmed for me another Canadian trait that I greatly admire. When chosen as leader of the loyal opposition in Canada in 1975, Clark had come to Washington to pay a courtesy call on President Ford. When I greeted him at the West Wing entrance of the White House, I was intrigued to observe that, with the exception of his driver, he had come alone, no coterie of escorts. I had grown up with the story of the single Canadian Mountie sent to quell a riot in the Yukon. He did so and when asked why only one Mountie had been sent he said; "There's only one riot."

There's a leaness to Canadian operations that offers an example for all who participate in the world of summitry. Canada had been represented at the 1974 NATO summit by the Honorable Paul Martin, Government Leader of the Senate, given that pressing domestic events had required the Prime Minister to remain in Canada. On the evening of June 26, 1974, the President had retired to the American Ambassador's residence in Brussels, with all the security and other supporting staff that his presence there required. That was the tip of the American iceberg. The lobby and the streets outside the Brussels Hilton were thick with the vehicles and personnel of the U.S. motor pool detail, U.S. security, and comet's tail of support personnel accompanying the American delegation. Having just returned from dinner, I was part of this throng. I watched Paul Martin emerge from his car and make his way alone to the reception desk to obtain his key and then alone into the elevator. While it ran counter to my sherpa's every instinct, I fully and deeply admired a man ascending alone to the summit.

End Notes

1. Carter, Jimmy. *Keeping Faith, Memoirs of a President*, Bantam Books, New York, 1982, pages 483–484.

2. Pearson, Lester B., Address at Notre Dame University, 1963, quoted in *Between Friends/Entre Amis*, National Film Board of Canada, Ottawa, Canada, 1976, page 36.

3. Saywell, John T., in *Federalism and the French Canadians*, Pierre Elliot Trudeau, Macmillan of Canada, Toronto, 1968, page vii.

4. Martin, Lawrence, *The Presidents and the Prime Ministers*, Doubleday Canada Limited, Toronto, 1982, page 241.

5. News Conference, At the White House with Ron Ziegler, December 6, 1971.

6. Exchange of Toasts Between the President and Prime Minister Pierre Elliott Trudeau of Canada, the White House, December 4, 1974.

7. Ibid.

8. Trudeau, Pierre Elliott, in Forward to *Between Friends/Entre Amis*, National Film Board of Canada, Ottawa, Canada, 1976.

9. Malcolm, Andrew H., *The Canadians*, Times Books, New York, 1985, page 19.

Bibliography

Acheson, Dean, *Present at the Creation*, W.W. Norton and Company, Inc., New York, 1969.

Brzezinski, Zbigniew, *Power and Principle*, Farrar Straus Giroux, New York, 1983.

Burns, James MacGregor, *Roosevelt: The Soldier of Freedom*, Harcourt, Brace Javanovich, Inc., New York, 1970.

Carter, Jimmy, *Keeping Faith, Memoirs of a President*, Bantam Books, New York, 1982.

Curie, Eve, *Journey Among Warriors*, Doubleday, Doran and Co., Inc., Garden City, New York, 1943.

Drath, Viola Herms, *Willy Brandt, Prisoner of His Past*, Chilton Book Company, Radnor, Pennsylvania, 1975.

Eisenhower, Dwight D., *Waging Peace 1956–1961*, Doubleday and Company, Inc., Garden City, New York, 1965.

Falk, Stanley L., and Bauer, Theodore W., *The National Security Structure*, Industrial College of the Armed Forces, Washington D.C., 1972.

Ford, Gerald R., *A Time to Heal, The Autobiography of Gerald R. Ford*, Harper and Row Publishers, New York, 1979.

Jobert, Michel, *Memoires d'Avenir*, Bernard Grasset, Paris, 1974.

Johnson, Lyndon Baines, *The Vantage Point*, Holt, Rinehart and Winston, New York, 1971.

Kennedy, John F., Public Papers of the Presidents of the United States, United States Government Printing Office, Washington, D.C., 1962.

Kennedy, Robert F., *Thirteen Days*, W.W. Norton & Company, Inc., New York, 1969.

Kissinger, Henry, *Years of Upheaval*, Little, Brown and Company, Boston, 1982.

Lewis, Finlay, *Mondale, Portrait of an American Politician*, Harper and Row Publishers, New York, 1980.

McCullough, David, *The Path Between the Seas*, Simon and Schuster, New York, 1977.

Malcolm, Andrew H., *The Canadians*, Times Books, New York, 1985.

Martin, Lawrence, *The Presidents and the Prime Ministers*, Doubleday Canada Limited, Toronto, 1982.

Muldoon, R.D., *Muldoon*, A.H. & A.W. Reed, Wellington, 1977.

National Film Board of Canada, *Between Friends/Entre Amis*, Ottawa, 1976.

Nixon, Richard, *The Memoirs of Richard Nixon*, Grosset & Dunlap, New York, 1978.

The Public Papers and Addresses of Franklin D. Roosevelt, 1941, The Call to Battle Stations, compiled with special material and explanatory notes by Samuel I. Rosenman, Harper and Row Publishers, New York, 1950.

The Public Papers and Addresses of Franklin D. Roosevelt, 1944–1945, compiled with special material and explanatory notes by Samuel I. Rosenman, Russell & Russell, New York, 1969.

Schlesinger, Arthur M., Jr., *A Thousand Days, John F. Kennedy in the White House*, Houghton Mifflin Company, Boston, 1965.

Trudeau, Pierre Elliott, *Federalism and the French Canadians*, Macmillan of Canada, Toronto, 1968.

Truman, Harry S. *Memoirs by Harry S. Truman, Volume One, Year of Decisions*, Doubleday & Company, Inc., Garden City, New York, 1955.

Tsetung, Mao, *Quotations from Mao Tsetung*, Foreign Language Press, Peking, 1972.

Vance, Cyrus, *Hard Choices*, Simon and Schuster, New York, 1983.

Wainwright, Jonathan M., *General Wainwright's Story*, Greenwood Press, Westport, Connecticut, 1945.

Walters, Vernon A., *Silent Missions*, Doubleday & Company, Inc., Garden City, New York, 1978.

Walworth, Arthur, *Woodrow Wilson*, Houghton Mifflin Company, Boston, 1965.

Index

The Author

A. Denis Clift is currently Chief of Staff, Defense Intelligence Agency, Department of Defense. He was born in New York City and educated at Friends Seminary, Phillips Exeter Academy (1954), Stanford University (1958), and the London School of Economics and Political Science, University of London (M.Sc 1967). He began a career of public service as a naval officer in the Eisenhower administration and has served in military and civilian capacities in eight successive administrations, including the positions of staff member Europe, National Security Council (1971–73), senior staff member Eastern and Western Europe and Soviet Union, National Security Council (1974–76), and Assistant to the Vice President for National Security Affairs, White House (1977–81). His awards include the Department of Defense Distinguished Civilian Service Medal, the Department of Defense Medal for Distinguished Public Service, and the President's Award, Rank of Meritorious Executive. He is a veteran of two Antarctic expeditions, including the 1961 Bellingshausen Sea Expedition. From 1963 to 1966 he was Editor of the United States Naval Institute *Proceedings*. His writings include the book *Our World in Antarctica*, and the novel *A Death in Geneva*.